WAY DOWN

PLAYING BASS WITH ELVIS, DYLAN, THE DOORS & MORE

THE AUTOBIOGRAPHY OF JERRY SCHEFF

WAY DOWN
Playing Bass With Elvis, Dylan, The Doors, And More
Jerry Scheff

This book is dedicated to my mother, Lois Scheff, and my wife, Natalie.

A BACKBEAT BOOK
First edition 2012
Published by Backbeat Books
An imprint of Hal Leonard Corporation
7777 West Bluemound Road
Milwaukee, WI 53213
www.backbeatbooks.com

Devised and produced for Backbeat Books by
Outline Press Ltd
2A Union Court, 20-22 Union Road,
London SW4 6JP, England

ISBN: 978-1-61713-032-8

Editor: Thomas Jerome Seabrook
Design: Paul Cooper Design

Printed by Regent Publishing Services Limited, China

12 13 14 15 16 5 4 3 2 1

CONTENTS

A Note To The Reader 5

CHAPTER 1   The Last Tour 7

CHAPTER 2   Viva Las Vegas 12

CHAPTER 3   Into The Fire 23

CHAPTER 4   Longhorns 38

CHAPTER 5   Mia, Paula, And The Karate Chops 48

CHAPTER 6   The Jungle Room 60

CHAPTER 7   Boogie-woogie And The Tuba 65

CHAPTER 8   Sacramento Dreamin' 74

CHAPTER 9   Mistaken Identity 83

CHAPTER 10   Les Buie And The Bugle 89

CHAPTER 11   The Sergeant's Lady 102

CHAPTER 12   Back To California 129

CHAPTER 13   Paying My Dues 137

CHAPTER 14   The LA Plunge 146

CHAPTER 15   And Then … 156

CHAPTER 16   Another Dimension 165

CHAPTER 17   Green In The Big Apple 175

CHAPTER 18   The Sunn Amp 182

CHAPTER 19   Changing Of The Guard 197

CHAPTER 20   Cleaning Up 208

CHAPTER 21   Country Roads 214

CHAPTER 22   Convicts And Confederates 222

CHAPTER 23   The Trap 229

Selected Discography 234

Index 237

Acknowledgements 240

A NOTE TO THE READER

Way Down is meant to be an overview of my life as a musician. It is not an autobiography in the traditional sense. You won't find anything about potty training or great-great-grandfathers here. These are my musical memories, complete with many old pleasures and a few old pains.

No one can remember exact dialogue from yesterday, let alone from 60 years ago, so I have paraphrased what was said where I felt it necessary for the most accurate accounting of my experiences and feelings at that time. I have not invented characters, but I have renamed a few of them for the usual reasons.

This is not written as a reference book, a history book, or a work of fiction. It is my life as a musician in the culture and counterculture of the music business. My Life!

Jerry Scheff
Planet Earth

CHAPTER 1

THE LAST TOUR

ugust 16 1977. I drove south on the Pacific Coast Highway watching as the blue Pacific Ocean disappeared in my side mirrors. I was on my way to start an Elvis Presley tour in Bangor, Maine. I was pissed off, red-eyed, and quiet on the way to the airport that morning. I always dreaded leaving my sunny Malibu beach apartment for arguments with pasty-faced night clerks keen to push me into a disinfected room with panoramic views of the dumpster.

As I boarded the tour plane, the first people I usually came in contact with were The Sweet Inspirations—the female singers who sang background vocals on Aretha Franklin's 'Respect' ("sock it to me, sock it to me!") and were amazing talents on their own. When I refer to the Sweets, I'm really talking about Estelle Brown, Sylvia Shemwell, and Myrna Smith. (Cissy Houston, the mother of pop diva Whitney Houston, was with the Sweets in the beginning but left to pursue a solo career in 1970.)

The Sweets loved to laugh. Their laughter was frequent, irresistible, and often naughty-sounding. They could laugh with joy at the coming of the Lord and still sound as if they were up to no good. They usually got tickled toward the end of some muffled, indistinct narrative where Myrna would interrupt with a few short bursts of flea-in-the-throat choking sounds: "Eh! Eh! Eh!" Whenever I heard that, I knew what was coming: the others would join in with a chorus of ascending air-raid-siren ooooohs that would eventually explode into window-rattling belly-busters. For me, a bummed-out bass player struggling down the aisle with my carry-ons, this was redemption at its finest. Add to that the grins and nods from my friends, and by the time I had belted myself in I was suddenly in the mood to tour.

From a relationship point of view, the Elvis Presley group in 1977 was analogous to a big, peaceful, acquiescent middle-aged couple that could still get it on. Actually, we'd gotten better over the years—eight of them, as a matter of fact—since we started playing together. We'd been through all the mock-conjugal bullshit, the old bones of contention had long been buried, and we were still ready to rock hard on a moment's notice.

It helped that none of us were big stars—well, maybe one or two of us thought we were—and that none of us was extremely wealthy (much as some of us liked to give that impression). And we all absolutely despised luxury jets with catered sushi and Dom Pérignon, so we usually traveled—courtesy of Colonel Tom Parker—in an old, slow, prop-driven Lockheed Electra with a closet full of Fig Newtons and Cheetos.

Despite all this, we had a kind of perverse fondness for the Electra. It was like a big comfortable bathtub with seat belts and it rode soft and slow like an old Cadillac. The seats were in standard airline configuration except for a horseshoe-shaped lounge area in the back, where we could stretch out for a nap or huddle together to tell stories as we smoked a reefer. Laughter usually permeated the airplane going out, while snores took over on our way home at the end of the tour.

The sheer size of our group set us apart from most touring rock shows at the time. Not counting the technical-support people, there were more than 20 of us traveling and performing together. We had eaten, drank, laughed, cried, partied, and—in the few instances—slept together, yet I can't remember a raised voice, let alone a serious blowup.

This was all the more amazing because of the diversity among us. We were men, women, Caucasians, African-Americans, Northerners, Southerners, Jews, Christians, alcoholics, teetotalers, drug addicts, hippies, rednecks, liberals, conservatives, tightwads, braggarts, a virgin (so we were told), sex addicts, and a drummer or two. Looking back, I think I more or less belonged in five or six of these categories, although some of my show-mates may think I'm being modest. Who would ever have thought that this conglomeration of misfits, jammed together within the close confines of a cramped tour itinerary, could keep from killing one another, let alone become a family in the warmest sense of the word?

It helped that Elvis approved of each and every one of us. If you wanted to fuck with someone you had to take into account what Elvis would have to say in the matter. (Unfortunately, in later years, when Elvis wasn't there, our band would disintegrate into the usual rock-group configuration of power politics. I just wanted to be left alone.)

Only part of the Elvis group was on board when we headed for Maine that morning. Some members of our group lived in other parts of the country, masquerading as normal people. For some strange reason, a small portion of our cast still felt convinced that they could pass for normal in Las Vegas. So we had to fetch them. We also had to pick up one of our comedians, either Sammy Shore or Jackie Kahane. In this instance it was Jackie Kahane. Orchestra conductor Joe Guercio usually boarded in Las Vegas, too, but Joe wasn't on the flight that day in 1977. He was getting singer-dancer Ann-Margret ready to start a run of shows. Consequently, one of our horn players, Marty Harrell, was due to take Joe's role for the tour's first show.

When we finally left Las Vegas I felt like I was on the road again for real. The bar was open (whatever we brought ourselves), slow R&B was usually floating around, and I could hear the buzz of stories being told around the plane—the same sounds you might hear at a family reunion. By that time I had surrendered to the one particular feeling that always kept me sane on the road: anticipation. You never knew what to expect on an Elvis Presley tour, and I certainly never could have dreamed how this one would end.

About an hour and a half after leaving Las Vegas we were bumping along over Pueblo, Colorado, when a bell rang and the seat-belt signs came on. The pilot had received an urgent message to land and call Memphis. The flight attendants came back to explain the situation and I remember thinking, as we dropped toward Pueblo: *Elvis must be ill. They're going to cancel the tour.*

Once we hit the ground, some of us left the plane and walked in the hot sunshine to a small, private air terminal. The tarmac was deteriorating and weeds were invading. The air shimmered, reeking of aviation gas and goldenrod, and the ratchet sounds of yellow grasshoppers were deafening as they hopped out of our way.

As I see them in retrospect, the people walking over the tarmac are quiet, faceless shadows as someone—probably trombone player Marty Harrell—makes the call to Graceland. Looking back, I sometimes see us outside the terminal, standing around a dusty, chicken-wire-glass phone booth. Other times we're in an office, leaning over a counter like crapshooters over a gaming table, straining to hear the voice at the other end of the phone. It's amazing what time and emotions can do to your memory.

In any case, when the caller hung up the phone, he turned to us, looked at the floor, and said quietly: "Elvis died this morning."

Elvis died this morning?!

We took turns calling home and then walked back to the shady protection of our plane's wing, where most of the other group members stood. Somehow, the word of Elvis's death was passed around, and, as I remember it, stillness settled over the scene. We waited as the others trudged across the tarmac to make calls home. I don't remember how long we all stood out there but eventually the crew appeared in the doorway of the plane and began the delicate process of coaxing us back on board for the return flight to Las Vegas and—with brutal finality—Los Angeles.

On the flight home I recall seeing people lodged in their seats like crash-test dummies. I don't even remember landing in Las Vegas. As we reached Burbank airport the plane rocked with turbulence and beads of rain streamed across the window, lit up like a blinking neon sign by the Electra's strobe lights and stray flashes of lightning. Finally, we wobbled in for a hard landing, and as we left the plane it was as if a strange barrier of embarrassment had grown between us—we who had been together for years. There was a lack of eye contact, total silence, maybe a need to be alone to digest the unthinkable.

I remember seeing my midnight blue Ford Thunderbird through a chain-link fence. It was parked under a lamp in the parking lot. As I walked toward the car, rain was pouring down my face. I sat in the driver's seat, turned on the windshield wipers, and as I watched my friends disappear into the haze I took a look backward, trying to make sense out of the bits and pieces of my past. What had led me to this place in my life?

CHAPTER 2
VIVA LAS VEGAS

I n early 1965, I arrived in Los Angeles driving a gold Ford Mustang Fastback 289 V8, which may sound romantic until I tell you that I had no musical instruments and no clothes. I had been playing dinner music at a hotel in Palm Springs, California, for the previous six months, living in a room at the same hotel, eating steak every meal, and making good money. One Sunday, on my day off, I left Palm Springs; when I got back Monday morning, the hotel was gone—burned to the ground. I lost everything: musical instruments; most of my clothing. I lost the Mustang, too, after a few months because I couldn't keep up the payments.

Let's jump ahead to 1969. In the intervening four years I had made a solid place for myself in the Los Angeles music scene, which at that time was right up with New York City as one of the most important musical scenes in the world. I'll cover that period later on in this book. In the meantime, my experiences with Elvis Presley seem like a good place to start.

In mid June 1969 I received a phone call from a guitar player named James Burton. He was originally from Shreveport, Louisiana, and had moved to Los Angeles to play in Ricky Nelson's band on *The Adventures Of Ozzie & Harriet*, one of the first TV family sitcoms, where never a discouraging word was spoken. I had only worked with James a few times in the studio prior to that, and I wasn't a fan of *Ozzie & Harriet*, so I didn't remember who he was at first. That would change fast. James told me that

Elvis Presley was putting a new band together and asked if I wanted to come down and play.

The problem I had was this: I didn't like Elvis Presley's music. I thought he was just some Southern white guy trying to sound black. I was into black rhythm & blues and modern jazz, and by this time I was enjoying some classical music, too. I had definite opinions about what was cool and what wasn't. Elvis wasn't.

"You won't believe this," I told my then-partner, Vivian Varon, when I got off the phone, "but I just got a call to join Elvis Presley's band." We both had a good laugh. "I want to go down there and check this guy out," I added, "but I'm sure I won't like it."

"You have to be kidding!" she said. "What a waste of time."

By then I had decided that if some last-minute session came up for the night of August 18, I would call James and bow out. Fortunately for me, nothing came up, so that night I showed up with my bass at RCA Studios in Los Angeles. The studio was a medium-sized room decorated with the then-popular 'earth colors' of browns, tans, light greens, and orange, with natural wood finishes and a low drum riser against the back wall. Off to the side a bunch of guys were standing around Elvis, who was sitting on a stool.

Elvis was wearing a V-neck sweater pulled over a sports shirt and a pair of chinos. I believe James Burton was standing with them but I didn't recognize him. The rest of the guys were Elvis's 'Memphis Mafia': Red and Sonny West, Lamar Fike, Joe Esposito, Charlie Hodge, and a well known LA session drummer named Gene Pello. I had worked with Gene before: we had done some Motown sessions together, and he was a clean, energetic drummer with a good sense of time. (James later told me that his first choice of drummer had been Richie Frost, but Richie wasn't available.)

I walked over to Elvis and said: "Hi, I'm Jerry Scheff, the bass player." I remember standing in a cloud of aftershave vapor—it's amazing the things that stick in your mind. He stood up politely, and as I shook his hand I gave him the once over. What really appealed to me straight away was his warm, genuine smile. He was like a host welcoming me to his party. I don't know what I expected, but here was this charismatic, great looking guy: well dressed in a slick sort of way, but not corny. I had long hair at the time, and I was very happy I hadn't worn my cut-off jeans and sandals.

I figured I might as well confess to him right at the start that I didn't know any of his songs.

"That's all right Jerry," he replied with a laugh. "We'll have plenty of time to learn the songs. Go get set up and we'll just play some blues to start."

I was starting to like this guy, but I still didn't think I wanted to play watered-down white rockabilly music.

By the time Gene had finished getting comfortable, I was tuned up and ready to go. Also present was a talented piano player, Larry Muhoberac, who had already been hired, and a rhythm guitarist named John Wilkinson, plus James Burton, of course—he was always the first player called. In a sense, Gene and I were auditioning, but I never felt that way—there were no other bass players there.

I was expecting some vanilla approximation of the blues, but when James started with a low, growly blues-guitar riff I began to realize that this was not going to be a rehash of 50s rockabilly. There was something different going on.

I have to say right here that I was completely ignorant about what to play. When I came in, I just relied on my experience of playing black music, but with more energy. I believe that saved my ass. Elvis told me later that he wasn't exactly sure what he wanted from his new band, but knew he would recognize it when it came. It seems that Sam Phillips of Sun Studios fame had told Elvis that what he needed for his comeback was a real kick-ass, high-energy band, so I am sure that energy was one of the components Elvis was looking for. At 27 years of age, I had energy to burn.

When Elvis started singing I couldn't believe how natural he sounded. Yeah, it was a little white-sounding, but when the words came out of his mouth I could tell that he was real. His phrasing wasn't mechanical, as it can be with a lot of white singers (and even some black singers). No matter what style of music we played, he always focused on the story of the song. It was like the words and melody went through his brain, then to his heart, and then came out of his mouth. He wasn't thinking about how he looked, or whether anybody was watching him; he wasn't smiling while he was singing sad lyrics; he wasn't singing stock blues licks that Aretha Franklin had already written the book on. He was just living the song, and I was damned impressed.

Later, I became aware that Elvis just loved to entertain people. If it was just Elvis and us, he would do the stuff he thought the band enjoyed. If, say, a woman walked into the room, he would throw in some songs he thought she might enjoy.

Then came the power. In that first blues song that I played with him, Elvis built up his vocal from a sad, low-keyed beginning; when the proper time came, he opened up with an angrier phrasing that caused us, the musicians, to open up as well, producing a feeling that I had looked for repeatedly over the years but found only on occasion.

After we had played for a while and run through some of his simpler songs, Elvis said: "Well, I guess this is it." We all shook hands and patted each other on the back, and I thought to myself: You *are* going to take this gig, aren't you? I sort of felt like I had a lot to learn, and now I was enrolling in school to learn it. Elvis was my instructor, but I had a few things to offer him in return.

Gene was standing over with the Memphis Mafia, who were slapping him on the back, when Larry, the piano player, went over, whispered something to Elvis, and pointed to the far corner of the room. I looked over and saw a figure I hadn't noticed before lurking in the shadows. Elvis, being the guy he was, got up and yelled, at the top of his voice: "Whoa! Whoa! We have another drummer here. He came here all the way from Dallas. Ronnie, you go ahead and set up your drums and we'll take a longer break."

"No hurry," Ronnie replied. "Those *are* my drums."

Gene hadn't even brought his own drums along. As I left the bandstand I looked over at Gene, who all of a sudden had lost his 'I know I got it' look. The Memphis Mafia guys were frowning. I suspect they were telling Gene not to worry—we'll get rid of this guy and then we can get along with our real business.

The Dallas drummer was Ronnie Tutt, a burly, bearded, dark-haired guy. We started off with a rock song. We had just played the same song with Gene, and I couldn't help but compare the two. Now, as I have already said, I was no expert in this kind of music, but I had already decided that I wanted to play a busier, more prominent role in the rhythm section, and Gene was what many people would call a tight-ass drummer. One of the problems you get with a lot of players is that the louder they play, the stiffer they play. The trick is to be able to play with force but to stay loose—which in turn would accommodate my conception of what the bass role should be.

After we got to where a little energy was needed in the song, I found that I could play a busier bass part around what Ronnie was playing. It is rare for rock drummers to listen to the rest of the band as much as, say, a jazz drummer would, and I don't think Ronnie was any exception. Even so, it was easier for me to play what I thought was needed for Elvis's music with Ronnie than it had been with Gene. Judging by the way Elvis smiled at us, and moved to what Ronnie and I were doing, I knew we were on the right track. Ronnie says that Elvis liked the way that he (Ronnie) paid attention to his movements. There was also the fact that Gene was a New Yorker, whereas Ronnie was a good ol' boy from the South.

As we finished the first song with Ronnie, I looked over at Gene and I knew that he knew he had lost the job. And that was it. The band was formed.

I went home in a daze. I walked in the door and Vivian was waiting for me with a big grin on her face. I think she had envisioned that we would drink a couple of bottles of wine while I tickled her with stories about the 'hicks.' Instead, I told her I'd taken the job.

"You're kidding," she said. She had the most amazed look on her face.

I shook my head. I knew she wouldn't understand until she heard what we were doing. I told her that I believed that I had just started school that night—that I had a lot to learn. I invited her to come down to the rehearsal the following night. She came, and Elvis conquered.

Thus began a series of rehearsals that lasted for weeks. About a year later, some of our rehearsals were filmed, and we can be seen in all our youthful splendor on the DVD *That's The Way It Is*, which should give you a pretty good impression of what we were up to. When I went to the first rehearsal I was very relaxed—I knew I wasn't going to take the job. I was still relaxed after I decided I really wanted the job—I just shifted gears and went into a very serious mode where my powers of concentration took over.

We spent a few weeks at RCA Studios before we left for Las Vegas. I was amazed at the amount of clowning around between Elvis and his Memphis boys. I, of course, didn't feel secure enough to join in the fun—I was never a grab-ass kind of guy anyway. Some of the Memphis boys had gone to high school with Elvis; others had been in the army with him. As always, I just wanted to be seen as cool. I never really knew whether I was cool or not, but I was never the target of water balloons or the various other shenanigans that seemed to be a part of the daily routines of Elvis and the Memphis boys. I was very happy about that.

I think the fact that I was the only Yankee in the band probably put me in a category of my own. I have been told that being from the South was seen by Elvis and the boys as a determining factor when it came to being hired. I never felt that to be the case, but I guess the fact that I could play— and that Elvis liked what I played—helped overcome any prejudices.

We learned a myriad of songs in those first few weeks. A number of Memphis characters have written books about their time with Elvis, and they often describe themselves as having been responsible, to varying degrees, for both the TCB Band arrangements and the vocal arrangements. Even some of the people interviewed in Peter Guralnick's Elvis biographies tend to blow their own horns a little too loudly. Well, this may be the first time that a true description of the process has been written. And the way I saw it was like this.

The TCB Band and Elvis would work out the arrangements for the songs. Even the old 50s songs were done differently. Elvis would set the energy level for any given song. He was our conductor—all we had to do was to listen to him, watch his every move, and play in such a way that what we did matched his interpretation of the song. Easy, right? Not always. We soon found that his interpretation of a given song could change subtly from night to night, so our approach had to change, too. There were even times when, in the middle of a show, Elvis would start singing a song we had never played with him before. He loved to play 'stump the band,' but fortunately one or two of us would always know the song in question.

In 1969, Elvis's energy levels were out on the edge. He wanted us to kick him in the ass at all times, and if he felt someone wasn't contributing their fair share he would turn around to that person and symbolically bowl them over with a tidal wave of encouragement (but never anger). This didn't happen very often—we were a very tight, creative little band, and he loved what we did.

When we started working on a new song we would start by listening to it on tape. Sometimes it would be a studio version. We'd listen to the song a few times and then start discussing how we were going to turn it into *our* version. Someone would make a suggestion; someone else would throw their two cents in. We talked about the tempo and the feeling; we tore the song apart and put it back together again. Elvis, of course, was a big part of this, but he almost never dictated parts to us. He left us on our own to sink or swim. And we swam.

Things changed again when we played the song with Elvis singing full out and we, the band, adjusted what we were doing to what he was singing. This process of refinement would go on until Elvis and everyone in the band was happy, and then we'd move on to the next song. As I said, Elvis and the band were responsible for most of the rhythm parts and arrangements, unless we were working from older recordings with parts that were crucial to the identity of the song. Most of the time, these older parts were transformed by us so as to be suitable for live performance and for our own individual styles of playing.

Next, Elvis would bring the singers into the equation. I have already introduced you to The Sweet Inspirations. At that time, a white gospel quartet by the name of The Imperials were the male vocalists, and Millie Kirkham, a soprano who over the years sang on most of Elvis's recordings, rounded out the vocal spectrum. They went through the exact same process with Elvis that we, the band, had been through, using our foundation as a platform. Sometimes the sound engineers recorded the TCB Band with Elvis, so that Elvis and the singers could use the recording to work on their vocals. As with the band, the singers (and Elvis) were responsible for the vocal parts, except for when they directly echoed parts of an existing recording. The keyboard players, of course, proved invaluable to the vocalists by playing chord inversions for the singers to try out.

According to Ronnie Tutt, Colonel Tom Parker had originally wanted Elvis's Vegas shows to be a 'Hollywood extravaganza'-style production. I can just see it: lavish sets with six-foot-tall barely-dressed female dancers with three-foot feather headdresses, troupes of male dancers in tuxedos with top hats and canes, and Elvis doing a soft-shoe routine while singing 'Hound Dog' followed by a medley of forgettable songs from his movies. (We did very few of those songs over the years, by the way.)

Later, I was told, Elvis had a dream, and in the dream he was on stage with an African-American quartet of women singing background vocals. His band was out in front right behind him, and he could interact with the band and the singers as the show went on. Evidently, when the Colonel told Elvis his ideas for the show, Elvis told him that he was doing it *his* way or not at all. We did it his way.

After several weeks of rehearsals we arrived in Las Vegas and checked into the International Hotel. We still had a week or two to do soundchecks and dress rehearsals in the show room. The rehearsals before the opening were especially enjoyable: the songs were coming together and the band was already fairly tight. We were hearing the vocal arrangements come together with our instrumental parts, and of course Elvis's vocals. This hitched the energy level to a new horse. The sound was incredible. Elvis was in a great mood, and as he heard the energy build, day after day, song after song, he became even more buoyant. He was wonderful to be around at that time— kidding around, singing naughty lyrics to songs, laughing all the while. The final step was to commission orchestral arrangements to fit the revised versions of the songs that Elvis chose for opening night.

In the meantime, we spent a lot of our time at the hotel. In the evenings I gambled a little bit, ate in the restaurant, or went out on the town with friends. There were still great lounges in Las Vegas that sometimes had great music. When we first came to town, in order to be allowed to work there we had to report to the police, who took our fingerprints and checked if we were bad people or not. Sitting in the waiting room at the police station were Ike and Tina Turner and their band. They were going to play in the lounge at the International while we played in the big show room. We all spent a lot of time in the lounge when Ike & Tina were there. Great music.

Meanwhile, there was the gambling. One man who had a heavy reputation for gambling was Colonel Tom Parker, Elvis's manager. I had met the Colonel once or twice at the rehearsals in Los Angeles, but my first actual contact with him came while I was playing a 25-cent slot machine in the hotel casino. The machine had a $650 progressive jackpot on it. I had been playing five quarters a pull for about ten minutes when the Colonel walked up with two of his cronies from RCA Records. They each had a large paper bucket full of quarters; they had hit a machine hard somewhere else in the casino.

The Colonel put his arm around my shoulders and said: "Boys, I want you to meet Elvis's new bass player, Jerry Scheff." We all shook hands, but then as they made a move to leave one of the RCA guys whispered something to the Colonel, and they all turned around and dumped their buckets of quarters into the tray of my machine. After counting it, I figured they had just given me close to $1,000. This, I told myself, is going to be the greatest gig in the world.

We were due to do our first rehearsals in the big show room the following day. I was backstage, completely alone, walking down a long hallway, looking for my dressing room. As I made my way down the hall, Colonel Parker walked out of a door and then right past me, without even looking at me or saying a word. He went from giving me a bunch of money to ignoring me. I was really upset.

Later, we were all getting ready to rehearse, when Elvis walked on stage. I went over to him and told him what had happened. Elvis broke into a big grin.

"Jerry," he said, "we had a meeting last night and the Colonel found out how much money you guys are making." Evidently, Parker had told Elvis that he could put chimpanzees up on stage and the people would still love him. He barely said another word to any of the band-members for five years—and even then it was mostly grunts and murmurs.

When we, the TCB Band, came to record live albums with Elvis, Colonel Parker made sure we didn't get our names on the albums. He was probably thinking he needed to keep those goddamn expensive, uppity musicians in their place. It was widely agreed that we were probably the highest-paid backup band around at the time, although I should add that the quote about my starting salary in Peter Guralnick's book *Careless Love* is not accurate. Elvis was proud of us and enjoyed telling people that he paid us well—he, after all, was the one who agreed to the salaries.

I was not one to bother Elvis with every little problem. Later, when I thought I should have a raise, I would tell Tom Diskin, Parker's son-in-law, who worked in his office. We had a little scenario that would play out each time I talked with him about money, usually on the phone. First, I would tell him I thought I deserved a raise to x.

"Oh, I am sorry, Jerry," he would say. "We are at the salary top right now."

"Well, Mr Diskin, tell Elvis I have really enjoyed working with him."

An hour later, Diskin would call back. "OK," he would say, "Elvis said to give it to you."

This should give you an idea of how cynical the Colonel was. This same thing happened four or five times over the years. I suspect that they wouldn't have dared call Elvis about something as trivial as a raise in my salary. But I was just trying to be fair—I wasn't asking for the moon.

During the time I worked with Elvis, I did get a couple of gifts from the Colonel. If I remember correctly, the first one was a model of an old-time automobile, made in Mexico out of recycled tin cans. The second was a painting of Elvis on velvet that didn't look very much like him. I gave it to the maid in our hotel room. She loved it.

Soon after that, I think it was 1970 or 1971, we were on the road in Portland, Oregon. It was Thanksgiving Day, and we pulled up to the hotel at the same time as the Colonel. He came aboard the bus and said he'd like to buy us all Thanksgiving dinner. He walked from the front of the bus to the back, handing a five dollar bill to each person. In effect, he was buying our beverages. I heard a few people say: "Oh Colonel, you really shouldn't have." I believe my line was: "What on earth did we do to deserve this?" I don't think he picked up on any of our sarcasm.

On another occasion we had just landed at an airport, and while we were getting our carry-on luggage together, Tom Diskin came on our plane and said: "The Colonel's Learjet just landed. It's his birthday and I want to bring him on board your plane and we can all sing 'Happy Birthday' to him." We all shook our heads. No one would sing 'Happy Birthday' to him. When the Colonel passed away in 1997, I received calls from quite a few newspaper reporters asking about my feelings about his death. I said I had no feelings about it. One reporter said: "That's amazing! That's what almost everyone I've talked to has said."

In all fairness, some of the people who worked directly for the Colonel on the business end have told me that he was very kind and generous to them. I suspect that, to him, the whole thing was a big contest, and he didn't feel like he was doing his job unless he beat every last cent out of everyone— Elvis included. No doubt he rewarded the people who helped him do it.

CHAPTER 3
INTO THE FIRE

Finally, after all the rehearsals—the last being full dress rehearsals—we were backstage at the International, dressing our minds and bodies for opening night. Thursday July 31 1969: this is it, no bullshit. Do or die. The orchestra members were tuning and warming up in the hallways. Trumpet players always try to impress each other with screeching high notes, whereas trombone players blast the lowest or highest notes they can play. The brass players in our orchestra were no different. String players played snatches of classical pieces, as if they were trying to show each other that they could actually play more serious music than the crap they were about to play with us; when drummers warm up, they beat on anything they can reach, from tables and chairs to the walls around them. The halls were ringing with this cacophony, and you'd best not go to the rest room for a last-minute whiz because saxophone players love to warm up in there because of the echo effect. I have heard and smelled them before many a show. Sometimes, when I couldn't see them, I assumed they must have been in the stalls, screeching and honking and running off John Coltrane and Charlie Parker riffs at the same time—a very funny picture if you care to visualize it. Well, maybe not.

Back to the opening. Before the show we changed into our 'bop suits,' as we called them, and headed for Elvis's dressing room. We had been told that we were welcome there any time we wished to come by, and I wanted to let him know that I was with him. The tension in the room was denser than the smoke in the air and my lungs. I smoked two packs a day at that time, as did a lot of people. Elvis occasionally smoked small cigars, most of The Sweet Inspirations smoked, and many of the Memphis boys did, too.

As I remember, Elvis's dressing room was always full of smoke before the shows, but he never complained. It was the same with drinking: he didn't drink but he didn't mind others doing it. I don't think he would have been happy to have a bunch of drunks on stage with him, though, and although I don't remember ever being lectured about it, we knew that any illicit drug use had to be hidden. Elvis did not approve.

Anyway, we were all packed into Elvis's dressing room, all trying to talk at once. I can remember Elvis sitting on a couch, his knee going up and down like a piston and his hands dancing like butterflies. (He had surprisingly delicate hands.) He tended to stutter a little at times of stress, and this was a stressful time for him: "I ... I ... I ... ." All of a sudden, The Sweet Inspirations got up, kissed and hugged Elvis, and went on stage. Like bagpipers leading the Scottish clans into war, they were the first in the frontline of fire.

The Sweets and their band got a warm reception. After they left the stage it was comedian Sammy Shore's turn. I have done a few monologues out there by myself under the spotlight, so I can imagine how thick-skinned Sammy must have been to talk to 2,000-plus people who had not come to see *him*. On top of that, Colonel Parker wanted a 'wholesome' show—poo-poo and ca-ca jokes were out, so Sammy had to make people laugh with his quiver half empty.

The intercom was on in Elvis's dressing room, so while we were hanging out we could hear Sammy on stage. He finally started his closing monologue about going into a restaurant and ordering a live lobster from a tank. Sammy told the audience that when he went over to the lobster tank, it suddenly occurred to him that he was actually playing God among the lobsters. All he had to do was point his finger at one unlucky lobster and that was the end of the line for her or him.

Just as we heard "God among the lobsters" from the intercom speakers, the stage manager walked in and told us that it was time for the band to go on stage. For the remainder of the shows we played with Sammy Shore—and sometimes even when we worked together later on—no matter where we were backstage, be it in Las Vegas or on the road, when the time came we would shout "God among the lobsters time!" and head for the stage.

Finally, it was our turn, and we made our way out to the stage where our instruments were waiting for us. Elvis had played Las Vegas before, during the early part of his career, when most of his fans were too young to get in the show rooms. I had heard that he got stuck in front of an older audience—probably Jimmy Durante fans or Xavier Cugat freaks. The show bombed and I think the humiliation still bothered him, all these years later. He had no idea how the audience sitting in the show room would receive him after such a long absence from live performance—and nor, for that matter, did the rest of us. Elvis had not done many shows in front of people since 1961, but I remember hearing voices in that Las Vegas dressing room repeatedly reassuring him that the people are gonna love you, man!

I don't remember having any doubts. I had worked with some great entertainers up to that time, and I knew that what Elvis was getting ready to do on that stage would be great. Certainly, we had all done everything we could to make the show as tight and musical as we could. Almost all of us were seasoned professionals.

The opening show was by invitation only: on the other side of the curtain, just a few feet from my face, sat 2,000 handpicked celebrities, newspaper columnists, and music critics, plus assorted Las Vegas big-shots. Among those attending were Nancy Sinatra, Sammy Davis Jr, Petula Clark, Burt Bacharach, Paul Anka, Sam Phillips, Angie Dickinson, George Hamilton, Ann-Margret, Tom Jones, Shelley Fabares, Wayne Newton, and many others.

Piano player Larry Muhoberac gave the orchestra their notes and everyone started tuning up. And I do mean everyone. If you are wondering whether Ronnie Tutt was tuning his drums, he was: *thump, thomp, thamp, schmeck*, over and over again, even though we had had a soundcheck that afternoon. Drummers have a certain tuning system that we mere musicians

25

have no knowledge about. They stuff pillows inside their bass drums, moving them around until they provide just the right amount of dampening to the sound. They have holes in the front of their bass-drum heads for a mic to fit into. They sometimes use tape on the drumheads. In jazz clubs ... oh, well, we were all ready to rock. The worst thing in music for me is having to wait for a show or a recording session to start. There's a corny old saying about striking while the iron is hot. For me, it's true.

Every single member of the TCB Band, The Sweet Inspirations, and The Imperials was in the zone: we were zeroed in on—and ready to react to—the thousands of little split-second intuitive decisions and reactions that have to be made by each musician or singer in order to hopefully make up not just a successful show but a memorable show that the members of the audience might one day tell their grandchildren about. All really good entertainers, singers, and musicians have the ability to refine their senses to such a point that they enter a state almost of clairvoyance during the actual performance of an opening show. If one has to wait in place before the downbeat, that feeling may be lost.

The way the stage was set up, the TCB Band was spread across the front, just behind Elvis, with the orchestra further back. Orchestra musicians have parts to read and a conductor to lead them, so they don't have to worry about remembering each note or even the order in which the pieces are played: it's right there before them in black and white. In 1969, the conductor was Bobby Morris (he was later replaced by Joe Guercio). The conductor's job was to convey what was coming from the front of the stage to the orchestra. We had our backs to him most of the time—Elvis was our primary conductor, and we didn't use written music. Everything was etched in our brain. This took sheer concentration, memory, and muscle recall. Some of us used our instincts to play as we felt it.

Because of my upbringing in jazz, I never memorized a whole bass part and played it the same way night after night. I was always working to make the part better. When a bass part worked, I would tend to repeat it, but I was always experimenting, trying to put together a better rendition of a song—and, of course, my ears were and still are open for a new stroke of genius coming from the other players, something on which to hang a new musical hat. As I said earlier, Elvis would change what he did, subtly, over a period of time, and I would feel compelled to try to match his energy and performance and maybe help prod him to new heights. If you were to listen to early live versions of a song like 'Polk Salad Annie,' for example, and then listen to the live versions of later performances of that same song, you would hear how almost all of us—musicians, singers, and Elvis—had evolved our parts from a medium-tempo swampy feel to an almost punk intensity.

Back to opening night: Bobby Morris, the house conductor, tapped his music-stand for silence. The lights went down backstage, and I felt like my face was smashed against the curtain a foot in front of me. I wasn't nervous but I wanted that curtain out of the way so we could get on with it. I looked over to the wings and saw Elvis get off the elevator with a couple of the Memphis Mafia. He looked wonderful but his face was a plaster cast. I could see muscles twitch in his face. He was laughing nervously at the grab-ass and snappy patter the Memphis boys were peppering him with. They probably didn't want to give him time to think.

All of a sudden the curtain went up and Elvis was on stage. We were starting with 'Blue Suede Shoes.' When he got to the 'one' in "Well it's-a ONE for the money," we in the rhythm section had to play our very first note with Elvis Presley in front of an audience.

BAM!

We hit the 'one' note exactly with Elvis's voice.

"TWO for the show."

BAM!

"THREE to get ready now ..."

Ronnie played a big drum fill under "... go cat go" and the rest us came in with the perfect walk-up to Elvis shouting "Don't you ... step on my blue suede shoes!" Pandemonium!

The audience flew to their feet, clapping their hands and moving to the beat. I watched Elvis's face go from uncertainty to confidence, the statue of doubt dissolving into a euphoric smile. He knew then that people still loved him. His natural instincts took over. We were rocking in a new era of Elvis

Presley—one that did not fade upon Elvis's death. In fact, unbeknownst to us or anyone else at the time, this new period of Elvis's stardom would continue to expand to this day.

For me, those 40 minutes seemed like the doppler effect of a rocket flying by. The whole show was a blur of sweat flying, song endings, song beginnings, and Elvis demonstrating that *he* owned that stage—and indeed the whole show room, maybe Las Vegas itself. The audience response at that first show is best described by Peter Guralnick and Ernst Jorgensen in their book *Elvis Day By Day*:

> *"The response to Elvis's performance is practically cataclysmic, as Elvis is bursting with energy, falling on his knees, sliding across the stage, even doing summersaults. The celebrity audience is on its feet for almost the entire show, and rave reviews come in from all over."*

I don't remember any summersaults.

Not everyone was happy with the new sound. There were—and still are—music critics, musicians, and fans who were disappointed that Elvis didn't come out with a little rockabilly band and imitate his 50s style. Even Ronnie Tutt complained to me that the feel and tempo of the music was too over-the-top and that he would rather the band be more laid-back.

I believe Ronnie mistakenly tried to do that when I took a two-year break in 1973 and he recommended Duke Bardwell as my replacement. Duke was a laid-back good ol' boy from Baton Rouge, Louisiana, who was and is a talented singer-songwriter and bass player. He and Ronnie first met while working with Jose Feliciano. I was told that the reason that Elvis and Duke didn't hit it off was because Duke's talents didn't lend themselves to Elvis's new high-powered style. That wasn't Duke's fault. Pairing him with Elvis Presley was like pairing a perfect dust-devil to a perfect tornado. Many critics and musicians wanted to pigeonhole Elvis in a time slot that he no longer lived within. This attitude sometimes kills entertainers—even bass players.

Ronnie went on to work with Jerry Garcia and The Grateful Dead, who regularly laid themselves back by smoking dope before a show. At that time, just as wine connoisseurs keep different kinds of wine on hand, Ronnie kept six or eight kinds of marijuana in his freezer—he showed it to me. When we started a run of shows with Elvis, I could always tell when Ronnie had been playing with Garcia—it would take him a couple of nights to get his mind back up to Elvis-level intensity.

As the shows continued I got to know the rest of the band.

Pianist Larry Muhoberac was originally from Louisiana. When he was 20 he joined The Woody Herman Big Band, so I am assuming he was playing his ass off even at that young age. Larry was a 'schooled' musician— his musical knowledge covered every musical genre, except maybe hardcore classical music. He moved to Memphis in 1969, but by then he had already done some work with the Elvis Presley organization, having appeared on some of the 60s movie soundtracks.

In late 1969, Larry left the band and Glen D. Hardin took over piano duties. Larry and I didn't hang out much off stage and he was only with us a short while, but after he was gone I really missed his smooth, inventive, adaptive approach to playing the piano. He was creative and he didn't just play 'parts' and 'licks'—he played songs. There was no ham-fisted left hand in your bass face, claiming all the mid-range.

When Glen joined us, however, he brought with him a powerhouse of funny stories and a wonderful 'live and let live' personality. Glen came from Lubbock, Texas, and had played with The Crickets after Buddy Holly died. He has given me permission to tell you about some of his escapades over our 35 years of our working together—and there were quite a few.

Firstly, I will give you a brief look back to the years before he came to work for Elvis. Betty Hardin tells me that even when they met in high school, Glen was different. He was, she says, the ugliest guy in school, but there was "something about him." He asked her out to the movies but she said no because he had a reputation for drinking. He asked if she would change her mind if he quit drinking and she said maybe, so from then on, every morning, he stuck his head in the door of her homeroom class and gave her a sign that meant: "I haven't been drinking."

After a few weeks of this, Betty agreed to a night at the drive-in. When they got there, Betty says, Glen sat against the car door and didn't say a word to her. Finally, when they graduated high school, Glen asked Betty to marry him. She said no. Then, after returning from a spell with the US Navy in the early 60s, he asked her again. This time she said yes.

Glen had been a radioman on a heavy cruiser and was completely self-taught on the piano. He didn't know how to read music so he played entirely by ear—mostly country & western and rock'n'roll. He and Betty settled in Los Angeles, where Glen got a job in the house band at a country nightclub called the Palomino. Our paths didn't cross very often—we played together for Gary Paxton a few times over the years but I didn't really get to know Glen until we came together in what would soon be known as the TCB Band.

One of my favorite Glen stories dates back to when he was playing piano with the late, great singer-songwriter Roger Miller. I knew Roger—I once gave him a pair of shoes right off my feet in a recording studio in Los Angeles. Everybody liked Roger except for when he used cocaine. Everybody did it back then, but some people just couldn't handle it very well, and Roger was one of those people. Glen says that they were playing at the Palomino Club one night when Roger said something that pissed him off. It was the final straw. Glen got up from the piano, walked out to the front of the stage, grabbed the mic from Roger's hands, and said: "I am giving you the Glen D. Hardin two-week notice."

"Yeah?" Roger replied. "What's that?"

"In two weeks, you will NOTICE that I have been gone for 14 days! Goodbye."

Glen may have been unschooled when he arrived in Los Angeles, but he had a style of playing that soon caught the ears of certain record producers. He told me that one of the big revelations he had in his career was playing with an orchestra in a recording studio. After seeing these string, woodwind, and brass players in action he went to a store to buy some books on how to read and write music. He was on his way. (He even wrote some of the orchestral parts for some of Elvis's show songs.)

Glen told me that after he and Betty started their family, he knew they would need to buy a house. They needed money. Glen had been doing sessions for a record producer named Snuff Garrett, who was producing a group called Gary Lewis & The Playboys—Gary being the son of the comedian Jerry Lewis. Glen wrote four songs and submitted them to Snuff, who in turn recorded them for the next Gary Lewis & The Playboys album, and Glen made some money. He then stopped writing songs. When I asked him why, he told me he didn't need the money any more.

Glen also told me about the time his wife confronted him about having to use bed sheets for curtains in the living room while he was spending money having his boat refurbished. At the same time, he said, they were having new siding put on their house, so when Betty went to the grocery store, he went out and got the siding contractor, pulled him into the house, pointed at a dining room window, and said: "See that window? I want you to make it disappear."

When Betty got home she immediately noticed the new drywall in the living room. When she asked Glen what he had done, Glen says he pointed to another window and said: "Betty, if I hear one more word about those goddamned drapes, *that* window is going to go next."

I haven't heard Betty's response to the story, but Glen seemed to think it was pretty funny.

Being in Elvis's band in Las Vegas was a fairly powerful position, although not all of us saw it that way. I personally never went to Elvis for help with anything. I knew, though, that he was there if I really needed him. Over the years, he helped many people from the show that really needed help.

The power was subtle but palpable. If I needed tickets to the shows—say, front row seats—I knew that the maître d' would not want to give me choice seats for my guests because he knew they would probably not tip him hundreds of dollars. On the other hand, he knew that if I went to Elvis and complained, it would make him, the maître d', look like a chump, so I never really had to play my ace in the hole.

After the shows, Glen liked to shoot craps at the casino. He made a big show of not drinking before the show—or at least not obviously drinking—but afterward he had the waitresses running back and forth with scotch and water. Before he passed out, Glen would take control of the crap table. He usually had chips flying all over the place, and his energy attracted people who wanted to be where the action was fast. One night Glen cozied up to a crap table and in a minute or two the table was jumping.

I was in my dressing room one evening before the first of two shows and Glen came in with his pants and coat pockets bulging. "Jerry Scheff," he said—he likes to call people by both names. "Look at this." He started pulling handfuls of black $100 chips from his pockets.

"Where in the hell did you get those?" I asked.

He said that he woke up in the afternoon on his bed with his clothes still on and he was covered from neck to belt buckle with chips. "I must have shot their eyes out at the crap tables last night," he said. "The security guards must have stood me on a skateboard and rolled me to my room, laid me on my bed, and poured the chips over me."

When he woke up and saw all those chips, he started counting them: $3,500, $4,000 ... and then the phone rang. It was Betty, calling from Los Angeles. According to Glen, she said: "Glen, I tried to phone you all last night and you weren't in your room! I bet you were gambling all our money away!" Glen carried on counting to himself: "$5,000, $5,500 ... yup, Betty, I gambled it all away."

Rhythm guitarist John Wilkinson and I were never close friends during the Elvis years, but I liked him. He was always very polite—to this day I have never heard him say a bad thing about anyone. I am a little confused as to how he became part of the TCB band. James Burton told me that he had called John for the gig, but John says that he had known Elvis for a few years prior to that, and that Elvis himself had called him about the job. That's good enough for me.

I think that John was probably the most conscientious person on stage with Elvis. If you look at videos of him on stage, he never took his eyes off Elvis. It was almost like Elvis might pull a gun and shoot him at any moment, and John had to be ready to duck.

As I have said before, James Burton was the guy who called me about the Elvis job. James grew up in Bossier City, Louisiana. I think it would be safe to say that he was considered a child prodigy. He was playing big-time professional country music in his teens. James invented a style of guitar-picking that influenced a great deal of the country and rock guitar sounds that you hear on the radio today, only he still does it better than anyone around.

When I think of James the first thing that comes to mind is his graciousness when he is on stage with other guitar players. In later years, after Elvis died, James and I did a show with Roy Orbison that was later released on film as *A Black & White Night*. Now, Roy Orbison was like an opera singer. His voice melted out of his mouth into the stratosphere and back. He never seemed like he was trying to sing, he just did it. I played double bass behind him for this show because an electric bass would have been overkill. Even though we played kick-ass music behind Elvis, we had all played enough different styles to be able to listen to the singer and the song, and we all knew how to provide what was needed no matter what singer we were backing.

We had a stage full of celebrities who loved Roy: Steven Soles, Bonnie Raitt, Jackson Browne, Elvis Costello, Bruce Springsteen, and then us, the TCB Band. We were all thrilled to contribute our talents to the show. We had spent three nights rehearsing with Roy and had everything down to a sliver. Perfect. The first time we rehearsed with the background singers, the string section, and the percussionist was at the dress rehearsal the day of the show. After the first song, Bruce Springsteen, who was also playing electric guitar, bobbed over and yelled at us: "Where's the heat! Turn up the heat!" In other words, he wanted us to sound like The E-Street Band: loud and raucous. That would have been all wrong for Roy Orbison. I remember telling Bruce that the heat would be there as and when it was needed. (Glen says that I was much more to the point.)

Anyway, Springsteen kept bobbing over to James during the guitar solos like he was challenging James to a shootout. James was exhibiting his usual good-natured style until Bruce finally left James no choice. James played a flawless solo that sent Bruce bobbing right back across the stage.

In another part of this book I cover Ronnie Tutt's earlier career. Here, I want to tell about a harrowing time for Ronnie—and an amazing, rapid comeback from the edge.

In 1999, while preparing to do a soundcheck with Neil Diamond in Bakersfield, California, Ronnie suffered a heart attack and a stroke. He was 61 years old. After all that could be done had been done for Ronnie, I rode to Bakersfield with Stig Edgren, the producer of our Elvis: The Concert shows, which we had been touring since 1997 and which featured Elvis on the big screen and the whole 70s cast backing him on stage. We had cameramen filming us, too, so the audience was able to see us on the screen with Elvis. The only difference was that the 'big screen' show was twice as long as any we had done back in the 70s with Elvis, and we were all 30 years older. Somehow, we made it through.

Back to Ronnie: I was the only one of our band who lived close enough to Bakersfield to go see him. His wife Donna and some of his children were there. Nobody knew then if he would ever play drums again—he had had a stroke and multiple bypass surgery. Donna told me that the stroke was the big question mark. Ronnie was then moved to Los Angeles for aftercare. (Neil Diamond paid for the whole thing, including a nice condo—way to go, Neil!)

We had a tour of Australia and New Zealand booked for later in the year, which was already being advertised. The plan was for Ronnie to come on the tour, but no one knew how much—if any—of the show he would be able to play. It was decided that a great Australian drummer, Mark Marriott, would learn the music and come on the tour in order to cover songs that were too strenuous for Ronnie to play.

The best I had expected was that Ronnie would come out to play some of the slow songs. It had, after all, been only four months since his illness. Amazingly, it ended up being the other way around: Ronnie played most of the show, with Mark sitting in for some of the ballads to give Ronnie a break. By the end of the tour, Ronnie was playing most of the show—he never looked back.

One night during the first run I was standing just in front of the drums. Charlie Hodge was standing just to the right of me. Charlie had a small table with water and 'Elvis Presley' scarves that he would hand to Elvis when Elvis turned toward him after certain songs. There were also towels, because Elvis was dripping wet the whole show. Unfortunately, there was no air freshener. That day before the show, I had eaten at a Mexican restaurant. Somewhere in the middle of the show, during one of Elvis's monologues, I farted. Elvis and the audience couldn't hear it, but Charlie Hodge did. He gave me a look like I was in church, but he didn't say anything. After the next song, Elvis turned around and walked right into it. He looked at me and said: "Goddamn, Jerry!" I pointed to Charlie and whispered: "He did it." By then Elvis was turning back to the audience. We laughed about that in later years.

Charlie Hodge and I did not have a close relationship, but there were no real arguments either. The closest we came to a flare-up was because of his guitar playing. Charlie had an acoustic guitar that he strummed during the songs. He played just so he wouldn't look idle. No one in the audience could hear him. During the ballads, though, I could hear him. In fact, he strummed so loud on the ballads that he was as loud as the drums—which were being played at a suitably soft level. I had asked him many times to please play softly during the ballads because he was interfering with my ability to hear the drums. He was always on top of the beat—'rushing,' in musicians' terms.

After a few months, it became clear to me that things were not going to change, so one night I brought some wire cutters out onto the stage and placed them in an accessible spot. Just before 'Love Me Tender,' Elvis came back for some water and Charlie threw his guitar over his shoulder, onto his back, where it was caught by the guitar strap. The strings appeared right in front of my face, almost as if by magic. I couldn't help myself. I reached down for the cutters and grabbed as many strings on the guitar as I could and—*sproing!*—I cut the strings. Elvis had just turned to head back out front, and although the noise was fairly loud, I think he might have thought that Charlie had just knocked the guitar against something. In the meantime, Charlie was grabbing at the tuners on my bass, trying to de-tune it, but I was laughing and holding him away. All of this was going on while Elvis was preparing to start 'Love Me Tender.' Charlie handed his guitar to a technician, who handed him a replacement. When he started to play again, he hit the guitar twice as loud as before. Something had to be done.

A little while later, we were touring in one of the southern states where there happened to be a bait shop just down the street from the hotel. The next day, I went down to that shop to see what it was like. As I walked in the door I saw a stack of containers with wire screening on parts of them. The sign said: "Bait crickets: 100 for a dollar." I initially thought about asking the bait shop owner to pour the crickets out of the cylinder and count them for me. (Can you imagine having the job of packaging them?) Then my mind flashed with a picture of crickets flying out of Charlie's guitar on stage. I bought 100 of them. I asked the bait-shop owner what one did to keep the crickets quiet. He told me to put bread in the cage and they would be too busy eating to make noise, but they'd start singing if I pissed them off. Again, I had a vision of a quiet guitar until Charlie hit his first chord—and then mayhem, like a plague of locusts.

Charlie's dressing room was right next to mine. I knew he tuned up and then left for Elvis's dressing room before the show, leaving his guitar for a later pick-up. I planned to sneak into his dressing room, pour the crickets into his guitar, put a few slices of bread in there for a snack, and wait for the fun. Unfortunately, a few of the guys saw me come out of Charlie's dressing room and asked me what was up. I had to tell them, and they in turn told others, and very shortly Felton Jarvis, Elvis's record producer, caught up with me in Elvis's dressing room and told me that he knew what I was up to.

"Please Jerry, don't do it," he said. "If those bugs fly out onto the stage, Elvis'll freak out. He'll start steppin' on 'em and slippin' around on their guts."

The thought of that appealed to me greatly, until I realized I'd be having to look for work the next day. I called it all off. Sadly, it wasn't the last time I was foiled by a snitch in the band.

Charlie has since passed away, but a few years ago, just before he died, we played together in Italy. After Elvis's death, Charlie seemed to go into a tailspin. I didn't see him for years, and when I did he seemed agitated and tormented. The Charlie Hodge I met in Italy, however, was different. I heard that he had married, but whatever happened to him in those last months or years had definitely brought him to earth, and he landed in a bed of flowers. RIP Charlie.

CHAPTER 4
LONGHORNS

In 1970, we finished a 27-night engagement in Las Vegas and left for Houston, Texas, to start a three-day, six-show run at the Astrodome. Our transportation was provided by a wealthy Texan friend of the Colonel by the name of Mr Rose. Wearing a huge cowboy hat, he flew us—quite literally: he was one of the pilots—to the venue on his large corporate jet.

If Federico Fellini had been a Texan, he would not have been able to create anything so bizarre as our first visit to the Astrodome. The scenes from the movie *The Right Stuff*, where Vice President Lyndon Johnson throws a Texas-sized barbecue in the Astrodome for the first American astronauts and their wives—complete with a fan dancer—are a model of sanity in comparison.

Our trip to the edge began when we landed at a private terminal, outside of which sat a huge bus with Texas Longhorns mounted on the front. The inside was like a living room, with all the couches and chairs upholstered with unborn calfskins. One by one, as we got on the bus, Mr Rose presented us with Swiss Army knives with 'Rose Trucking' printed on the side. It was very clear that Mr Rose was enjoying himself immensely. He was very friendly, and I liked him a lot.

Still wearing his cowboy hat, Mr Rose climbed into the driver's seat of the bus with the Longhorns on the front and sped away from the airport. I do mean sped away: we flew down the highway, grasping our seats, and when we exited the freeway, Mr Rose did not slow down—instead, he turned on a siren and flashing lights and blew his horn at people. We were going at least 60 miles per hour on downtown streets when another siren emerged from behind us. A police car pulled up beside us and the officer driving smiled and waved at Mr Rose, beckoning him to follow. We now had a police escort. Connections!

On the day of the first show, Mr Rose drove us to the Astrodome, down a tunnel, and out onto a dirt surface where Colonel Tom Parker was waiting—in front of 17,000 people—to goose us with his cane as we got off the bus. This was the matinee show, and he literally tried to stick his cane up my ass, through my clothes. The reason that the whole vast Houston Astrodome floor was covered with dirt was because we were part of the halftime entertainment for the Houston Livestock Show & Rodeo, complete with the sounds and smells of cow and horse shit and dust. At showtime we all climbed aboard a portable stage and were hauled to the middle of the Astrodome like a bunch of yearlings for branding. We were all holding onto something. The stage was lurching and everything was falling over. The dirt floor of the Astrodome was wet from the water used to keep the dust down but I noticed after the show that my bass and amp both had a film of dust on them.

It was a strange feeling, being out there by ourselves. We couldn't see or even hear the crowd because of the distance between us and them. When we were all set up and ready to go, a Red Chevy Blazer—I had a sky-blue Blazer just like it at home—roared out with Elvis standing up, waving to the crowd from the back. When we started playing, there was a two or three-second delay from when we played a note to when we heard it come back to us. Bob Lanning was subbing for Ronnie Tutt for these shows, and when he hit a drum, it would sound small on the stage—*smack*—but then a few seconds later an enormous explosion would roll back at us. Multiply that by the sounds all the rest of us were making and it was like the world was coming to an end.

We repeated the whole thing five more times over the next three days for a total of six concerts for 200,492 people and then flew back to Las Vegas.

I didn't have too much of a social life in Vegas. I hated it. Sometimes my partner, Vivian, came to stay. I was provided with a nice room at the International (renamed the Las Vegas Hilton in 1971), but I was not comfortable having to walk through the casino—assaulted by the ringing of slot machines and the general din that blanketed the place—to get there. It was like having to walk a mile to a coffee shop or restaurant just to get a sandwich.

Vivian had a friend, Chic Masi, who was an old friend of the baseball player Joe DiMaggio. Chic had been DiMaggio's personal chef when DiMaggio was married to Marilyn Monroe. At the time he was the maître d' in the dining room of a small hotel on the Las Vegas strip called the Castaways, owned by the billionaire Howard Hughes. Chic arranged for us to move into a suite of rooms in the very back of the Castaways that had been converted for Howard Hughes's second-in-command, Robert Maheu.

Maheu was a former FBI agent and a veteran of CIA counter-espionage activities. His duties for Howard Hughes included intimidating would-be blackmailers and obtaining information on business rivals. Maheu was the go-between between the CIA and Mafia bosses Sam Giancana and Johnny Roselli in their plan to assassinate Fidel Castro in Cuba. He and his wife had lived in our Castaways suite while they waited for their home in Las Vegas to be built. We had a living room, dining room, kitchen, two bedrooms, and a fenced-in patio in the back. If we didn't want to cook, we just walked to the dining room where Chic would always have a table for us. The food was superb.

The second day we were there I discovered that all the rooms were linked by an intercom controlled from a master panel in one of the bedrooms. As Maheu had been an FBI and CIA agent, I shouldn't have been surprised, but I was. Anyway, I decided to turn the intercom on one night and listen to what Otis, our African grey parrot, was saying or singing in the next room. What I heard was a door slam and a woman screaming at a very contrite-sounding man: "You son of a bitch! I saw you stick your tongue in the ear of (so-and-so) when you were dancing with her!" The woman went on and on, with the man begging her for forgiveness until she finally gave in. The screaming gradually turned into sighs and moaning, at which point Vivian made me turn off the intercom. By then we had had a lot of laughs, however. Evidently, Maheu was so paranoid that he wanted to know what kind of people were in the whole hotel—either that or he got off on eavesdropping on other people's lives. I can assure you that, having had the chance, it is very difficult to stay away from an intercom. What you hear is mostly boring, but it's very difficult to stop.

One evening we arrived in the dining room for dinner and I noticed a lobster tank with various sizes of lobsters. One stood out. I decided to play God among the lobsters. I pointed to it and said I would like to have it. Chic laughed and said: "That lobster weighs five pounds. If you can eat it all, I will buy it for you." I did eat it all, but I couldn't eat lobster again after that for a year—and I still like prawns more.

Otis the parrot lived on top of his cage and talked up a storm. I taught him to whistle my favorite jazz song, 'Straight, No Chaser.' I bobbed up and down while I whistled it to him. He only learned the first phrase, but he repeated it over and over and over, imitating me bobbing up and down as he went. One day, Vivian and I got back from grocery shopping one day and heard Otis whistling the song, but from the wrong end of the suite. We put the groceries and Vivian's purse down on the table and followed the sound into the bathroom, where we found Otis in the toilet, bobbing and whistling. He seemed relieved to see us, and right then I realized why, because as I walked out of the bathroom I saw a man running for the back patio. Vivian's wallet, which had been in her purse on the table, was lying on the flagstones; all of her cash and credit cards were gone. I surmised that the thief had been waiting behind the door when we came in and had then grabbed the purse and riffled through it on his way out to the patio. He was over a six-foot wall before I even got outside—a cool customer!

It seemed obvious that the robbery was an inside job and that it was time to move on. I almost moved much further than I had initially planned.

Somewhere around this time I got a call from my old friend and LSD-taking buddy, Stan Bronstein, in New York. He had co-founded a band called Elephant's Memory, which had subsequently joined up with John Lennon and Yoko Ono. They needed a bass player, and John Lennon had heard me with Elvis, so Stan told me the job was mine if I wanted it. I thought about it, but I was a California kind of guy, and I was pretty happy doing what I was doing, so I turned it down.

Elephant's Memory didn't last very long with John Lennon. Who knows what kind of relationship he and I might have formed, or what working with him would have meant to my career. I will never know one way or another, but then I have never been good at what-ifs anyway. What a choice, though: stay with Elvis in Las Vegas, or join John Lennon's band in New York?

I decided to stay, and I have no regrets. As it happened, we ended up moving only to a small apartment close to the International, the Paradise Inn, which had housekeeping suites, a very large lawn area, a tennis court, a swimming pool, and something else that was and still is very rare in Las Vegas: quiet. We checked in and the place soon became home. Vivian and her son Marlo arrived with a birthday present for me: a Shetland sheepdog puppy named Moon. Moon was the perfect puppy: he intuitively knew what he was supposed to do and he did it—in the right places.

Glen D. Hardin and his wife Betty soon moved in next door with their two wonderful daughters, Laurie and Karen, who spent a lot of time in our apartment, probably because of Moon and Otis. Those were good times between the Hardins and me. Eventually, Kathy Westmoreland, the soprano singer in our show, moved to the Paradise Inn as well. We were like a little family of normality in our little hideaway in the middle of unreality. Even though we could have had free rooms at the Hilton, we chose to get out of that environment. Besides, the only time we went back to the Hilton, Otis chewed up all the phone cords.

Soon after moving into The Paradise Inn, I was asked by Nancy Sinatra to do a 30-day engagement at The Las Vegas Hilton, back-to-back with the Elvis show. Nancy wanted to use the core of the band that had played on her most recent recordings, which included probably the most prolific drummer in the history of the Los Angeles recording scene, Hal Blaine, who even managed to get his name on the Hilton marquee for the show. Also present was another icon of the LA studio system, pianist Don Randi, along with a full orchestra conducted by Nancy's record producer, Billy Strange.

The entire orchestra—and band—were to wear black-tie tuxedos. I was playing only double bass—no electric bass—as the whole show was to be 'uptown,' so to speak. Nancy was married to a Hollywood choreographer and Broadway dancer, Hugh Lambert, who produced the show. Unfortunately, in my opinion, Hugh took Nancy Sinatra on a detour away from her tremendous strengths as a pop performer.

The other guests on the Nancy Sinatra show were Frank Sinatra Jr, the great boxer Sugar Ray Robinson—tap dancing—and The Muppets. Basically, what Hugh Lambert tried to do was move Nancy into the big-time showbiz world of supper clubs and New York elegance that were, in fact, no longer big-time.

Hugh was also clearly unprepared for dealing with two of the biggest jokesters in Los Angeles: Hal Blaine and Don Randi. Hal, Don, and I had played on Nancy's most recent recordings, but Hal and Don had also worked on a lot of other projects with Billy Strange, so I guess this made him fair game for one of their pranks. During the rehearsals, they noticed that Billy kept six or seven small bottles of Perrier water lined up on the conductor's music stand. Between the dress rehearsal and the opening downbeat that night, Don and Hal emptied all the bottles of water and refilled them with vodka.

The curtain went up and we started the show, our 40 or 50 tuxedos forming a backdrop for Nancy, who was singing her songs, wearing custom-made gowns, and ballroom dancing with her husband Hugh. All of this was right out of a 30s movie. After Nancy and Hugh finished waltzing to their wedding song, Billy reached down and grabbed a bottle of 'water.' The whole orchestra knew what was coming next as vodka came flying out of Billy's mouth and splattered all over his musical scores. He must have thought that only the first bottle had been tampered with. Choking and coughing, he grabbed the second bottle, and—*sploosh*!—it was raining vodka. All of us—band, orchestra, and Muppets—were howling.

When the curtains came down, Hugh Lambert chewed us out and informed us that if he saw even a slight smile the rest of the month, we would all be fired. Someone asked if we could smile during the Muppets part of the show. Absolutely not!

I really have to flash forward here for a moment because of my admiration and affection for Nancy Sinatra. In 2002, the TCB Band played a poorly produced concert in Vienna, Austria. It was publicized as an Elvis-type show but also included Nancy Sinatra and her band. I had not seen Nancy since our show together in Las Vegas. Her pianist in Vienna was none other than Don Randi, who is at least as old as I am. We had a wonderful reunion and I was greatly moved by the occasion, especially when it came to listening to and watching Nancy on stage. Her band sounded great and—because the only time I had seen her on stage was in the Hugh Lambert production—I was amazed at her talent in a modern scenario.

Back in Vegas, we were always invited to Elvis's suite after the late shows, although I have to confess that I only went there a few times. I remember one visit when I walked into a crowd of people milling around with drinks in their hands. I got my own drink and sat down on a couch and just watched the proceedings. Elvis was not there yet, but there were many beautiful women standing around waiting for him to show up. Most of the women had their hair teased into the kind of bubble styles that Priscilla Presley was wearing at that time, as opposed to long, straight 'hippie' hair. When we were on tour we looked out across the audience at a sea of bubble hair-dos. (As time went by, this suddenly became a sea of Farrah Fawcett Majors hair-dos.)

Backstage, I noticed that a large number of the bubble-headed women in Elvis's suite were ignoring the men in the room. There was no eye contact, and anyone who did approach them—I didn't—would get the cold treatment. They were waiting for Elvis: when he appeared they became animated and bright, putting on their best show. I have to say that I never saw him do more than exchange a few words with these women. But after a certain time, when they had finally given up on the idea of The King spending all eternity with them, they turned their attentions to other pursuits: us.

Now, I have never been a prude—if you haven't figured that out by now—but then, and still today, I have a certain amount of masculine pride. If I had met a lovely woman with interests similar to mine, and a heart for the world, and I knew for sure this bright lovely woman was not there just for Elvis, I might have been tempted. But unfortunately—or, who knows, maybe fortunately—that was not to be. We all had women approaching us in casinos saying things like: "I would do *anything* to meet Elvis." Not my style!

Anyway, here I was entertaining myself on the couch in Elvis's suite when a six-foot-tall natural-blond woman came over and sat down next to me. She introduced herself and I did too. She was beautiful. I asked her what she did for a living and she said she worked at Circus Circus—one of the more family-oriented casinos in Las Vegas—at the Bed Toss.

"What is the Bed Toss?" I asked.

She said that every night she dressed in a skimpy nightgown and would lay under the covers in a bed on the casino floor. The object of the game was to hit a target with a one-dollar bill—if anyone could, the six-foot blond would be dumped out of the bed so that everyone could 'appreciate' her.

I know that everyone has to do something to get along in life, so I didn't let this put me off. I asked her where she came from, and she told me she came from Sweden but had grown up in Wisconsin. That all sounded fine until she pulled some pictures from her purse. The first one was of her standing with a rifle in hand, next to a tree from which was hanging a dead deer, tongue hanging from its mouth.

"Oh, very nice," I said, my irises disappearing into my eyebrows.

"Look at this one!" she continued, pulling out another picture that was very similar except that this time the victim was a bear with its tongue out. I assured her that if ever I needed a beautiful woman to bring home the meat, I'd be in touch.

Around this time, just before I decided to move away from Las Vegas, I received an invitation to have supper with Elvis and Priscilla at their home in Holmby Hills, Los Angeles. This was my first and only chance to spend time with them without any of Elvis's entourage around. My partner Vivian came with me and we had a very nice evening.

This was right at the time when Elvis had his big infatuation with law enforcement—and especially guns. The house was completely different from Graceland; I believe that Priscilla supervised the decorating, and from what I remember she did a very tasteful job. This is only my opinion, of course— I have never been noted for my proficiency in the decorative arts.

Priscilla and Elvis greeted us at the door and I remember thinking it was odd that Elvis was wearing a suit when we were told to dress casual. We walked through the dining room past a stand on which was perched a gorgeous, huge macaw. Priscilla asked us if we liked chili as we all sat down at a seating arrangement of a couch and easy chairs. Elvis immediately took over and, opening his coat, drew out a pistol. We all laughed and then Elvis started pulling guns out from everywhere: from under his coat, from shoulder holsters, from his ankles—he even pulled a couple out of his sleeves, which shot out on extensions when he pushed a button. Finally, out of nowhere, he produced a regulation police flashlight that squirted mace. (Not at us, fortunately.)

He was being humorous with all this, of course, and actually I was very entertained and glad that he had broken the ice. After the whole exhibition was over, Elvis got up and said he would be right back. We had just started talking to Priscilla when we heard a door shut right behind the wall we were sitting against. Then we heard a metallic *clunk*, then another, and then another. After a few more *clunk*s, Priscilla started laughing and said: "Sounds like a knight taking off his armor!" We were still laughing when we heard the toilet flush and, after a few minutes, Elvis appeared from around the corner. Priscilla let him in on the joke and we all had a good laugh together. They were both very charming, and Vivian and I soon felt at ease. I left with the feeling that—given the chance—Elvis and I could become friends.

The other scene from that night that I carry with me to this day is of a dimly lit hallway that we could just see to the end of from where we sat. At some point during the evening, Vivian gave me an elbow jab and nodded her head toward the hallway, and along came Lisa Marie, maybe three years old, wearing her nightgown and walking slowly toward us, rubbing her eyes. Anyone who has been around children has been charmed by such a scene as this. The difference in this scene was that, when she got closer, we noticed that this little girl slept with her diamonds.

CHAPTER 5
MIA, PAULA, AND THE KARATE CHOPS

I n 1973, the Elvis show went to Hawaii to film a television show that was one of the earliest to be broadcast around the world by satellite. It was watched by more than a billion people.

For some strange reason, around that time I had developed an extreme fear of flying. On January 12, however, my doctor prescribed some tranquilizers, and I was soon fuzzy in my seat and on my way across the Pacific to the Hilton Hawaiian Village hotel in Honolulu, which was right next door to the convention center where the concerts were played.

I had played in Honolulu some years earlier with Delaney & Bonnie at the Waikiki Shell so this was all somewhat familiar to me. The city had to pull the plug because the crowd would not let us get off the stage. After the Delaney & Bonnie concert, we all were invited to a large house up on the mountain to a rocking big party. At about 2:00am I wound up on the other side of the island with a lovely young blonde lady, watching the sun come up. No hanky-panky, though—just a beautiful morning in a lovely lady's arms.

My room at the Hilton Hawaiian Village looked out over the armed forces' R&R facility. I went down and had dinner before opening all the sliding glass doors, crawling under the covers, and falling asleep. I loved the feeling of the tropical breeze gently wafting over my face as I slept.

Early the next morning I awoke to the air-conditioning roars of about 20 buses idling on the street below. Every room was sold out, so I was stuck in a cocoon that could have been anywhere, as I had to keep the doors shut the rest of the time.

The rest of my time in Hawaii was fairly uneventful. By this point in my career I had played a few filmed or recorded concerts and this was, to some extent, just another concert to me. In my opinion, however, the *Aloha From Hawaii* show was one of the most consistent that we recorded. Elvis was in very good shape and his spirits were high. I played my best in this situation but, at the risk of sounding blasé, it never really occurred to me that we were playing to such a large television audience.

When I got back from Hawaii, I decided that I needed to take a break—not from Elvis, necessarily, but from the whole circus atmosphere surrounding him. I did one more Las Vegas run before telling him I had to take some time off, citing personal reasons. He took it well, but he demanded loyalty in return: if I had been leaving to tour with someone else, Elvis wouldn't have worked with me again—a point he proved by the way he dealt with Glen D. Hardin a few years later. In the mid 70s, Glen played with Emmylou Harris in between tours with Elvis. By 1976, however, Emmylou had become so hot that Glen had to make a choice. He chose to go with Emmylou. (James Burton had to make the same choice, and he opted to stay with Elvis.) Later, when we needed a piano player and Glen was available, we asked about bringing him back, but Elvis replied with a quiet but firm no.

It was during my last Vegas run in '73 that a very funny thing happened to me, and in the mind of the press I became a karate expert, according to a story that went out via UPI and appeared in the *Las Vegas Review Journal* among other places.

> *Back in his fighting-weight days, Presley could actually deliver the karate chops that he choreographed into his performances. In March 1973 he demonstrated that he didn't need all of those bodyguards that kept a watchful eye on his Vegas shows.*
>
> *It was the midnight show at the Hilton Hotel, before 1,750*

fans. Presley and his bass guitarist, Jerry Scheff, also a karate expert, immobilized and knocked to the stage floor four men who had climbed on stage. ... Presley and Scheff executed a few effective chops and punches.

The four men were then set upon by hotel security guards who were routinely stationed in the wings and at the edge of the stage. The four were arrested on drunk charges. Neither Elvis nor Scheff were injured and neither pressed charges.

"I'm sorry, ladies and gentlemen," Elvis told the audience. "I'm sorry I didn't break his goddamned neck, is what I'm sorry about."

When I read this I was afraid that some hotshot punk was going to choose me out, and not really being a karate expert I would spend a few weeks in the hospital or even worse. What really happened was this. A well-dressed man tried to climb on stage to shake Elvis's hand. Due to the fact that there had been serious threats to Elvis's life, everyone on stage was on edge. J.D. Sumner—the bass *singer*—planted his size 14 foot into the man's chest, sending him backward onto his party's table and causing food and wine to explode all over the rest of his similarly well-dressed friends.

The male members of his party were furious and charged the stage. Elvis was at the other end of the stage, standing next to me and Charlie Hodge. Charlie was holding onto Elvis's arm and, with security men doing their best to subdue the marauders, Elvis was swinging at clear air next to me, yelling "lemme at 'em," seemingly unable to break loose from Charlie, who was about half his size. Then the security guys came in and mopped up.

So how did I wind up on the front page with Elvis? I think that reporters, after the fact, must have heard 'bass singer' and assumed that I, the bass *player*, was involved. Then they did what reporters do best: they manufactured a story. I was just a victim of circumstance.

During the mid 70s, I spent several years living in Salt Spring Island, British

Columbia (more on that later). I still commuted occasionally to Los Angeles and spent a fair amount of time in Vancouver, playing record sessions and writing and playing on jingles. That continued until April 1975, when I left Canada and Vivian behind and moved back to Los Angeles, with only two suitcases to my name, to make a fresh start.

Elvis had remained very loyal throughout my two-year absence, and I had received several calls from him and from the Colonel's office during that time. This time, when he asked me back, I said yes. I moved into a studio apartment with a beautiful patio and a swimming pool. The patio was like a jungle full of tropical plants with a small flock of Double Yellow Headed Mexican parrots. It was the perfect place for a period of bachelorhood.

My first concert back with Elvis was in Macon, Georgia, on April 24 1975. There were no rehearsals and we never did soundchecks, so the first time I saw Elvis after two years was on stage at the start of the show. I don't remember thinking anything negative about his appearance or personality, but my memories of the intensity levels with which we had played certain songs in the past kicked in automatically right at the beginning of the first song. I believe it was 'That's All Right Mama.' I jumped on it fiercely just as I would have done in the past. Elvis turned around and said: "Whoa, whoa." I realized then that I was way out in front of everyone else. This all happened in the first two or three bars of the song. The whole mood of the show had changed since I had been gone. I believe that that was one of the only times that Elvis ever said anything about my playing.

It was also around this time that Elvis started saying things on stage about the soprano singer Kathy Westmoreland. They had been close at one time but had since separated. Evidently, Elvis asked her to resume the relationship, but Kathy declined. He started insinuating on stage to the audience that Kathy was being overly friendly to various members of his band. Somehow, Elvis had heard that Kathy and I were seeing each other. One night, while introducing the band, he said: "That's Ronnie Tutt on drums and Jerry Scheff on Kathy Westmoreland." Kathy was very upset by all this. Elvis was acting out his feelings of rejection on stage.

Despite his karate training and his interest in guns, I never saw or even heard of Elvis getting physical with anyone. I don't think that was part of his nature. I think he was like the kid who, angry at his parents, goes to his room and beats the feathers out of his pillow. Of course, in Kathy's case, he threw a little public humiliation into the mix. Elvis still had fun on stage, and most of the time his singing was very good and sometimes spectacular.

Elvis loved to play practical jokes on people but didn't like to be the butt of the joke himself. Ronnie and I spoke about this one night after I rejoined the band. Elvis had thrown water on Glen and Ronnie during the show the night before. We were trying to come up with ideas about how to get back at him. This was during the time when Elvis incorporated karate moves into his shows, particularly during 'You've Lost That Lovin' Feelin'.'

I started the song with a slow, simple, almost dirge-like bass part. Then Elvis would come in with the first line of the song, quiet and soulful, drenched in sorrow. The song would build over time but never get out of hand, until at the end it dwindled back down to the same quiet bass part I played at the beginning, with quiet *ohhh*s from Elvis and the singers. It would seem to the audience that the song had ended—until Elvis's right hand shot up in the air, accompanied by a loud shout, at which point he would explode across the stage like a Tasmanian devil with hemorrhoids, chopping away in a fit of anger, while Ronnie followed him on the drums.

Ronnie followed Elvis's karate moves in the way a burlesque-show drummer would accompany the bumps and grinds of a dancer. After a few minutes of this, Elvis finally raised his hand in the air and stopped: there was dead quiet for a few moments, until suddenly Elvis's arm struck down through ten imaginary karate bricks toward the floor, at which point everyone—orchestra, vocalists, band—played and sang the final chord as if it was the end of the world. I would not have wanted to be the person that had lost that lovin' feelin' for Elvis. Maybe Priscilla was on his mind.

How to get back at Elvis for his practical jokes? I suggested to Ronnie that during the big finale of 'Lovin' Feelin',' when Elvis brought down his hand for the death blow, instead of an enormous loud chord, everyone would play: nothing. Silence. Zip. Ronnie suggested that he play one quiet note on the bell of his cymbal—*plink*. So Ronnie and I went to speak to the conductor, Joe Guercio, and he in turn told the Sweet Inspirations and The Stamps Quartet. When we went on stage that night, everyone except Elvis knew what was up.

When I started up 'Lovin' Feelin'' on the bass, I had a huge urge to giggle. I couldn't even turn around on stage because I was afraid if I looked at anyone else we would all collapse like a bunch of hyenas on laughing gas. Elvis started singing. It was too late to call off our prank. The song continued as an exercise in melancholy until Elvis shot his hand in the air with a bellow. The anger came out in Elvis's voice and the karate chops grew in intensity until he was a blur flying across the stage. Finally, drenched with sweat, he lifted his arm. Silence held for a few seconds until, with a mighty blow, Elvis sent his fist flying toward the stage lights, and—*plink*.

The audience had no idea what was happening. Elvis stayed low and looked back at us. Everything was quiet, but his look said: "I am going to do this one more time, and if you don't play the loudest final chord in the history of music, I'll kill you!" And so Elvis started his karate moves again, Ronnie played the accompanying drum fills (although perhaps a bit harder), and the rest of us looked around: some of us wanting to go for another *plink*, others shaking their heads. But we didn't have the guts to do it again. When Elvis's hand came down this time, we blew the roof off the place. Once again, Elvis had had the last laugh, but he never said a word about the incident.

This is not a book about sex and drugs, but there are a few stories that I think belong here just because they describe the atmosphere of the time and the sorts of characters I met during my time with Elvis. One time in the late 70s, we were playing a concert in Milwaukee, Wisconsin. When we finished the concert and came back to our hotel, Ronnie Tutt and I were approached in the lobby by a young girl and two women in their thirties. The younger one introduced herself as Mia, and said the other two were her aunts. Mia was beautiful but she looked very young. She told us that her father owned some jazz clubs in town and asked Ronnie and I to go to one of them with her. We thought that sounded great, so we went to our rooms, changed out of our rhinestone-studded bop suits, and came back down to meet the ladies, who in the meantime had hailed two taxis.

As we pulled up to one of the clubs, we noticed a long line of black Cadillacs with Italian flags out front. A wave of very well played light jazz wafted over us as we entered the club. The décor inside the club was like that of an upscale American steak house—it was a familiar scene for me. There was a long bar across the side of the room where ten or more beautiful women stood. I noticed right away that tall dark men in dark suits and shades would go over to one of the girls, whisper something in her ear, and then they'd go out through a side door. That explained the Cadillacs.

Mia pulled Ronnie and me over to a bland-looking man—think a balding Robert Duvall in his fifties—and introduced him as her father: the head Mafioso in Milwaukee. She told him who we were, too, and he immediately summoned someone to show us to a table that looked like it was reserved for special guests. Mia and her aunts joined us and we were served with drinks and antipasto right away.

There was an Afro-American jazz trio playing that night and Ronnie and I enjoyed listening to them. Then came the cruncher: we were introduced by the piano player as Elvis's rhythm section, whereupon everyone in the place urged us to get up and play. Little did they know that Ronnie and I had been in this situation many times before. We weren't just rock'n'rollers.

After we had survived the trial by fire, we could do no wrong. We played a few songs and then left the bandstand to waves of applause. Mia's father was very congratulatory. He asked where we lived and we told him Los Angeles. He gave us both business cards with his name and phone number on the front and 'The Golden Cockatoo, Long Beach, California' on the back.

"If you ever need *anything*," he told us, "call these people and tell them who sent you."

Ronnie and I said goodbye to Mia, her father, and her aunts, and we were given a ride back to our hotel in one of the black Cadillacs with an Italian flag on the back. We had had a great time and had acquitted ourselves favorably but thought that would be the end of it. We were wrong.

The next morning my phone rang. It was Mia. She said she knew we'd be in Chicago the following night and that I should expect her at my hotel there at noon. I was floored.

"How old are you, Mia?" I asked.

"I'm 16 but don't let that bother you," she replied.

"Don't let that bother me?! Don't you dare show up in Chicago. If you do, I won't know you!"

She didn't show up, and I was greatly relieved.

Flash forward six months. We were back in Las Vegas and had just finished a show when a waiter came backstage with a note. "Jerry: this is Mia from Milwaukee. My father and I are out in the main bar. Please come and have a drink with us."

At that time, when I had no business reason to be in Las Vegas, I retreated to an elegant A-frame house 90 miles away in Mount Charleston, Nevada: big trees, wild horses, ice caves, and skiing in the winter. I loved to see the herds of wild horses running across the painted hills in the moonlight. I wanted to get back there but I decided to stop by the bar for a quick hello-goodbye.

Mia looked fabulous. Her father seemed like a very gentle man but I suspect he had an 'in' with the Las Vegas concrete manufacturers. They invited me for a drink but I was already a little high on mescaline and I had a long way to drive.

"I'd love to go with you and see where you live," Mia said after I'd explained all of this. I was ready to tell her that I didn't think that was a very good idea when her father grabbed my arm and nodded as if to say: "Go ahead, it's all right."

I was floored: OK, how do I get out of this gracefully? I decided to drive Mia up to Mount Charleston, offer her a Coke, and then get her straight back to Las Vegas before her father could imagine any scenarios of sex and debauchery with his underage daughter.

I had to go to my dressing room and grab my toilet kit. Mia insisted on going with me. Her father gave me a smile that said: "Go ahead, you're a smart boy."

Twenty minutes later, Mia and I were headed north on the Tonopah Highway—a very dark, deserted Tonopah Highway at four in the morning. Some stretches of the road are so straight that you can see for miles in every direction. About 15 minutes into our drive, I looked into the rear view mirror and saw headlights far behind us. I started to get worried. When I slowed down, the headlights slowed down; when I sped up, they sped up.

Eventually I called Mia's attention to the situation. She was infuriated. She told me to pull over right away, but I had heard too many stories about people disappearing in the Nevada desert. I kept my foot on the accelerator. Mia screamed at me until finally I stopped off the road. The headlights pulled up behind us.

Mia jumped out of the car and ran screaming at the two men sitting in the car behind us. Before she was out of my hearing range I heard every swearword and insult in her arsenal. The two men turned their car around and sped away, back toward Las Vegas. I knew then that if I touched Mia I was a dead man. She was a very spoiled little girl.

Keeping an eye on the rear view mirror, I floored my Blazer toward Mount Charleston. I didn't have that lovin' feelin' on my mind—I was terrified! We turned off the highway and headed up the straight two-lane road to the house, past the herds of wild horses, past the ice caves, past the big trees. My treasured early-morning drive flew by and I didn't see any of it.

I unlocked the kitchen door and we walked into the house. It was cold—not freezing but uncomfortable. I got Mia a Coke out of the refrigerator and had a stiff slug of vodka from the freezer. I showed her around the place until we got to the bedroom, where she saw the fireplace and wanted me to build a fire. Underage girl, father with connections, bedroom fireplace? Hello, dummy! Get the fuck out of here!

I hustled Mia into the Blazer and raced back to the Las Vegas Hilton, where her father was still waiting for us in the lounge. Mia was very angry with me but her father was all smiles—he gave me the thumbs-up as I left. I never saw either of them again.

▬

I had another encounter with 'the boys' in Florida around 1975. I had just rejoined Elvis's band and we were in Lakeland to do a concert. The night before, someone had met two young ladies on vacation from Detroit, Michigan. I was sitting by the hotel pool when a member of the band—let's call him Dan—approached me with the two girls. They were both beautiful, but the one that was free was one of the loveliest women I had ever seen. Her name was Paula.

I immediately surmised that Dan and the other girl had set this up so that, if Paula liked me, they could leave her with me and go do whatever they were going to do. I guess she felt safe with me because she gave the nod to them and all of a sudden we were alone. We ate dinner together that night and Paula told me about herself. She was a 22-year-old divorcee of Polish heritage who worked as a belly dancer in an Arab club to put herself through court-reporting school and was the mother of two little girls. A Polish belly dancer? How exotic is that? She had been through one failed marriage to a Mexican man, had since been dating an Arab guy, and was now suggesting that I get a deeper tan.

I should have seen the brick wall as I ran toward it with my head lowered, but I was smitten: blonde hair, high Slavic cheekbones, green eyes, great personality, and a wonderful laugh. About what followed, no explanation is necessary.

The next day, Paula and her girlfriend followed the Elvis tour to Atlanta, Georgia. We had to part ways there but I had Paula's phone number in Michigan so I laid in a supply of suntan lotion and basted my way through the rest of the tour.

A couple weeks later, with the tour drawing to a close, I called Paula and told her I'd like to stop off in Detroit to see her on my way back to Canada. She was lukewarm about the idea but I wouldn't take no for an answer. There I was, a lily-white bass player smelling like cocoa butter and chlorine pursuing a Polish belly dancer with a preference for Mediterranean-looking men.

I knew that the tour's comedian, Jackie Kahane, was also of Polish extraction, so I had him teach me a few endearments in Polish. Jackie told me he knew some people in Detroit who would take care of me while I was there. I was all set. When the tour ended I flew straight up to Detroit and Paula picked me up at the airport. She dropped me off at a hotel and told me she was tied up until the following evening.

In the meantime I called the Lindell Athletic Club to arrange to meet these friends of Jackie's. When I told him who I was, the guy on the phone said: "Get your ass over here so we can get a look at you." I grabbed a cab and found myself in a bar decorated with pictures of the most famous Detroit athletes of years gone by. The smell of the grill was overpowering: burgers, fries, hotdogs, steaks. The Lindell AC was not quite like the sports bars of today but it may well have been one of the first. It was opened in 1949 by the Butsicaris family, although somewhere along the line a local 'businessman' with certain connections invested in the club.

A man came out from behind the bar and introduced himself as Jimmy Butsicaris. Right away Jimmy was impressed that I played with Elvis. He was extremely nice to me—it was as if he was a long-lost uncle. He kept offering me food and drinks and when some of his friends gathered around I answered questions and we laughed a lot. When they found out I was from California, they started to give me a bad time about the 1974 World Series, which was between two California teams, The Los Angeles Dodgers and The Oakland Athletics.

Jimmy showed me around the place, pointing out the memorabilia on the walls between the pictures: signed hockey sticks, baseballs, footballs, even a bronzed jockstrap that had belonged to Wayne Walker of the Detroit Lions. Another famous football player connected to the club was Alex Karras, the Lions lineman suspected for making bets on football games. He was initially ordered to stay away from the Lindell AC but instead ended up buying a share in the club and tending the bar there. Later, he became an actor, most famously playing Mongo, who knocks out a horse with one punch in *Blazing Saddles*.

After eating two steaks and drinking what must have been half a bottle of gin plus a few shots of grappa I went back to my hotel, where I had been told to have my date meet me in the lobby at 8:00pm. Paula was on time, and we were sitting talking in the hotel bar when a man in a black suit walked up and asked us to follow him. He led us out front to a black limo that had in it a freshly opened bottle of Italian sparkling wine. And off we went.

The driver took us to a small, elegant Italian restaurant where we were greeted by the owner, the maître d', and three waiters all in a row. Their faces were naked with lust for Paula. We were escorted to a secluded table and asked about what we'd like to drink. Paula opted for Asti Spumante, an Italian sparkling wine, but after tasting it she said she preferred the wine from the limo. It was on our table in under two minutes. Later, when I asked for the check, the waiter told me it was on the house. I tried to leave a large tip but that too was refused.

The following evening I went to the Arab club to watch Paula dance. She was beautiful and obviously admired by the Arab clientele. I had had an interest in Arabic music for quite a few years and had hung out with Arab students from UCLA and USC in a club in East Hollywood, where the dancers were accompanied by a four-piece ensemble consisting of a male singer, an oud player, a doumbek drummer, and flautist. They sounded very soulful—if I closed my eyes I could imagine being in the desert with the Bedouins. As Willie Dixon almost said: "Arabic music has the same feel as the blues."

Paula, on the other hand, danced to a recording of an Arab orchestra with violins and clarinets. She was a much better dancer than the 'Hollywood starlet' types you'd get back in LA, but this was still not quite the real thing. After we left the club I suggested she might like to start dancing to a recording of a smaller, more primitive ensemble, because I liked to smell the camel shit when I listened to that sort of music. She laughed but I'm not sure whether she ever changed it or not.

By now I knew that I had made a mistake in coming to Detroit. I had not been allowed to meet her daughters or invited into her private life in any way at all. The next morning I made plane reservations and told her I was leaving. She apologized for her aloofness and asked me to stay, but by now the fog of wishful thinking had lifted and I knew it was all wrong. She drove me back to the airport and I never heard from her again.

CHAPTER 6

THE JUNGLE ROOM

O ne night in 1976, we were flying somewhere on Elvis's jet, The Lisa Marie, when I asked why he hadn't recorded more rock songs. "I can't find any I like," he said. Right then and there I decided that I was going to write a new rock song for Elvis. I went back to the beach in California, sat down on the balcony, and about two hours later had written 'Fire Down Below.' (This was before the Bob Seger song of the same name came out.)

I wasn't aware that, for months, Elvis's record company, the Colonel, and record producer Felton Jarvis had been trying to get him back into the recording studio. Elvis, it seems, had been very elusive—evidently lagging behind in his obligations to provide a certain number of finished songs to RCA.

As far as I could see, it had been some time since Elvis had truly wanted to sing his hits from the 50s. When we rehearsed songs like 'Blue Suede Shoes' and 'Hound Dog' he tended to want to put them together as a fast-tempo medley, as if to get through them as quickly as possible. Over the first year or two, he added a few more raucous songs to the show—'Polk Salad Annie,' 'Suspicious Minds,' 'Burning Love,' plus some old blues songs like 'Steamroller Blues' and 'Never Been To Spain'—which we did in a very tough way that the audiences loved. Very few new 50s-style songs came to light, however. It was very apparent to me that the 1969 Vegas opening was

Elvis reinventing himself as a more mature entertainer. He had no desire to go back to 50s rockabilly.

When I brought 'Fire Down Below' to Felton Jarvis, he said: "Jerry, this will be another 'Burning Love.'" It had not occurred to me that Elvis might have decided to further refine—at least in his mind—his choice and style of songs. He had already switched to doing songs like 'My Way,' 'What Now My Love,' 'The Impossible Dream'—it's not that they weren't good songs, but if he really wanted to reinvent himself one last time, singing Vegas show room songs was not the way to do it. Rock fans and critics were less than thrilled by this change, with some accusing Elvis of selling out to Las Vegas.

The hybrid effect of the jumpsuits didn't help. I don't know how Elvis felt about wearing star-spangled outfits that accentuated the *normal* middle-aged spread that everyone has to deal with, but they screaming to be changed as he sang songs like 'Softly As I Leave You' or 'Bridge Over Troubled Water.' The jumpsuits gave me the impression of a bullfighter using his cape to maneuver Bambi to a violent death.

And so it was that, in presenting Elvis with another macho, strutting song that didn't really suit a man entering his forties in pursuit of legitimacy, I wound up accidentally in cahoots with the Colonel, Felton Jarvis, and all the other hangers-on in whose interests it was for Elvis to keep riding a dead horse. What would Frank Sinatra have done if he was being pressured from all angles to sing 'Strangers In The Night' right up to his death? (By all accounts, Sinatra hated that song, and had been trying to sabotage it with silliness when he added the 'Scooby Dooby-Doo' part at the end—only for the song's producer, Sonny Burke, to declare that he loved it and decide to keep it in.)

The only way to get Elvis back into the studio, it seemed, was to bring the studio to him, hence the Jungle Room sessions, as they later became known. Elvis had a room in his home that was decorated with animal prints, with a leaky waterfall at one end. The plan was to bring in a 16-wheeler filled with state-of-the-art recording equipment, park it next to the house, and run cables through the windows and doors into the now infamous Jungle Room, where all of the musicians and singers were sitting or standing in front of their allotted microphones, ready to rock.

Now, I am a little hazy about dates and what happened when, but I remember the actual events. The first time I had to travel to Graceland to record, I was booked into a Los Angeles session during the day and had to grab a flight to Memphis straight after that to get me there in time to start recording with Elvis—who had always been a night owl—after dark.

I was driven straight from Memphis Airport to Graceland, but when I got there Elvis wasn't ready yet, so I ate some dinner and shot pool for an hour or two in an adjoining room. Finally, somebody announced that Elvis was on his way down. I went back to the Jungle Room and tuned my bass. Apart from a few hours sleep on the airplane, I had been awake for about 20 hours by now and I was ready to drop.

I was quite close at the time with David Briggs, one of the keyboard players, and I asked him if he had any amphetamines. He reached into his pocked and handed me a pill, which I stuffed straight into my mouth. David then went around the room and told everyone, including Elvis, that he had just given me a Quaalude (muscle relaxant) and that they should watch me melt into my seat. We started the first song and I kept looking for that first rush from the pill but soon realized that I was heading the wrong way. My mind was telling me what to play and when to play it, but my arms and fingers were playing to their own instincts. Finally, my hands just slid off the fingerboard of my bass, and as I looked up I could see everyone laughing their asses off.

As it happened, that take of the song—I think it was 'Way Down'—was great except for the bass part, so somebody picked me up and brought me some coffee and an amphetamine. After a break I replaced the original bass track, which had sounded like snakes crawling across the strings.

There were a few other incidents of note during the second group of sessions at Graceland. It was then that we tried to record 'Fire Down Below,' which as I've said already was a throwback to the type of songs Elvis had recorded in the late 60s and early 70s and probably no longer wanted to have anything to do with. Today, I'm sure with all my heart that Elvis just wasn't comfortable with singing this sort of song this late in his career—it just didn't fit his image of himself. Nevertheless, we started rehearsing it and worked for an hour or two before Elvis said he needed a break, and I headed down to the pool room.

About an hour later, Charlie Hodge came and told me Elvis wanted to see me in his bedroom. He told me that he was too tired to go on but if we laid down a good track he promised to put a vocal on it. He never did, of course. We went to Nashville months later and sat waiting for hours for Elvis to show up. He finally got there, walked around a little bit, picked up some headphones (which he hated), threw them down, and walked out the door.

Felton Jarvis's wife later said that Felton had carried the master tape for my song with him for a couple of months in the hope that Elvis would put his vocal on it, but it just wasn't to be. I was very sad at the time but I now understand what he was going through. Having to sing 'Fire Down Below' in a spangly jumpsuit in 1976–77 would have been a double indignity for him.

Jumpsuits aside, what Elvis did like to wear was a police uniform. On the last night of the Jungle Room sessions, Charlie Hodge told me that Elvis wanted to see me again. I knocked on the door of his room and was welcomed in to meet five or six officers from the Denver Police Department who were sitting around the bed. Elvis was dressed in a captain's uniform with a cap full of gold braid. He introduced me to the officers before asking me to step into the clothes closet, which was about the size of my living room in California.

Elvis looked through some clothes until he came to five or six suits all alike except for their color. He pulled a green one off the rack and told me to try it on. The suit was a *Super Fly*-type suit with fur cuffs and a hat to match. The hat was fur-trimmed with a rhinestone pilgrim-style buckle on the front. I asked Elvis where he got the suits, and he told me that he and the Memphis Mafia had been walking down a street somewhere when they passed a shop window.

"Hey, look at those suits!" he had said. Three days later they were in his closet, but he had never worn them. Fortunately, the suit he pulled out was too big for me, so he picked out a velvet jacket for me instead. He had not quite given up on the *Super Fly* suits, however, and soon found out that they did fit J.D. Sumner and The Stamps Quartet. By the time Elvis had finished dressing everyone, none of us could keep a straight face—there was police captain Elvis, the *Super Fly* Stamps, and the rest of us who knew we were not going to get anything else done that night. The sun was coming up and Elvis started arranging everyone's transportation home. When it came to J.D. and The Stamps, he told Charlie Hodge to go get a white stretch limo and pull around to the front porch. He then presented the keys to J.D. and told him the limo was a gift.

As the sun rose we all escorted J.D. and The Stamps—all still in their suits and hats—out to the limo and waved with tears of laughter as they headed back to Nashville. J.D. later said that they had gotten hungry on route and pulled into a McDonalds. As they left, the person in the drive-thru window said: "Y'all be cool—no, wait, you already cool!"

CHAPTER 7

BOOGIE-WOOGIE AND THE TUBA

I n 2004, my wife Natalie and I were standing on a hill overlooking the neighborhood where I lived from when I was two until I was fourteen. I pointed out various landmarks as we walked through Sunrise Memorial Cemetery past a Spanish Civil War monument with cannons protruding from its concrete base and short stubby mortars at ground level that we, as children, used as urinals. The whole area had been one big playground when I was a child.

We Scheffs lived in a housing project on a hillside in Vallejo, California, during and after the waning years of World War II. Our neighbors were mostly government workers at Mare Island Naval Shipyard, which was just across the hills from us, hence our project's name: Federal Terrace. Everybody knew everybody there, so our parents gave us a little more freedom to roam than most children have today. If we happened to get in a tight spot, there was always someone from the neighborhood to pull us out.

Amazingly, Federal Terrace looked almost exactly the same in 2004 as it had in my childhood, except that the old houses, including ours, had been turned into condominiums. The old wartime grittiness had given way to flowerbeds and fresh paint.

Natalie and I were in town to have lunch with my Federal Terrace Elementary School music teacher, Douglas Fehler, and my Vallejo High School and Vallejo Junior Symphony conductor, Virl Swan. They were both in their nineties. It was a sweet reunion after all those years, and a very timely one, as it turned out, because we lost Virl shortly thereafter. He died of prostate cancer, about which he and I were able to compare notes before he died. I had received the same diagnosis seven years earlier, but my surgeon had been able to adeptly remove the cancer. I told Virl the story of my diagnosis and he and I laughed knowingly in the way that only two marked men can.

My cancer story starts in the 80s, when I was touring with John Denver. Every year we did a Christmas tour. John lined up a children's choir in each city to sing carols along with us and the audience. At the soundcheck each afternoon, the children would practice coming on and leaving the stage, and some of them would be standing on risers right behind the piano player, Glen D. Hardin. He and I loved to tease and make faces at the kids.

In one particular city I noticed a little girl of about six or seven who had a cast on her leg. Her mother was helping her out onto the stage, and they ended up standing right behind me. I couldn't resist—I had to make contact. I walked over to her and asked: "What happened to your leg?" This was when I was starting to lose my hearing, plus it was noisy on stage, so when her mother mouthed something to me, I heard "cancer." I felt as if the weight of the world was falling in on me.

After the soundcheck, I looked at Glen and said: "Isn't that terrible about that little girl having cancer?" Glen looked me in the eye and beneath the laughter I heard him say: "Jerry, her mother said 'soccer.'" I got a lot of laughs out of that story.

Fast forward to the 90s and my older brother Bill calling to tell me he had been diagnosed with prostate cancer. Not only that, but we had a first cousin who had been diagnosed with prostate cancer, too, but he had died of heart failure before the cancer could get him. It looked like we had some hereditary genes that weren't behaving.

"Jerry," Bill said, "pardon the pun, but you better get your ass to the doctor and have a checkup."

Finally, after about two weeks of bitten nails, my doctor called and gave me the news: he had found several tumors but they were still very small.

"Book me a bed," I said, "and let's get rid of them."
Later that evening, after I had mulled the whole thing over, I called Glen.
"Guess what," I said. "I have soccer."
He knew exactly what I meant.

On the way to lunch with my 90-year-old music teachers, Natalie and I drove past Federal Terrace Elementary and found that it was still functioning. The sight of it took me back to 1949, when I was first infected with the music virus.

One day that fall my mother, Lois, took me to meet Mr Fehler, who in turn introduced me to the tuba. Looking back, I think maybe he was an excellent salesman as well as a music teacher: he *needed* a tuba player for the school orchestra. Maybe, if I'd been older, I would have chosen an instrument more suitable to advertising my masculinity and scoring with girls—the drums, say, or a baseball bat. To my eight-year-old eyes, however, that glorious hunk of coiled brass was the most magnificent thing I'd ever seen, and I was thrilled to have it.

The school orchestra rehearsed every Friday. I won't even try to explain what we sounded like—even Stephen King would have been at a loss for words to describe the dismal *screech* and *squawk* as we tried to develop our latent muscle-memory. It must have been hard for our parents, who couldn't escape our astringent little monthly recitals. We cleared their sinuses, I think—or at least I seem to remember them blowing their noses a lot.

The tuba stayed at home all week until I had to wrestle it into school on Friday mornings ready to play 'Twinkle Twinkle, Little Star.' My memories of my journey to school that fall have me slogging through the soggy, orange leaves that coated the sidewalks and clogged the gutters. I usually walked up Selfridge Street, with its rows of trees and institutional two-story buildings overlooking ragged lawns that sloped down to the sidewalks below. Each building housed four families, each family shared a covered stoop, and every Friday morning I looked forward to seeing the smiles and pointing fingers of hair-netted housewives sitting outside in their house robes and slippers, smoking cigarettes, drinking coffee, and maybe flashing a little thigh here and there. They watched me struggling along with my tuba, and I knew they thought I was cute.

I, of course, was hoping to impress whoever was looking. With no case to protect it, the tuba was usually wet at that time of morning, and my clutching and grasping as I walked along playing caused the slippery horn to slide down my legs to where my knees tried to catch it as the mouthpiece bumped up and down against my mouth.

One morning, as I was staggering along blowing foghorn sounds, an angry man threw a shoe out of a second story window and told me to shut the fuck up. His aim was accurate. My mother told me later that she had received some complaints, too—some people worked all night, she said, and were trying to go to sleep in the morning. That was the end of my early morning concerts.

As I approached adolescence, I started to wonder how it had all started: how did prehistoric audiences discover the connection between rhythmic sounds and the bump'n'grind? For a rhythm & blues musician, this can be like reading the first description of the theory of relativity. Can you imagine the first attempts? Perhaps 10,000, 50,000, or even 100,000 years ago, one of our ancestors was the first hominid to wiggle his or her ass to music. Maybe it happened in the trees—a sort of slam dance in the canopy.

I still think about these things because, for a large part of my life as a musician, I've profited from my forebears' discoveries, both monetarily and in my personal life. Without getting into the old argument of which came first—the music or the ass-wiggling—I think it's safe to say that my earliest music-making predecessors discovered through trial and error that log-beating, stone-rattling, stick-scraping, gourd-shaking, gut-twanging, and ululation produced sounds and rhythms that encouraged people to throw little all night community sock-hops, after which they bashed or fucked each other's brains out, depending on their mood at the time.

So how did I—an innocuous little approval-seeking, pimple-faced, white tuba player—become an aficionado of 'black' music in the 50s, go on to embrace the 'make love, not war' sex-and-drugs culture of the 60s, and eventually wind up playing bass for Elvis Presley, The Doors, and Bob Dylan in the 70s? The answer's simple: I reached puberty and discovered that girls weren't sexually attracted to tuba players.

There were other influences along the way. We had a piano at our house—a black upright built at a time when elephants were considered expendable. One day in 1951, when I was ten years old, I heard my brother Bill stomping his foot and playing what was, to me, a new kind of music. I believe this was the first time in my life I ever wanted to wiggle my ass to the beat.

When I asked Bill what he was playing, he said something like: "This is *jigaboo* music—it's called boogie-woogie." (Knowing Bill, he probably jumped up and scared the crap out of me on the word 'jigaboo.') Later, I know I ran around our all-white neighborhood shouting "jigaboo" and "boogie-woogie" at my friends who, after a lot of smirking and finger pointing, added those words to our standard racist jargon. Needless to say, we lived in segregated housing back then.

Bill learned to play boogie-woogie from his friend Jerry Cunningham, who had been affectionately nicknamed Toad by his family on account of his hunched back (probably the result of tuberculosis). At 14, Toad was already an accomplished piano player. I became a fan from the first time I heard him, and I begged Toad and Bill to teach me, but I couldn't play with enough precision to make me want to tap my toe, let alone wiggle my ass.

When I talk about moving to the rhythm of music, I'm not talking about the way people move and pat their toes to polkas and hoedowns. I once heard a fiddler describe this kind of toe tapping by shouting: "We're gonna piss a puddle and stomp it dry!" To me, the kind of Caucasian rhythms that cause people to piss a puddle and stomp it dry are 'up and down' rhythms: they make people want to move their bodies as one unit, usually in up and down motions. (The old expression about people dancing like they've got broomsticks up their asses comes to mind.)

Boogie-woogie, on the other hand, is played with what I would call 'sideways' rhythms, like jazz and blues, which cause dancers and onlookers to spontaneously move selected parts of their bodies from side to side and front to back, usually in a loose, sensual manner. In fact, since the early 20th century, whenever they've had a choice, most white adolescent Americans have chosen African-influenced 'sideways' rhythms as a means of advertising their sexuality. Their parents have not always approved. (Take one Elvis Presley on *The Ed Sullivan Show*, for example.)

Don't get me wrong: over the years I've developed a great love for country and bluegrass, and I think European folk music and social dances have their own charms. In my adolescence, however, I was like most young people—I was interested in the 'mating ritual' aspects of social dancing. (Whoever heard of two horny teenagers jumping into the back seat of their car when Earl Scruggs or Lawrence Welk came on the car radio?) To me, it always came back to these mating rituals. Polkas, two-steps, and cotton-eyed joes paled in comparison to the sideways movements of the jitterbug. The crux of the matter is this: with the exception of the hula, folk dancers don't wiggle their asses. I don't remember ever seeing anyone waltz while cleaning the house, but I know plenty of people who shake their booties to rhythm & blues or rock'n'roll as they vacuum their wall-to-wall carpets.

In my house, I might've been taking a bath while Louis Jordan's 'Choo Choo Ch'Boogie' came chugging through the walls, or making my first feeble attempts at playing the tuba to the tune of 'Caldonia.' Thanks to my brother Bill, black music gradually slipped under my skin and became a familiar and necessary part of my life.

Bill and Toad got into black music by listening to the black radio stations from Oakland, California. I naturally followed their lead. When they heard a song they liked, they headed over to Love's music store on Lower Georgia Street in downtown Vallejo. Love's was the only black record store in town, and even though they didn't carry a big stock of records, Bill's collection grew. To this day, he remembers songs like Amos Milburn's 'Chicken Shack Boogie,' Hadda Brooks's 'Swingin' The Boogie,' and Roosevelt Sykes's '"44" Blues.' When his tastes expanded to include artists like Muddy Waters and Howlin' Wolf, Gene Ammons and Earl Bostic, Jimmy Forrest and Louis Jordan, I was right there with my ears and my heart wide open.

I consider these memoirs to be a blueprint of my musical growth, rather than a standard autobiography, but I feel I should mention the rest of my family. My father, William Graham Scheff, did not play a prominent part in my musical nurturing—if he had, I would have become a tuba player for Lawrence Welk. He was an engineering draftsman who worked for various companies around the San Francisco Bay Area during and after the war. He came home mostly on weekends, always dressed in a sharply pressed suit with matching fedora, and when he walked through the door he usually carried a large paper bag full of candy bars for us to fight over. He was always surrounded by a cloud of Old Spice, Seagram's whiskey, and Sen-Sen breath mints, the aromas of which, along with the paper-bag smell of the candy bars, have distilled to become the essences of my early childhood memories about him. Whenever he picked us up, cuddled us, kissed our cheeks, or yelled at us, he reeked of those odors.

My dad had been part of a surveying crew marking out future highways in Colorado when he married my mother. Years later, her eyes softened as she told me stories of them climbing the Rocky Mountains on horseback as newlyweds. She gave me a familiar look that I knew meant 'you better believe what I am telling you here,' and she told me that if she had to it all over again, she would not change a thing. My dad's good side was very sweet and loving; his down side was unfortunate. This was the first time that I knew for sure that, despite all the ups and downs, my mother loved him deeply.

I have two older sisters, Gloria and Walda, and a younger sister, Melva. They were—and still are—very important to me, but like my father they have no place in the musical scheme of things. That leaves my mother, my brother Bill, 78-rpm recordings, and radio broadcasts as the key musical influences in my life at that time.

I've read about the lives of many musicians, and the phrase 'child prodigy' often appears. I was not a child prodigy, and even if I had been, the word would never have been used in our house. Just as some Native American mothers molded their babies' skulls with 'cradle boards,' my mother saw young egos as pliant things to be bent and shaped to her will—and she willed our egos to be smooth and small to the point of invisibility.

We, of course, had other ideas, which I like to think added spice to our lives—and flyswatters to our butts.

In my defense, I think my mother mistook my attempts at manipulating approval for outright bragging. Yes, there's a difference: at 12 years old, I didn't really believe I was the greatest tuba player in the world—I just wanted her to tell me I was, and of course she didn't. I'm sure she was afraid that I would grow up to be a pompous, overblown braggart. I doubt that I'm as shameless a braggart as she feared I might become, but she nonetheless withheld superlatives until she passed away at 97 years old—just in case I ever got any bright ideas about myself.

This is a book about the music in my life, but I'd like to give you a brief non-musical perspective on my mother. When she was in her forties, she knew that she would be able to depend on my father, who by then had fallen ill. So she went back to school, got her college degree, and then went to work as a counselor to teenage boys in a state reform school. She continued on as part of the law enforcement community until she retired at the age of 65. (My father had passed away by then.)

When she was about 90, my mother came down with Bell's palsy, which causes one side of the face to droop out of control. It mimics the effects of a stroke. When a doctor who hadn't seen her before came by, he said: "90 years old—you probably don't smoke."

With one half of her face, my mother said: "Oh yeth, I thmoke."

The doctor looked at her with amazement. "Well, how much do you smoke?"

"Oh, I've cut back to a pack a day," she said.

"I can't believe it!" he replied. "How long have you been smoking, Mrs Scheff?"

"Oh, about theventy-fithe yearth," she told him.

The doctor called in the head nurse. "When this woman wants a cigarette," he said, "day or night, you get her on a gurney and take her outside right away."

A few years later, when she was 97, my mother lost the ability to swallow. They gave her two choices: they could put tubes down her throat, or she could go home to my sister Melva's house, be medicated, spend time with her family, and pass on peacefully in about three days' time. She looked at the doctor and said: "Where's Dr Kevorkian [aka Dr Death] when I need him?" He had to smile.

All five of her children, most of her grandchildren, and many of her great-grandchildren were with her when she died. She died like she lived: in control. She could be a pistol at times, but when it came to encouragement and sacrifice to allow me to pursue my musical interests, my mother was my champion, as you will see later on.

My brother Bill left home in 1953, just as I started the seventh grade at Vallejo Junior High School. I inherited some of his older records, which I played on the family phonograph. Coincidentally, the school orchestra happened to have a spare double bass. Suddenly, everything was starting to come together.

Vallejo Junior High School was a small-town school, grades seven through ten, but it had a music program superior to any I have seen to this day. It was conceived and run by the aforementioned Virl Swan and Wilfred Yeaman. They, along with my grammar school music teacher Douglas Fehler, were the unsung heroes of my musical life. They were the ones who told me: "Jerry, if you want to be a real bass player, you have to learn to play string bass."

There were no electric basses at that time. Within a year, Mr Yeaman recommended me for the Vallejo Junior Symphony, which was conducted by Virl Swan. Mr Swan then invited me to play in the combined high school and junior college orchestra.

I enjoyed playing in the orchestra very much but something was missing. As part of such a large group of musicians, it was impossible to get attention from any pretty girls who happened to be in the audience.

I continued to play tuba in the concert band and double bass in the junior symphony, but I would also listen to jazz and blues recordings on the Oakland radio stations at home, pick out the bass parts, and play them the next day on the school string bass. As people started to listen to my rhythm & blues and jazz basslines, I noticed that buttocks were inclined to undulate here and there—a few of them female. This, more than anything, made me think I might be on the right track.

CHAPTER 8
SACRAMENTO DREAMIN'

We left Vallejo and moved to Sacramento, California, in 1954, when I was 14. There were two children left at home: my sister Melva, who was nine, and me. As it turned out, my mother had more time for me after the move, and, as I mentioned before, she became my main musical influence without ever being a pushy stage mother.

My mother understood the nurturing of young musicians. In the late 20s, her oldest sister, Velna, a singer and piano player, had married a trumpet player named Dean Miller, who was the brother of the soon-to-be-famous bandleader Glenn Miller. Dean later went on to become a dentist, but at that time, he and Velna were young and were playing music professionally. My mother, who was still in her teens, sometimes traveled with them to ballrooms around Colorado and Wyoming.

Velna and Dean's daughter, my first cousin Velna Lou, changed her name to Wynne and moved to New York in the 50s, where she built a career on Broadway, starring as the lead in *Li'l Abner* and other hit musicals. She also acted in soap operas and sang at the Metropolitan opera and in European opera houses. She married an Austrian count and at the time of writing still lives with him in Manhattan.

With this background and the understanding she gained from her early exposure to music, my mother knew all about my passions and desires. She drove me to clubs where I worked on weekends at the age of 15 and would pick me up at 2:00am when I was finished for the night. Later on, I became an adept liar and worked my way out of having my mom around, but I have often wondered whether, if the occasion had arisen, I would have done the same thing for my children that my mother did for me. In any event, my mother understood my musical ambitions and saw to it that I was exposed not to the music she liked but to the music she knew I loved and wanted to play: black music.

After we moved I started hearing about concerts and clubs around town. My mother took me to see Lionel Hampton's band, where I saw Monk Montgomery play the first Fender electric bass I'd ever heard. We also went to see Jazz At The Philharmonic, where I heard my first bass-playing hero, Ray Brown. I fell in love with Ella Fitzgerald at one of those concerts, and even though we were sitting so far back in the Memorial Auditorium I couldn't see her, I didn't have to. I knew by listening to her voice that she was beautiful, no matter what she looked like.

I was fortunate that my mother was able to provide some musical exposure at that time because the music program at my new high school, El Camino, was sadly behind the times. There was a concert band and a small classical orchestra, but the head of the music department was an unimaginative man who didn't care about what we, the students, wanted to play. Instead he waved his baton of boredom as we slogged through civil-war songs and ghostly, watered down versions of the same old John Philip Sousa marches I'd played in grammar school. There would be no ass-wiggling here. The clubs and after-hours sessions in Sacramento and San Francisco offered much more exciting ways to learn and prove myself, and I gradually lost interest in school.

Once I was in the musical pipeline I started to hear about the various musical events that were taking place around town. I was 14 years old when I heard about a weekly Sunday afternoon jam-session at the Tropical Cellar, a dilapidated bar located in downtown Sacramento. It was a seedy part of town but my mother took me there anyway. The club was starting to fill as we walked in, and as I looked around I felt a little underdressed. Most of the crowd was dressed sharp, like they had just come from church, whereas I—

in my white shirt, black tie, and black trousers—looked like a pimple-faced, undernourished Mormon missionary with a duck's ass haircut. I felt like I was eavesdropping on some secret ceremony.

I spotted the house bass player across the room kneeling next to his string bass and unzipping the long canvas cover. He was an African-American man of around 35 years old, and he was wearing a bartender's apron—he did double duty. While my mother got us a table, I walked over to him and mumbled: "I'm a bass player."

He unfolded up to about six-foot-two and my eyes worked their way up to two gold teeth with a toothpick between them. "No shit," he mumbled back, and I probably said something lame like: "Do you let people sit in and play?"

"Why'nt you listen to us for a set," I remember him saying, "and then lemme know if you still wanna play."

I walked back to our table and tried to pretend that my mom didn't exist. I was 14 and green. I had no idea how to act at a jam session.

I watched a skinny black drummer adjust his drums. He looked up and smiled at a white piano player who was standing on top of the piano bench with a tuning hammer in his hand, trying to make a beat-up upright sound decent. This same piano player, Jerry Murphy, had taken me under his wing early on and had shown me how jazz basslines moved against different chord changes. He must have been pretty sure of me because, now that I think about it, he was the one who invited me to come down to the jam session.

As I sat there trying to look cool, a saxophone player, backlit by blinding sunshine, came through the back alley door by the edge of the small stage. He had on shades and a pork-pie hat and stood in the open doorway for a moment while the sunbeams turned smoky and his eyes adjusted to the darkness. *He* was cool. He shut the door and walked over to the bass player–bartender who was already holding out his arms in welcome. They laughed and joked while they unpacked and wiped the dust from their instruments. I could tell they had played together many times. Watching them, I was overcome by loneliness, as if I were walking alone and hungry in a strange town and could see people sitting down to dinner behind sheer-draped dining room windows. They could have been axe murderers but I'd have given anything to join them.

A hard-looking waitress came over to take our order. She hardened up even more when she saw me sitting there. I knew she was going to ask me to leave. Then my mom made eye contact with her. That was all it took—not a word was spoken. I ordered a Coke and my mother ordered coffee. The waitress smiled and disappeared. I was amazed.

The bass player walked up to the mic and announced the first song. The drummer played a few bars of introduction and then the rest of the group joined in. Every hair on my body stood to attention. This was not like the 'little kids' combos I was used to playing with. These guys were good! I was elated and terrified at the same time—thrilled to be hearing great players burning it up right in front of me but terrified at the thought of playing with them.

Halfway through the set, a middle-aged black woman with a Liz Taylor hairdo asked if she could join us at our table. She introduced herself as a singer, Maxine. I would end up playing bass behind her quite a few times in the next few years. She had a voice like Sarah Vaughan.

When the band took a break, the bass player came over. "You still wanna play, kid?" he asked. "Go talk to the piano player and tell him what songs you like."

Maxine looked at me. "What do you play?" she asked.

The bass player–bartender got in before I had a chance to reply. "He says he's a bass player!"

"Now don't you cats be layin' no bullshit on this boy," she told him.

That started me thinking. I had only known a few of the songs they'd played—mostly jazz standards with complicated chord changes. The bass player was good, but he had botched some of the changes. Either he didn't know them or he didn't have the ear to play them in the first place. Had he been on the same level as the rest of the group, I probably wouldn't have played but, scared as I was, I thought: if he can do this, so can I.

When I saw the other players heading back to the bandstand I caught up with Jerry Murphy and asked if we could play a straight 12-bar blues in F.

"Sure Jerry," he smiled. "You start it."

I didn't have a clue that I was being set up for a trial by fire.

The bass player came over to the bandstand to make sure I was comfortable with his bass. Then, while I was adjusting the bass and checking the tuning, I noticed that three new horn players had joined us on stage. The horn section now included an alto sax, two tenor saxes, and a trumpet, the significance of which only became apparent to me after we started playing. The bass player introduced the new horn players to the audience, who seemed to know them already, and then said: "Ladies and gentlemen, it gives me great pleasure to introduce to you—ah, whatchoo say yo name was boy? Uh, yeah ... Jerry Scheff!"

There was some light applause, and a few derisive wolf-whistles.

"Jerry says he's a bass player," the bass player continued. "Show us, Jerry."

Oh, shit. I knew I was supposed to start a blues in F but I hadn't thought about whether to play a fast blues or a slow one. Everyone was waiting for me, ice clinking in their glasses. I took a deep breath, closed my eyes, and started walking the blues chord changes in the low register at a fairly fast clip.

It starts like this:

De-doom doom doom doom

All of a sudden I realize no one else is playing. I'm completely exposed.

Doom doom doom doom doom-be doom doom doom

My mouth is dry, my legs are shaking. I'm afraid to look up.

Doom-be doom doom doo-be-de doom doom doom

Well, I think, at least this bass feels great. I start to tap my foot, shake my ass a little. And then—*wow*—there's Maxine smiling and snapping her fingers.

Doom-be doom doom doom doom-be doom doom

I sneak a look around: people are diggin' it! Then, as I come to the end of the first chorus:

SNAP!

The drummer comes in. I jump up to a higher register.

Ping ping ping SNAP! Ping ping ping SNAP!

Every hit on his cymbal and snare rim are right with me. His eyes are saying: I hear you. I dig where you are. Let's ride it!

Whompity shmecketa CRASH!

The horns and piano come in with a Charlie Parker line called 'Now's The Time,' and suddenly I'm filled with a surge of power, like a piston in a large locomotive. The four horn-men, playing in unison with a throaty, masculine sound, make me feel like I'm ten feet tall.

I play a little bass riff at the end of a phrase and the drummer accents the end of it. It's like he's reading my mind! How did he know where I was going?

Chuck-eta chuck-eta chuck-eta de-de-da CRASH!

The alto sax player starts a low, simple solo. I follow, trying to listen to everybody at the same time. Jerry Murphy looks up at me at one point and plays a different chord change—one I've never heard before. I wait until it comes around again and then try to play it with him. I get the whole thing right except for one note. Jerry the piano player looks over and winks at me. Maybe I do belong here!

Before long we've been playing for 15 minutes. My fingers are getting a little sore. I'm still trying to get into the other players' heads—trying to anticipate what someone will play, just like the drummer did with me. It's a wonderful feeling when it works: a feeling of unity, complete communication, almost telepathy.

The trumpet player starts his solo by staying on one note softly, changing the rhythm every bar or two. Everybody pulls back to give him room for growth and expansion, but the groove stays the same. The audience is sucking up every nuance. It seems like we—the band—have given them something to grab hold of and they don't want to let go.

I don't want to let go either, but my fingers are hurting. It's a relief to ease off for a bit, but I'm starting to understand what's coming. If the trumpet player, alto sax player, tenor sax player, and piano player all do ten-minute solos, my fingers will be lunchmeat.

I try to hold back, keep something in reserve, but it's like I'm caught in a rip tide and I can't help but go with it. The drummer is really laying it down now—when he feels me drop off he looks at me with a questioning look. I can't let him think I'm a lightweight. I start leaning on it with him, riding on the top of the feel. Fingers or no fingers, I am not going to give up.

Gradually my fingers start to go numb. Thank God! As we come to the end of their solos, the last horn player leaves the stage and I take a four-bar rest so the piano player can play an introduction to the first chorus of his solo. The drummer is soaked; I'm dripping. I turn my right hand over and discover two huge blisters on my middle and index fingers. I feel a cramp coming on and shake my left arm. I'm a mess!

There's a sense of relief as we near the end of the piano solo. Twice more through the head (the starting melody) and we'll be done. A dull, throbbing pain radiates up my right arm and I feel the blisters break on my fingers, but I'm happy—I made it.

After the piano player finishes his solo I expect to see the horns come back on stage. Instead, he says: "Take it, Jerry!"

I stand there dumbfounded, my mind rapidly running through the few alternatives at my disposal. I either have to start playing or walk off the stage with my tongue between my legs.

I remember hearing Ray Brown take a solo at a Jazz At The Philharmonic concert where he didn't play like a horn player—he just walked around a regular bass part. It started simply, staying on the root note until it was time to change. With every chorus it would get slightly more complicated. I knew I could never begin to play the way Ray did at the *end* of his solo, but I could at least play like he did at the beginning and take it as far as possible.

On the first downbeat of my solo, the drummer slams one note on the snare—*BAM!*—as if to say: "Shut up and listen to this kid!" Faces in the audience snap to attention as if a gun has gone off.

I start soft, playing the simplest part I could think of. The drummer smiles and plays a soft rhythm on the hi-hat. People start to get caught up in it. This was a very hip crowd and I can only think that they were digging it more for the spectacle than for my musical genius. I don't think many skinny 14-year-old white kids sat in on bass.

So, now what? I have to do something different the second time around or I'm going to lose them. I play a little bit harder, accenting various notes here and there, and people start tapping their feet and snapping their fingers.

After that I know I have to build the solo some more, but how? I'm just about ready to give up when the drummer holds up four fingers and then points at me and back to him. He wants to 'trade fours,' which is where one musician solos for four bars, and then another musician solos for four bars, and they go back and forth until they decide to stop. He must have sensed that I'm out of ideas. He's saving my ass.

I stop. The drummer plays a simple rhythm for four bars, which I then copy, adding a little bit to it. He then spends his next four bars playing something else for me to copy. When I start my next run, I jump high up on the fingerboard so that what I play matches his high cymbals. He understands what I'm doing and plays his next four bars on the bass drum. I follow suit with some low bass notes.

By now the crowd has caught on to what we're doing and applauds every time we each finish another four bars. I know I'm not playing anything groundbreaking, but I'm working hard and sweating my ass off, and the people in the audience know that the skinny, sweaty white kid they're watching has a lot of heart, at least, and maybe a little more.

Finally, I just can't play any more. I lay the bass on its side and walk off the stage. People are smiling and clapping, and with that all my anger about having pimples and being shy with girls fades without a whimper into its proper place.

Instead of walking over to my mother—God forbid—I went to the bar where the other musicians were hanging out. I swaggered over to them, checking out their postures, wanting with all my heart to look like one of them. They ignored me. I stood there a few minutes, with my hands in my pockets, listening to the drummer solo his heart out. He was the best I had ever played with. I was probably snapping my fingers and trying to look cool. As the drummer finished his solo, the crowd exploded. He stood up and waved and walked off the stage.

The intermission started. People in the audience looked over at me, smiling, nodding. I nodded back knowingly. Someone handed me a beer. I didn't know what else to do so I started to take a sip and then heard an angry whisper.

"Hey, you little motherfucker! You tryin' to get this club closed down?"

It was the bass player–bartender. He took the beer out of my hand and glowered at me. I was just about to cry when he started to laugh. I looked at the other guys standing at the bar—they were all cracking up. They mussed up my duck's-ass hair and headed to the men's room before the start of the second set. I felt great.

Then, for the first time since we'd stopped playing, I looked at my fingers. They were a bloody, throbbing mess. The friction from rubbing the bass strings had broken the blisters and rolled the ragged edges of my skin down over the tips of my fingers. I wouldn't be able to play for a week or two.

I went back over to our table.

"You were very good, Jerry," my mother said. "But the next time you play, why don't you smile?" I knew she was proud of me.

Maxine smiled and said: "You are gonna be a great bass player!"

My spirits fell. I wanted her to tell me I was already a great bass player.

CHAPTER 9
MISTAKEN IDENTITY

By the start of my senior year of high school, I was leading a double life. I had a few non-musical friends in school, but in reality we were worlds apart. I sat alone eating my peanut butter and jelly sandwiches in the school cafeteria while 'Be-Bop-A-Lula' and 'Rock Around The Clock' blared out of the jukebox.

I was scornful of the bunch of white idiots who listened to this poor imitation of the real thing. To me, Bill Haley and Gene Vincent were hicks with the hiccups who moved like puppets. I was into Hank Ballard & The Midnighters and Little Willie John. These white guys definitely didn't sound right. It's safe to say that, out of ignorance, I had developed an attitude.

I saw some great rhythm & blues shows at the Sacramento Memorial Auditorium: groups dressed in sharp clothes, their movements smooth and synchronized. There were no phony sneers on their faces, no jerky movements. They were cool. To them, rock'n'roll meant sex. To me, standing in the middle of a mostly black crowd when one of these shows started was an intoxicating revelation.

As the band kicked in, the crowd started moving together, swaying like a wheat field in the wind, singing the words to the song, gradually picking up speed until, by the end of the song, most people were dancing with the shine of perspiration on their faces—myself included. It was impossible to stand still. The first time I became immersed in one of these steamy rituals I can remember thinking: why can't white people be cool and sexy like this?

Looking back, it's easy for me to see what my problem was. I was caught in the middle of two different mating rituals. I wanted to participate in both but I didn't belong to either one. Even if the popular kids in school had accepted me with open arms, the status symbols required for belonging to their group were beyond my reach. I didn't own a car—I didn't even have a driver's license. My vocabulary was filled with the jargon of another tribe: hipster jazz musicians. And I was totally ignorant when it came to the little nuances and signals that provided for the smooth running of the in crowd. Instead of attending sock hops, drinking Kool Aid, and dancing with my sweetheart to songs that would trigger nostalgic memories in our later years, I was at the clubs and after-hour sessions in Sacramento and San Francisco, studying how to be black.

There was only one problem ...

I wanted to be black with all my heart. I studied black people to the point of obsession—if there was a magic formula for being black, I would have found it and made the transformation right then and there. I probably looked ridiculous as I walked down the halls of my all-white high school, doing my best impersonation of some cool black guy I had seen in a club the night before. (I know now that I was a scrawny little white kid trying to affect the speech and mannerisms of people who had spent their lives coping with cultural influences and pressures that I could never comprehend if I lived to be 100.)

I didn't have the money to buy the clothes I needed for my metamorphosis—I didn't even own a suit, let alone a cool suit. My usual costume in the club environment was black slacks, black tie, wrinkled white shirt, and wedged sandals. I wore huaraches—the Mexican open-toed sandals popular among young men in California at the time. We always wore them with white socks. We would take them to the shoemaker and have him remove the heel and then build up the leather sole, layer by layer, until they were an inch and a quarter thick. We called them wedged soles, as in "I just got my kicks wedged." Add taps to the heel, toe, and sides and people could hear you coming for a block or two. They were especially deafening in school hallways.

All of this was topped by a crew cut with long sides pomaded back into a duck's ass. I was trying to fit into both worlds, you see, but I was making a poor showing. The button-down Ivy League styles were popular at El Camino High School at the time. I was never the button down type.

One night when I was about 15, I was in San Francisco with a piano player I had met at a jam session. We'll call him John Beardsley. John was a very hip dresser. He was also a junkie. I had watched him cook, tie off, and shoot up. I begged him to show me how. He refused and told me never to ask again. I told my mother I was spending the weekend with a friend—and I was, just not the sort of friend she had in mind.

I first learned about musical taste from John. Every note he played seemed to be engraved in granite like an artifact that had laid buried, waiting for him to uncover it. This only applied when he could stay awake, however.

John took me to a great jazz club in San Francisco called the Black Hawk. John Coltrane—who I would later hear live with Miles Davis in Washington, DC—was playing there with his band. At the end of an amazing set, after the standing ovations died down, John Beardsley walked up on the empty bandstand and started moving things around. There he was on his hands and knees under the piano, like he was looking for something. That's when the bouncers grabbed him. As they escorted John to the door he shouted: "I know it's up there, man! He played his dick off and I know it's up there!"

Now and then, I played bass with a piano player named Flip Nunez at an after-hours club called Jimbo's Bop City on Post Street in San Francisco. Flip was a young Filipino man who had been exposed to black music for some time. He had lived with the Montgomery brothers—Wes, Monk, and Buddy—all of whom went on to become big names in the jazz world. They called Flip Cousin Ugly, but I never could understand why.

If the Black Hawk was the premier jazz venue in San Francisco at the time, Jimbo's was the premier after-hours club. The atmosphere was made up of perfume, cigarette smoke, disinfectant, stale beer, body odors, cooking grease, and darkness. During the day it was a chicken-and-waffle joint, but from 2:00am until 6:00am the place was jammed with hip people either playing or listening to bebop. Flip was one of the hippest.

I almost never went to Jimbo's with other kids my age, but I did go once or twice with my friend Gene Copeland, a budding young drummer back then. Gene told me recently that he was once stopped by a bouncer who pointed at me and said: "He's OK, but don't let the tall kid in," meaning Gene. We were both underage, of course.

The first time we went to Jimbo's was with Flip. I had met Flip at an after-hours jam session at the ILWU Labor Union Hall in Sacramento, and he asked me to play with him at Jimbo's the following Sunday at 2:00am. I told my mother the usual tale about spending the weekend with a friend, borrowed the school's string bass, and lined up a ride to San Francisco with Gene.

That Sunday, as we walked through the door, I was half hidden by my bass, so the first time John 'Jimbo' Edwards, the owner, got to look at me I was already on stage tuning up. He knew I was underage but he never called me on it. He would just shake his head and smile. He was a very nice man, and he loved musicians, but he wouldn't tolerate any funny business—especially racism. In later years, he talked in interviews about the kids who came to the club all the way from Sacramento. I like to think he meant Gene and me.

One morning, when I was on stage at Jimbo's with Flip and a couple of other musicians, a very large black woman came up to sing. I remember her perfectly because of her size and because she had on a drab brown skirt, a Pendleton work-shirt, and high-topped clodhopper boots. Flip introduced her as Big Mama Thornton. I hadn't met any other Big Mamas at that time, and she really was big: six feet tall and over 300 pounds.

She said "blues in B flat," stomped her foot, and then *whomp whomp whomp whomp*, the dust flew out of the carpet and up into the spotlights as her enormous voice filled every crevice of the club and probably a half-block radius. I had no idea at the time that she had anything to do with the song 'Hound Dog' and didn't make the connection until years later, when I was working with Elvis. At the time, though, she made overwhelmingly clear the amount of humor, pain, and honesty one human voice can carry.

Speaking of pain, no matter how cool and grown-up I tried to be back then, reality would eventually set in and my inner smarm-alarm would go off. In other words, I was very self conscious—and I often ended up in pain because of it.

One morning I was at John Beardsley's pad, which was in a rooming house that smelled of cabbage and cat piss. He had an early morning gig— 6:00am!—at a café in the tenderloin district and he wanted me to play with him. I was waiting for him to get dressed. John only owned two suits and two pairs of shoes, but as far as I was concerned they were the coolest suits and shoes I'd ever seen. I asked him if I could wear some of his threads to the gig. I wanted to be cool like him. John said something like: "Hey, knock yourself out, baby." He had a soft, poetic-sounding voice—it was common for bebop musicians at the time to use terms of endearment like 'baby' and 'sweetie' without any sexual connotation.

The only mirror in John's room was a small one hanging by a string on the wall, and there was no way that I could use it to gauge the impact of the fashion statement I was making. In my mind's eye, as I dressed myself, I was really seeing John in the clothes. I put on his baggy, black, pinstriped pants with pegged legs and pencil-thin cuffs. Then, as I slipped into the matching jacket with oversized shoulder pads, I noticed a horrible smell.

"Oh, my old lady got sick last night," John told me. "Here, throw some of this shit on it." He tossed me a giant bottle of Bay rum and I dumped half of it on the coat.

Now for the kicks: they were black-and-yellow wingtips, and I was counting on them as a badge of cool. I tried to slip into one of them but it was too small. I stripped off my white socks and tried again, but at that moment John looked over and I knew it was hopeless, so I slipped back into my huaraches.

It was just before 6:00am when we pulled up to the Seven Eleven Café in John's car. It was the kind of place where hookers, pimps, drug dealers, musicians, and beatniks came for breakfast—or maybe something more. The Seven Eleven regularly hired a jazz trio to provide the lullabies required to rock this crowd to sleep after a long hard night, and that morning John, a vibes player, and I were it.

I got my bass out of the back seat of John's old Chrysler and headed across the street. The sun was just beginning to illuminate the morning fog, but it was still dark and moist down on the street, the only light coming from neon signs. As we approached the place, I caught a glimpse of my reflection in the window and realized I didn't look anything as cool as John. In fact, I looked like a circus act. I was devastated! The shoulder pads made me look like a junior-high football player; the baggy pants revealed about three inches of white socks; and the pegged cuffs were so tight around my ankles, they made my wedged huaraches look like snow shoes. All in all, I looked like something out of *1001 Arabian Nights*, and I smelled like a rum factory with a hint of vomit. I kicked off my shoes, thinking: damage control—better no shoes than these shoes. I remember telling people I had to feel the drums through the stage to stay in the groove, and I couldn't do that with my kicks on.

I continued playing in jazz clubs and at after-hours sessions in and around Sacramento and San Francisco until I left home. As my reputation as a bass player grew, my grades at school dropped. I was failing everything—even the band instructor was failing me because I wouldn't play at football games on Saturday nights. I had better things to do.

Finally, after I disappeared for a whole week, the ultimatum came from my mother: get serious about school, get a regular job, or join the military.

CHAPTER 10
LES BUIE AND THE BUGLE

I n the fall of 1958, I arrived in San Diego for boot camp with the US Navy. Like everyone else, I was miserable. On the third day the company commander pulled me out of formation and told me he'd seen in my records that I had some musical experience.

"The color guard has a bugler graduating in a week," he said. "You do play the bugle, don't you?"

"Oh yes, sir," I lied.

The company commander took me over to the color guard's room, where a large group of sailors were standing around in dress blues with white belts and leggings. Some of them were armed with silver swords; others were carrying long lances with little pennants hanging from them. There was only one bugler, and he walked over to greet me carrying a big, shiny, silver bugle dripping with gold braids and tassels.

The Naval Training Center ceremonial color guard appeared at graduations and change-of-command ceremonies. The rest of the time we did drills and attended whatever classes were required for graduation from boot camp. We were not required to participate in cleanup details or mess duties, and we had the privilege of going to the head of the line at mealtimes. In short, things were looking up.

At first I spent most mornings by myself in a small battleship-gray room practicing calls on a small brass bugle. In the afternoon I sat smoking unfiltered Camel cigarettes outside on the bleachers with the other newcomers. When we could stay awake we watched the A team go through their drills in preparation for the time when we would take their places.

You'll notice that there was a large silver bugle and a small brass bugle. The mechanics of blowing into them, while similar, are slightly different, and playing the tuba—my *real* brass instrument—is a whole other story. When you play the tuba, the mouthpiece covers most of your mouth and you have to flap your lips back and forth within it to produce the required low frequencies. This high-speed flapping is called buzzing. With a bugle, however, the mouthpiece is tiny, and requires you to flap just the tip of your lips at a much higher rate.

I had one week to teach my lips to flap accordingly, and I did very well. I got to where I knew exactly how much pressure to put behind my lips in order to make that little brass bugle speak. Within a few days, I was rattling off every bugle call like a pro.

The purpose of a bugle in our ceremony was to relay the commanding officer's orders to the troops. I guess this was a holdover from the days before the loudspeaker was invented. In our ceremonies, the commanding officer would say: "Bugler! Sound attention," and the bugler would play the call for attention with one loud note at the end. On that last note, hundreds of men would snap to attention. The men were trained with great precision to do whatever the bugler called for them to do—that is, as long as they could understand what the bugler was playing.

My first ceremony was a Naval Training Center graduation. I spit-shined my shoes and my uniform sparkled. My predecessor was graduating that morning, and with great ceremony he presented me with the big, shiny bugle with the gold braid. I loved it. I had waited all week to get my hands on it. It never dawned on me to try and play it. I remember something about not having my white gloves on, and not wanting to get fingerprints all over it. Whatever: I was filled with self-importance and couldn't wait to show everybody how the bugle should be played.

As I marched out onto the field with the other members of the color guard, I found myself looking out on the martial splendor of hundreds of recruits standing at parade rest in their dress blues, their rifles slashing from their right hands to the ground like italic exclamation points. We took our positions in front of the troops. The color guard, with their sabers and lances, lined up ten feet in front of the rest of the field, and I stood conspicuously by myself, five feet in front of them all. We faced a podium where our commanding officer held court in front of 100 or so guests who were sitting on the bleachers, perfectly placed to see the slightest offhand movement or ass-scratch.

As I stood there on that beautiful warm San Diego morning, I noticed the sun glinting from the gold-braided officers' caps in the front row of the bleachers. We were later told that the reviewing officers that day included Secretary of State John Foster Dulles as well as three flag admirals. The rest of the audience comprised family and friends of the graduating recruits.

The whole scene was like a painting: women in brightly colored sunbonnets, seagulls riding the breeze in the blue skies above us, and me, with all these sailors waiting obediently for my bugle calls. I have to admit I felt slightly drunk with pride, cradling the bugle under my right arm like a football. Suddenly, I heard the commanding officer.

"Bugler!"

My right arm snapped straight out in front of me with the bugle.

"Sound attention!"

My mind immediately started flashing muscle-memory instructions to my lips and diaphragm. The problem was: at my lips—with hundreds of men waiting to hear it—was the large silver bugle. The signals I was getting were for the small brass horn. I might just as well have been trying to blow up an inner tube.

Burble burble blat pfff.

Instead of the precision sound of hundreds of men snapping to attention, I heard hundreds of feet shuffling in confusion: men going to parade rest, men going to order arms, men turning to their left, men turning to their right. I saw an admiral in the bleachers laughing so hard he had to take off his glasses to wipe the tears from his eyes. At that moment, with my bladder about to prepare me for my flight to safety, a little voice whispered: you're trying too hard—relax. I resisted the temptation to use the bugle as a shovel and instead returned it to my armpit.

"Bugler!"

Snap!

"Sound attention!!"

Ta ta ta ta—taaa.

After boot camp I arrived home thinking of myself as the conquering hero. Most guys would look up their school chums and strut around in their uniforms. I immediately ditched my military garb and went looking for my friends in the clubs. A good friend of mine from the Navy, Randy Fendrick (now a retired symphony trombone player) reminded me recently that I took him down to Jimbo's Bop City around this time. Charles Mingus—another of my bass-playing heroes—was playing, and at one point Flip Nunez went up and asked Mingus to "get the white boy up to play."

If you had the guts to get up and sit in at a jam session at Jimbo's and you weren't cutting it, the musicians would ask you to leave—sometimes right in the middle of a song. I had seen it happen. So it was that I shakily took Mingus's place, playing his own bass with his own band. I was in musical heaven.

According to Randy, I played a few songs, and Mingus told him to tell me to get in touch if I was ever in New York. As you'll soon see, I ended up spending the next few years in the US Navy's music program, eventually winding up on the West Coast, so I never did meet him. I played the rest of the set that night, and by the time I'd finished, Mingus had gone.

It seemed back then that everywhere I went I found myself in the middle of important people and important situations for a budding young musician. I believe that I owe everything to the people who accepted me, looked out for me, steered me in the right direction, and gave me approval when I desperately needed it. Most of them were very sweet people just trying to make some sense out of their lives, and one of the sweetest of them all was a 21-year-old black guitar player named Les Buie.

I first met Les at one of the after-hours sessions at the ILWU Labor Union Hall in Sacramento, where we all showed up at 1:00am to help set up tables and chairs. He was in the Air Force and was one of my early mentors. He knew most of the standard songs that jazz players liked to play and taught me how basslines should weave in and out of the various chord changes that nobody I had met before knew how to play. Les was a great rhythm & blues guitarist as well, and he went on to become a part of the great James Brown's band of the early 60s—the *shang-alang-alang-alang* guitar part was Les. He later became a studio musician in Los Angeles, after which I lost track of him.

Les was the first black person whose blackness disappeared in my mind. He was just a friend. This phenomenon became the backdrop against which the bigotry and ignorance of 50s America would kick me hard in the ass. My father was a bigot. My brother was a bigot. I was a bigot. I had never heard my mother say a derogatory word about anyone, but my dad made up for it. If you have followed me so far, you will know we lived in a segregated housing project, and, as innocent children, we would repeat all of the racist slang we heard. If my mother heard me saying those words, however, she would at least have yelled at me, if not spanked me with the flyswatter.

For quite some time—even though I had black friends, thought that black culture was so cool, and secretly wanted to be black more than anything—I still clung to some of my old racist views. I even once wrote my mother a letter complaining about the "negro problem" in Washington, DC. Later, when I was delivering a tirade against racism to her, she brought out the very same letter, asking whether the 'problem' I had mentioned was that there were too many black people in Washington. Immediately I understood: there I was, trying to brag about how far I had advanced, but I still had a long way to go, and before she gave me her approval my mother wanted to remind me of that.

I ended up in Washington because, by coincidence, Les was getting out of the Air Force at the same time I came home from boot camp. He was going home to his mother's house in Washington, and I had orders to report to the Navy School of Music nearby, so it was settled: we would drive across the country together in Les's Buick, sharing the driving and the expenses.

On the morning of our departure, Les picked me up at my house and my family stood in the yard to wave us away. This was my first trip out of California as an adult and I had a lot to learn. Les suggested we travel in our uniforms—he thought that people would be more amenable to boys in uniform than they would be to a suspicious looking interracial pair with God knows what on their minds. And he was right. Our only other strategy for staying out of trouble was to drive straight through to Denver, Colorado, where we would seek refuge at my paternal grandmother's house. As we drove, we talked about everything and swapped stories about music and our childhoods. We only stopped for gas at twenty cents per gallon and ten-cent hamburgers. Most restaurants wouldn't serve us because Les was black.

It wasn't long before we lost the black radio stations from California and were left with polkas and 'How Much Is That Doggie In The Window?' I wanted to turn the radio off but Les told me to wait a minute while he scrolled through the frequencies until he landed on a country music station.

"You don't listen to that shit, do you?" I asked. In truth, however, the only country music I had ever heard came from the jukebox at the Valano Lunch tavern in Vallejo. In order to explain my opinion of country music as a 17-year-old, let me tell you about the Valano Lunch. Situated at the bottom of the hill on Sacramento Street, it was a five minute walk from our house in Federal Terrace. On summer evenings when I was 11 and 12, my friends and I would hang around out front. It was a typical 50s bar fronted by diamond-patterned Naugahyde doors with round portholes. My friends and I would sit on the warm sidewalks breathing in the smell of melted tar oozing in the cracks between the cement slabs. Every once in a while a drunk would push through the swinging doors, and Hank Williams's 'Hey Good Lookin" would blare out at us. We lagged pennies for the half-smoked butts that these drunks discarded between the tavern and their taxis. Then we smoked and did mocking, nasal impersonations of country singers.

Back in the Buick on the way out of California, Les tried to explain why he liked Hank Williams. I wasn't buying it. This should have been an eye-opener for me as far as my musical prejudices were concerned, but it wasn't quite time for the scales to drop from my brain.

Just when I thought I would go crazy from listening to country music, we went up into the Rocky Mountains and lost all radio reception. It was about 2:30 in the morning and the moon lit up the snow on the side of the highway. I was dozing off when I felt the car slow to a stop.

"The car's overheating," Les told me as he opened the hood. He checked the hoses and the belts—they were fine. He checked the oil—also fine. "Must be the thermostat," he said. I probably had a worried look on my face because he immediately reassured me by pulling blankets out of the trunk.

"We've got these and our heavy coats," Les said. "We'll be fine." He had seen a sign that said Steamboat Springs was 25 miles up the road. We would sleep in the car and try to thumb a ride in the morning.

It seemed like I had just gone off to sleep when I heard a rapping on the window. I sat up, cleared the fog off the window, and found myself staring straight into the face of Wyatt Earp, complete with Stetson, six-shooter, badge, and an enormous handlebar mustache. I froze.

"You boys having some trouble?" he asked. I started to speak and was shocked to hear myself singing soprano. Les jumped in and, in a very dignified way, explained our situation. You could gauge how serious Wyatt was by how far his frozen breath shot out. He told us to stay there by the side of the road and wait for him. A few minutes later he came back and said he'd found somewhere for us to stay. I thought I knew just what he had in mind.

In 1958, Steamboat Springs, Colorado, was nothing like the resort it would later become. It was about 4:00am when Wyatt drove us up to the front of what looked like the best motel in town. We followed him into the office, where he introduced us to Miss Kitty.

Miss Kitty looked to be in her fifties. She was wearing a sheepskin coat over her nightgown with bare feet peeking out. Her mink-colored hair was up in rollers, partially hidden by one of those hairnets that look like they're covered with black bugs. Her eyes were filmy with tears and she didn't look happy at being awakened at four in the morning.

"You boys look like you chased a fart through a keg of nails," she said, or words to that effect. Wyatt wheezed into a smoker's laugh. Les and I simply smiled and nodded. I was just getting ready to confess our poverty when she tossed Les a room key, which he started to hand back.

"I don't want any arguments," Miss Kitty told us. "You come back and pay me when you can."

Les unlocked the door to our room. The lights were on, and at that time I don't think I had ever even been in a motel at all, let alone one this nice. There were two twin beds, a nice bathroom, and some sandwiches and milk on the dresser. Les and I looked at each other and started laughing. Hot showers were heaven.

A young girl woke us the next morning and took us to Miss Kitty's kitchen. Just as we finished our bacon and eggs, Wyatt Earp walked in.

"I had the boys from the service station go out and hot-wire your car this morning." he said. "I don't suppose you could pay for the thermostat?"

We were in a euphoric mood the rest of the way into Denver. We sang Hank Ballard & The Midnighters' 'Annie' songs—'Work With Me Annie,' 'Annie Had A Baby.' We were on our way to Grandma's house.

Grandma Scheff remains a shadowy figure in my memory. I was two years old when my parents left Denver, heading west for wartime jobs in the shipyards of California. As I have said before, money was scarce at times during my childhood, but every Christmas, like clockwork, large boxes would arrive from my dad's family filled with toys, oranges, candy, clothing, and bath cloths for the children—always bath cloths, as if the Scheffs would never wash otherwise.

My dad's family took on a Santa Claus-like aura in my mind. I have distinct memories of being spoiled rotten by my father's family on a Greyhound bus trip to visit my grandmother in Denver when I was eight years old. Of course, that time I didn't show up on the doorstep with Les.

It was getting dark as we pulled up. We had stopped at a gas station to shave, change clothes, and buff our shoes. We looked like pretty good specimens of young American manhood. I knocked on the door, and after a minute or two the porch light came on. Les was brushing the snow from his clothes in anticipation of being invited in. The door opened a crack and a small scratchy voice said: "Who is it?"

I would tell you what my grandmother looked like at that time—except that I never saw her. She got a clear look at the darker of the two young men on her porch and the door moved back to being almost closed.

"It's me, Grandma," I said. "It's Jerry."

"How are you, Jerry?" she croaked through the crack.

"Fine, Grandma."

A pause, then: "You must be tired."

"Yes Grandma."

Another pause. "Are you hungry?"

"We're starved Grandma."

A longer pause. "I'll be right back."

The door closed softly, but the sound of the deadbolt cracked like a gunshot. I walked over and sat down on an old porch swing.

Before the snow on the swing could melt under my butt, the door opened slightly, and a small white hand holding Velveeta cheese sandwiches on white bread snaked its way through the crack. How had she gotten to the kitchen and back so fast? Looking back, I have to laugh, thinking of my white-haired Grandma flying through the house, flinging the refrigerator door open, throwing the cheese and bread together, and heading for the finish line clutching the sandwiches in her hand. The depth of her fingerprints in the sandwiches should have made it clear how uncomfortable she was—it looked like a toddler had carried them around in clenched fists. It was obvious she wanted to get rid of us as soon as possible.

After assuring Grandma that it had been wonderful to see her, Les and I got in the car and threw the sandwiches in the back seat. I think Les knew he had just witnessed a death in the family, because we sat in silence for what seemed like a long time. Finally, Les reached over and put his hand on my shoulder.

"Come on, Jerry," he said. "Let's go find that Chinese restaurant we saw on the way into town. I'm gonna buy us some dinner."

Ten minutes later we pulled into an empty parking lot covered with fresh snow. I was sure the place was closed—there were no tire tracks in the snow—but Les pointed out that all the lights were on, and he could see someone through the curtains.

Although I considered myself an expert on chow mein and egg rolls at the time, I still thought all Chinese people ate out of paper cartons, so I was amazed to see a large room full of empty tables set up with table cloths and matching napkins. I took off my sailor's hat and saw an elderly Chinese man coming toward us. He had thinning black hair that looked like it had been painted on one strand at a time. He was just reaching for some menus when he noticed Les. His smile remained unchained but an almost pitiful look appeared in his eyes. He motioned me behind a screen.

"I sorry," he whispered. "We no serve colored people in here. White people see colored, they no come here."

Sensing the situation, Les had already gone outside. As we walked to the car I told him the restaurant wasn't open yet. He just smiled and put his hands in his pockets. We had struck it rich in Steamboat Springs but we were striking out in Denver. We started up the car, put the radio on, and ate my grandmother's sandwiches on the way out of town.

Three more uneventful days of driving and sleeping in the Buick brought us to Washington, DC. We pulled up in front of a three-story walkup in a black neighborhood at 10:00pm. There were still kids playing in the puddles on the street. They recognized Les's car immediately and quickly started grabbing things to carry as they welcomed their hero home. Les had already talked to his mother, Florence, about me staying with them for a couple of days so, baggage in hand, I followed them up the stairs.

Florence Buie was a dignified woman in her mid forties whose husband had died when Les was a teenager. She received me with polite caution. I knew she was checking me out. I didn't mind—I was a 17-year-old kid in a strange apartment in a strange city, the first black home I had ever been in. I was checking everything out, too.

Les hugged his 16-year-old sister Cynthia, who everyone called Little

Sister. She was taller than Les but there was a softness about her that was very feminine. I was to have some very unbrotherly thoughts about her.

Later, after the neighborhood kids had gone home, we drank coffee around an old white wooden table in the kitchen while Les told Florence and Little Sister about the latest twists and turns in his life. Les sounded different when he spoke to his mother. Unlike most of the black women I had come into contact with on the West Coast jazz scene, Florence didn't use the hip slang of the era, and now Les seemed to be avoiding it, too. As a musician, I was used to memorizing tones and cadences, and I immediately started filing away the subtleties of what I was hearing.

When the conversation started to slow, Florence turned to me and said: "So, Jerry, Les tells me you're a bass player."

I didn't know who I should be in this particular situation, but I wasn't sure that being myself would be enough. I reached into my bag of linguistic tricks, broadened my drawl, dropped some consonants, and said something like: "Yeah, I been playin' the colored joints out of 'Frisco."

All of a sudden, Les was studying something deep at the bottom of his coffee cup. I knew I was blowing it. I tried to salvage the situation by adding something like: "Yeah, we only got eyes to blow East Coast bop out there. You know: Thelonious Monk, Mal Waldron, Dizzy ... cats like that." I didn't even know the word 'stereotyping' back then, and it had never dawned on me that these people might not actually care about the current jazz scene.

With what I believe now to have been great compassion, Florence assured me that she would like to hear all about it in the morning. As she stood up to clear the coffee cups from the table, I knew right then that she and Little Sister thought I was a phony. After that, I felt relieved when Les held up his end of our usual joking and kidding around as I made my way down the hall to a small bedroom. (One of the many things I loved about Les was that, even though he was four years older than me, he always treated me as an equal.)

Later, while I was using the bathroom, I heard Little Sister and Florence talking.

"Mama, what that white boy talkin' about?"

"Shush. He might hear you."

"I don't care," Little Sister whispered. "It's like he's trying to sound colored or something."

"He don't sound like no colored I ever heard," Florence replied. The pair of them laughed, and then Florence added: "He's our guest, and Les likes him, so let's give him a chance."

When I got back to the bedroom, Les was making up a palate on the floor next to the bed. He insisted that I take the bed, and as my head sank back into the pillow, I noticed a large black-and-white print on the wall. In it was a group of black men, women, and children in ragged clothes. They were gathered in a small, poor-looking room around a soldier, who seemed to be reading from an official looking paper.

I don't know why, but I sensed that this was something I needed to know about, so I asked Les about the picture. Standing there in his underpants, he added another layer of enlightenment to my young and uninformed mind. The print had come from his grandmother, whose grandparents had been slaves in South Carolina, he told me. When Les was a little boy, his grandmother had repeatedly gone over the picture, one face at a time, and even though the people in the picture were the invention of some long dead artist, Les's grandmother had a name for each person in the picture, and she could even tell Les what each person was feeling.

The black soldier was from the Union Army, and he was reading and explaining the Emancipation Proclamation to a group of former slaves. I didn't even know what the Emancipation Proclamation was, let alone what it would have been like to be a slave. I had flunked history class. Now, Les told me about the whips and the chains, the broken families, and only then did the reality of being black sink in. As I fell asleep that night, one of the biggest frustrations in my life disappeared, and I abandoned all hope of ever becoming a black person.

The following day, I went with Les to meet some of his friends at the Howard Theatre, where Count Basie was playing a matinee show. The featured vocalist was a young singer named Della Reese. We had good scats in about the fifth or sixth row. I just sat back and let the waves of energy wash over me. The audience talked throughout, yelling to the musicians, egging them on. I had never seen anything like it.

That evening, we were back at the kitchen table eating the best pork chops I had ever tasted. I hugged Florence and Little Sister after the meal and then Les drove me out to the Navy School of Music, where I was due to report for duty in the morning. Les and his old Buick were the last remaining ties to my childhood. Even though we swore we would stay in touch, I somehow knew that we wouldn't. But I was wrong.

In the car, I told Les that I felt like the biggest asshole that ever lived, and that I just knew his mom and sister thought I was a phony. Les pulled something out of his pocket and there, inside a gum wrapper, was a wallet-sized school photograph of Little Sister.

"What about your mother?" I asked.

"She liked you, Jerry."

"How do you know?"

"Because my mama can't be buying pork chops for just anybody."

CHAPTER 11
THE SERGEANT'S LADY

I n 1958, the Navy School of Music was based in Anacostia, in Southeast, Washington, DC, and was part of a small land-locked base called the Naval Receiving Center. There were students and instructors from the Army, the Air Force, and the Marines—only the most gifted musicians were accepted. I had auditioned for the school at boot camp in San Diego.

The draft was in effect back then, and a common way for professional musicians to fulfill their military obligations was to spend two years teaching at the Navy School of Music. The school was really two schools: half martial music, half pop and jazz, with instructors from both backgrounds. Some of the other less talented musicians handled the administrational duties. (The school has since moved to Virginia, where it is now called the School of Music.)

On my first morning at the school, dampened by a cold rain, I pushed my way through a pair of fogged-up glass doors into a chow hall full of rows of blue dungaree uniforms topped by crew cuts, all hunched over pancakes floating in maple syrup with bacon and powdered eggs. A haze of real unadulterated cigarette smoke artfully obscured the smell of coffee and artificial vanilla flavoring. I was looking forward to contributing to the smoke.

I put my metal tray down next to a big guy in a blue denim uniform with a musician's lyre on his sleeve—imagine the wimp in glasses sitting down next to Burt Lancaster in the prison cafeteria in *The Birdman Of Alcatraz*.

He ignored me. Out of the corner of my eye, I noticed him frantically digging through a mountain of scrambled eggs. He eventually narrowed his search to one large lump, carefully lifting a flap of egg to reveal one well done, inch-long, perfectly preserved cockroach. Scraping the offending tidbit to one side, he triumphantly declared: "I knew I saw that little fucker." I had just met Musician Second Class Maxwell Anderson, the school's military percussion instructor.

Max was a high-school music teacher from Wisconsin who had joined the Navy to avoid the draft. At the time, many musicians chose the Navy because their prospects were better here than in other branches of the military—a phenomenon that brought some very hip players to the Navy School of Music. Maxwell Anderson was not one of these. His musical vocabulary consisted of words such as 'precision' (as in marching), 'strict' (as in tempo), and authorized (as in these songs have been authorized for performance by the US Navy's music department). As I sat there trying to eat my food I was bombarded by discourse on toeing the line, military discipline, and—most incongruously for a sailor—not making waves.

Finally, as I stood to leave, Max gave me two or three once-overs.

"You need a haircut, Jerry," he said.

"Yeah," I mumbled, looking down at the cigarette butts sticking out of my eggs. "I know that, Max."

"I'll help you get squared away this morning."

"I don't want to take advantage of your time, Max."

"We'll have you shipshape in no time."

"Good, good … uh, Max? How long have you been in the Navy?"

"I came aboard 16 months ago," he said, straightening up, "but my father was a career Marine."

Max would become very disappointed in the months ahead when he came to realize that, for me, laying down a solid bassline under 'I Got Rhythm' chord changes was much more important than splicing a line or rendering a taut sheepshank knot.

After morning roll call, I followed Max to the concert band rehearsal room where my first class was to be held. These rooms have a very distinctive odor, so I felt right at home. First there is the oil used to lubricate the moving parts of the brass instruments, which permeates the hands, clothes, and even the breath of the players. Then, more subtly, there is the smell of saliva. Most of the people in a 30 or 40-piece concert band coax sounds from their instruments by buzzing their lips inside or over mouthpieces of various sizes. This technique is very similar to spitting, but while the average spitter takes between one and ten seconds to gather and expel the unwanted mass, a virtuoso trombonist will spit into his horn for a solid five minutes or more—the amount subject to the length of a given piece of music and how addicted he or she was to amphetamines.

If you multiply that by 20 or 30 people rehearsing for an hour or more … that's a lot of spit. Which brings us to the question: where does all the saliva go? You would think that band rooms would provide spittoons. Sadly, that's not the case. In each horn there is a valve placed at the lowest point in the horn. When the musicians notice that they sound as though they are playing underwater, they just reach down, open the valve, blow hard into the horn, and the collected saliva runs out onto the floor. Spit valves are notorious for leaking, however, and I have seen trombonists whose spit valves are located at the very end of their slides drive away whole sections of unsuspecting clarinet players sitting in front of them.

Because of the way tuba players hold their horns, the spit valve is right above their crotches. I myself have experienced the wet crotch phenomenon many times. Whenever I go to the symphony, as the musicians rise to take their bows, I immediately inspect the tuba player. If he has a dark spot on his tuxedo, I know he's probably not incontinent but rather lax in the care of his instrument.

In summary, then, band rooms the world over are united by pools of saliva evaporating from the floor and commingling with the sharp smell of lubricating oils.

My first chore that morning was to choose a sousaphone: the big brass instrument seen coiled around players' shoulders in marching bands. The sousaphone took the place of the tuba in marching bands back in the late 1800s because marching with a tuba caused back problems—imagine the difference between carrying all the weight of a garden hose out in front of you and coiling it around your neck with the weight supported by your shoulders.

At the Navy School of Music, the sousaphones could be found resting on padded wooden saddles in the instrument room. Some were silver, others were brass; some were dented and beaten up, others were pristine. They looked quite impressive, hanging in a row on the wall. Quite a few of them were already spoken for, so I had to make my choice from what was left.

The first thing I always do with a new sousaphone is stick my arm down the bell as far as I can, then give it a shake to see if there are any foreign objects beyond my reach. People are always using sousaphones as trash cans—in high school, I found stale half-eaten sandwiches, candy wrappers, and even a mummified mouse down there. At the Navy School of Music, the most curious object I found down there was a pair of women's panties. I still wonder how they got there, especially since we were an all-male outfit at the time. Maybe a cross dresser was caught red-handed in the instrument room, or maybe a couple got hot and bothered at a parade.

Speaking of parades, the only one from that time that sticks in my mind was when President Ferdinand Marcos of the Philippines came to Washington. They sent our concert band to stand on Pennsylvania Avenue and play as his motorcade passed by. The temperature was below freezing and snow was falling. Before we left the base, someone showed me how to cut the fingertips of my gloves so that I could play with minimum exposure. Nobody told me to keep my mouthpiece in my pocket when I wasn't playing. If you have ever put your tongue against an ice tray, you'll know what happened. My mouth and tongue were sore for days—and I still had to play.

At boot camp, I had managed to avoid most of the humdrum military duties, so it was a shock when I got to the Navy School and was required to stand on guard duty or found myself on the roster for the kitchen police. My good luck held, however, and I was assigned to a classical double-bass teacher from a major American symphony orchestra who didn't know how to wiggle his ass. Let's call him Jack. He was a very nice guy, confident in himself with nothing to prove—his career was already evident in his mastery of the bow.

During my first lesson, Jack asked me to sight read some exercises using the bow. He was not very impressed. He then asked me to sight read a few big-band jazz charts. Now he was impressed. He called a friend of his, US Army Sergeant Rom Ferry, who played jazz piano and taught musical theory at the school. Rom turned out to be my theory instructor.

Jack asked Rom to play a few bebop tunes with me, so Rom and I jammed for a while before lunch. Rom was a fabulous piano player. He was a friend of the great jazz pianist Bill Evans and was already experimenting with the new and innovative modal styles that Bill had been playing with Miles Davis. I had no idea how I fitted into this new environment, and I was scared shitless. I knew that people liked what I played—most of the time—but as always I half-thought that a lot of the praise I received was for the novelty of my being a teenage white boy in a black club, and I worried that there would be players like Ray Brown out there waiting to embarrass me. (Nowadays, I start to wonder whether some of the praise I get is because I'm an old man who can still play.)

Rom and Jack kept talking about the faculty jazz band, and I finally worked up enough nerve to ask about it. The band was made up of the premier jazz players in the school. Most of them were on the faculty, hence the name. During my next lesson with Jack, he asked me if I would like to take his place in the band. I was floored!

Jack knew his playing was stiff and that during the solos he could only read the written bass part over and over. He struggled with improvisation and felt that he was holding the other players back. Then he told me that, by being in this band, I would be taken off the duty rosters. No standing watch, no scrubbing toilets, no kitchen police—I'd been saved again.

One day, Rom Ferry invited me to go to the Spotlight Club in Washington, DC, to see Miles Davis perform. By now, I had played with some great players, but these were the big boys. Listening to Paul Chambers

THE SERGEANT'S LADY CHAPTER 11

play bass that night and on record had an influence on my playing that continues to this day. Bill Evans's piano playing was mind-blowing, and likewise his touch and phrasing had a huge influence on my own. John Coltrane, one of my all-time favorite tenor sax players, took modal jazz to great heights—and on that night at the Spotlight he was doing it right before my very ears and eyes. All because of Rom Ferry, I was able not only to hear those musicians that night but also to hang out with them. I don't remember saying a word. I was in shock.

After a few weeks of playing with the faculty jazz band, I started to get calls about paying gigs at officers' clubs in the area. I usually played with small combos or at most eight-piece bands. One night I was part of a small group at the NCO (non-commissioned officer) club at the Marine Corps Base in Quantico, Virginia, around 30 miles from Washington, DC. It was late on a Saturday night and the crowd had thinned out quite a bit. One sergeant and his lady had been drinking and dancing body-to-body all night. The sergeant had his hands on his partner's butt, pulling her close while she writhed against him. At times it seemed as if she was putting on a performance for us. She looked to be about 30 or so—a bit old for me, but when you're 17 years old ...

We were playing on a small stage with an upright piano positioned diagonally across one corner. As you stepped off the stage on that side you came to a small hallway that led to the restrooms. I stood with my string bass partially hidden behind the piano so that only my head and the scroll of my bass were visible to one side of the dance floor. The body of my bass blocked the view of the rest of me to the other half.

As the show continued, we leered as discreetly as possible at the sergeant's lady and alerted each other to the spectacle. At one point I noticed that she was giving me the eye and I'm sure I rushed the tempo of whatever we were playing. When we finished the song she got up and smiled at me on the way to the ladies' room.

About ten minutes later, midway through another song, I noticed the sergeant's lady crawling across the bandstand on her hands and knees, hidden from the view of those on the dance floor. She got to me and then calmly unzipped my pants. The piano player's eyes popped out of his head. About two or three seconds later—it wasn't long—she zipped me up and crawled back out into the hallway. Then, after hiding out for about five minutes, she made her grand re-entrance and went back to the dance floor as if nothing had happened.

We could hardly play after that, and the few remaining people in the club were looking at us strangely, wondering what was so funny—especially after the lady planted a big, wet kiss on the sergeant's mouth. I guess you could call that episode one of the perks of being a musician.

As well as performing at officers' clubs, I also played at civilian jazz clubs in the DC area, usually as part of a small trio of vibes, string bass, and drums. Once in a while, when we couldn't find any other paying gigs, we would play an after-hours show at a nearby house of ill repute in the basement of a three-story brownstone, complete with a red light (yes, really) on the door. Inside was a large, dimly lit room with a bar and women in various stages of undress sitting on faded, overstuffed couches. Being a skinny teenager, I would receive an exorbitant amount of teasing from the more worldly ladies who worked there. "I bet you're a virgin," they'd say, or: "Ain't it past your bedtime, lover?" or maybe: "How'd you like to come upstairs with Lulu and me and let us learn you the ropes?"

I had to work out some logistical problems in order to play these gigs. It was against Navy regulations for me to work in civilian clubs, and I didn't own my own bass. I had to arrange for my (civilian) drummer to pick me up at the school in his station wagon, and we would then smuggle an Official United States Military Property string bass into the back, covering it up with a blanket.

It's amazing I got away with it for as long as I did, but eventually, of course, I was caught. One evening, the guards at the gate asked me what was in the back of the station wagon. I later found out that I had been turned in by my favorite drum instructor, Max Anderson. I was shut down for a while, or at least until I found an old but decent-sounding German string bass, which I bought for two installments of $100 (two months' pay) and stored at the drummer's apartment.

It wasn't long, however, before I had to make a decision. I had graduated from my nine-month course and the Navy was trying to decide what to do with me. At one stage, I heard from my string-bass instructor that they were thinking of offering me one of the plum positions in the Navy music system: a role in the United States Military Academy Band in Annapolis, Maryland. This would have meant an automatic promotion to petty officer second class —a jump of three grades. I still had the moonlighting and using Navy property without authorization hanging over my head, but Rom Ferry told me that they were probably going to overlook that if I kept my nose clean.

Well, I tried.

One night I arrived back at base at around three in the morning, fresh from working in a civilian club, and saw a friend standing in the shadows outside the school building. He was supposed to be standing watch inside the building but had stepped outside to smoke a joint. When I got nearer I smelled the marijuana.

"Are you crazy?" I asked, but he told me he smoked it every night and not to worry.

Just then, the duty officer heard our voices, came around the corner, and busted us. It was Max Anderson. I have never been more scared in my life than I was that morning. Back then, smoking marijuana was serious business: Robert Mitchum had been sent to jail for the same thing a few years earlier, and I could be looking at up to five years behind bars just for a first offense. Being beaten to death sounded better than spending five years in jail.

We eventually convinced Max that I had nothing to do with the drug, so he agreed just to write me up. My friend, meanwhile, was sent to the brig to attend a court-martial. After lying awake all night, I went to my faculty jazz band rehearsal and told Jack, my string-bass instructor, what had happened. He was pissed off but he said he would see what he could do.

The next morning, Jack sat me down and told me an interesting story. He had been talking to another member of the faculty—let's call him Dave— about my problem. Dave was bisexual and had seen Max on the gay nightclub scene around DC. Dave and Max made a deal: Dave wouldn't expose Max's sexual orientation if he let me off with a misdemeanor hearing for something like, say, distracting a sentry. Back then, of course, being outed as gay in the military was almost as hazardous as being exposed as a drug addict.

Although this put paid to me being sent to Annapolis, I was thrilled to escape spending time in a federal prison. I was pleased also that part of the agreement between Max and Jack was that Max would say he only *thought* he smelled marijuana, which meant my friend the sentry managed to avoid the court-martial and got off with scrubbing pots and pans for a few weeks as punishment for the lesser offense of briefly abandoning his post.

Shortly thereafter, I was officially informed that, since I would not be going to the Military Academy in Annapolis, I was instead going to be sent to the Naval Amphibious Base in Coronado, California, where I would be joining a 19-piece big-band jazz outfit that had just returned from a worldwide goodwill tour for the USA. This was, in theory, my 'punishment,' but people in the know told me I was going to heaven. And they were right—I had been through boot camp in San Diego and loved the climate, so I was very happy to be going back.

In the meantime, back in DC, Christmas was coming and I was scheduled to go home to California on leave. After my leave, I had to go back to DC for a few weeks before transferring to Coronado. There was only one problem: I had to find a way to get my big double bass out to California. I asked around in the slim hope of finding someone who was driving to California, but the best I could do was an army drummer who was going home to St Louis, Missouri. I decided to chance it. I didn't know what I would do from St Louis onward, but I finally decided to try hitch-hiking from there. Worst come to worst, I'd spend all my Christmas money on a Greyhound bus ticket to Sacramento.

The army drummer and I hit it off right away. He was Italian and his family owned a restaurant in St Louis. We got there in the middle of the night and his elderly grandmother met us in her robe. She lived in a small apartment above the restaurant while the rest of the family were out in the suburbs. She gave us red wine and cookies and then went down to the restaurant to heat up some dinner. "Mangia, mangia!" she yelled. "Eat,

eat!" She also let me sleep in a cot at the back of the restaurant. My clothes smelled like garlic for two days afterward. I loved it!

The next morning the army drummer took me out to the main westward highway, and I was suddenly alone. I laid my string bass on its side in the snow, sat down on it, pulled my wool peacoat collar up around my ears, and stuck out my thumb.

In those days, the US military still had a shining image. Because I was dressed in military uniform, and even though I had this enormous instrument with me, I got a ride almost immediately. A black army sergeant in a station wagon on his way to report for duty in Washington State took me as far as Salt Lake City. He and I faced the same problems with discrimination that Les Buie and I had had on our way to DC the year before: very few restaurants would serve us, so we lived on takeout hamburgers for two-and-a-half days.

The drummer dropped me off at a Greyhound bus station just outside Salt Lake City, where I decided to go in and have something to eat. I carried my bass in and stood in a corner where I could keep an eye on it. The restaurant was crowded, so I sat at the counter next to a young family of four. The father and I started talking, and it turned out he'd been in the Navy, too. One thing led to another and he pointed to a large sedan with a small trailer hitched behind. He and his family were going to live in San Francisco, he told me, and if I didn't mind tying my bass to the trailer, the main highway was only two blocks from my mother's house in Sacramento. Sometimes I really do lead a charmed life.

My father was working as an engineer at Mather Air Force Base at the time, and at the end of my leave he arranged some space for me aboard an old C-47 bound for Washington, DC. Nicknamed Gooney Birds by pilots, C-47s were the two-engine transporters that flew over the Himalayan mountains during World War II. They were configured for paratroopers and on each side of the fuselage had a run of hard metal benches with indentations for your buttocks, although because there were only a few of us on the plane we all commandeered parachutes for padding (not that packed parachutes are particularly soft).

There was no soundproofing on the plane, so the engines were deafening. There was also very little heat, so once we were up to altitude, we all had columns of frost coming out of our mouths. After landing and refueling several times, we got caught in violent thunderstorms over the Southwest—people were vomiting and the plane felt like it was going to come apart. We ended up having to make an emergency landing at a small out-of-the-way Air Force base in Oklahoma, where we were stuck for two days—which in turn meant that I would be late reporting back for duty in DC. I was in trouble again.

I think the administrating officers at the Navy School of Music were relieved when I finally left. It's not that I was a bad person—I just wasn't suited to a regimented existence. Fortunately, my next port of call was a magic kingdom where I would take up a position in what was probably the least regimented outfit in the military.

ABOVE: Jerry aged two in Denver, Colorado.
RIGHT: Sailor Jerry. **BELOW**: Playing jazz at age 15.
The guitarist in the background is Les Buie.

On stage with Elvis at the International Convention
Center in Honolulu, Hawaii, January 14 1973.

ABOVE: The baby TCB Band, c.1970.
Left to right: Ronnie Tutt, Jerry, James Burton,
John Wilkinson, Glen D. Hardin. **RIGHT**: Playing
for The King c. 1975.

LEFT: Recording *LA Woman* with The Doors, January 1971. *Left to right*: Jerry, Mark Benno, Robby Krieger, Jim Morrison.
RIGHT: On stage with Elvis, mid 70s.
BELOW: With Bob Dylan on the US leg of his 1978 World Tour.

Madison Square Garden, September 30
1978. *Left to right*: Billy Cross, Ian Wallace,
Bob Dylan, Jerry.

TOP LEFT: Band meeting with Bob Dylan, 1978.
Left to right: Jerry, drummer Ian Wallace, guitarist
Billy Cross, vocalist Steven Soles, Dylan.
BELOW LEFT: Taking off with John Denver, mid 80s.
ABOVE: Playin' and smokin' with Roy Orbison for *A
Black & White Night Live*, 1989.

ABOVE: With Elvis Costello & The Confederates outside the Royal Albert Hall, London, England, 1987. *Left to right*: Jim Keltner (drums), James Burton (guitar), Costello, Jerry, Benmont Tench (keys), T-Bone Wolk (whatever else was needed).
RIGHT: Playing the tuba with Elvis Costello & The Rude 5, 1989.

LEFT: Jerry the bass terrorist, 90s.
ABOVE: On stage in Chicago for Lakland
Basses with four other monsters of bass.
Left to right: Duck Dunn, Jerry, Joe
Osborn, Darryl Jones, Bob Glaub.

FOLLOWING PAGE: Getting way down,
mid 2000s.

BACK TO CALIFORNIA

oronado, California, sits at the north end of a long isthmus. It is almost an island. On one side is San Diego Harbor and on the other side is the Pacific Ocean. Back in 1959, there was a regular ferry service from San Diego. I remember stepping off the boat and getting my first view of the place. Suddenly, all was right with the world. This was my Shangri-la.

I rode the bus past the naval air base, with its huge, gray aircraft carriers, into a street lined with palm trees and jacaranda. The pace of life seemed to slow down automatically. At the end of the road was a large white Victorian building: the Hotel del Coronado. It's still there, and it's still just as beautiful. You can see it in numerous movies, from *Some Like It Hot* to *My Blue Heaven*. Beyond the hotel to the west there was nothing but miles and miles of unspoiled beaches—the Silver Strand, as it is known. To the east was my new home, the Naval Amphibious Base.

As I stepped off the bus I was shocked out of my reverie by the sight of panting, grunting men wearing nothing but shoes and shorts and running around with huge logs in their arms. For a moment I worried whether this was the exercise program for the band, but it turned out that I had been stationed at the West Coast training center for what used to be called Underwater Demolition Teams (now known as Navy Seals).

When I got to the band room, I met my new bandmaster, Sid Zaramby.

He was the oldest enlisted man in the Navy at that time—he never told anyone his age, but we knew he had joined up in 1917. He looked like Jimmy Durante, with a huge nose that hung down almost to his lips and a cigar always on the go. Even when we played at very solemn naval ceremonies, Sid would still have a cigar sticking out of the side of his mouth. If ever we got to play at a less solemn occasion—a ship full of Marines headed out to the Middle East, for example—Sid turned into a vaudevillian. He would put on a brightly colored 'Top Banana' hat and oversized clown shoes to belt out Cab Calloway's 'Minnie The Moocher.' Nobody messed with him. He was on first-name terms with the admiral and was almost untouchable.

Once in a while we would play a military ceremony on the base. There were only 20 of us, but that was more than enough to wreak havoc with the troops. We had a drummer named Bill Cady who had been in the Navy a long time. Bill smoked a lot of dope and didn't take anything too seriously. The one time we went out to sea while I was in the Navy—a two week sail to San Francisco and back—Bill brought with him a small fruitcake tin filled with pre-rolled joints. Most of the other band-members brought sunglasses and cheap canvas deck-chairs so we could sunbathe on the fantail. The sailors hated us. When we stood in line for chow, the servers would give us the smallest cuts of meat they could find. Finally, we complained to Sid, who suggested we take a small rock'n'roll combo to the chow hall for an hour at lunch every day. That did it—from then we couldn't do anything wrong. The ship's sailmaker even put heavier canvas on our deck chairs. We ate well and developed our tans.

Back on land, when we played ceremonies we would stand off to the side so that the rest of the troops from the base could march to and fro, thereby putting on a smart exhibition for the top brass. If the marching got sloppy, the officers responsible for training these men would get the blame. We tried to make it as difficult for them as possible.

Our day-to-day routine was usually very lax. We had to be at the band room at 8:00am, but Sid usually came in around 10. There were 19 of us, and at least half of us were addicted to double-deck pinochle. When we got in at 8, we would change into our Navy dungarees and T-shirts, sit down four to a table, and then someone would yell: "Deal 'em!"

Often, when Sid eventually rolled in around 10 or 11, he would simply look around and say: "Aw, for Christ sakes, get the hell outta here!" For me, getting the hell outta there meant going back to the beach, where I would cultivate my tan while the frogmen busted their asses. At night, some of us would carry cases of beer over to the beach and build a fire to roast hotdogs. It was a hard life.

This routine was interrupted on occasion, however, when the admiral in charge decided that morale in his offices might be boosted by our appearing outside the windows to play music at 8:30am, starting with 'Oh, What A Beautiful Morning!'

Sid had to come in early for these performances, too, of course, so he wasn't too thrilled about having to do them either. Our drummer had a bird whistle that tweeted loudly when filled with water, and Sid would instruct him to stand in front of the band and tweet as loud as he could while the rest of us played softly. He then came up with the idea of having us follow 'Oh, What A Beautiful Morning!' with our most raucous marches. Sid had spent many a night drinking with the admiral and rightly suspected that there would be a few sore heads in the building. When we got to the marches, windows soon began to slam shut. We were back to pinochle the following morning.

Before long I started meeting local musicians and playing in San Diego clubs. I played string bass with a few different groups, one of which was a modern jazz group featuring the late great drummer John Guerin, the wonderful pianist Mike Wofford, a fantastic trumpet player named Don Sleet, and a great tenor saxophone player named Gary Lefebvre.

These guys were heavily into the modal jazz I'd first heard in Washington, DC, as played by the Miles Davis Sextet. This was a much sought-after learning experience for me. We were playing in a very energetic way, right on top of the beat. My string-bass chops were probably at their peak.

One time we played at a club in La Jolla, California, called the Pour House, where two giants of the Los Angeles music scene, flautist Buddy

Collette and drummer Earl Palmer, came to sit in. Earl was originally from New Orleans—he had played with Little Richard and Fats Domino, and was now one of the top session drummers in Hollywood. (Among many other things, he's on 'You've Lost That Lovin' Feelin',' 'La Bamba,' and the soundtrack to the TV series *M*A*S*H*.) Buddy meanwhile had played with everyone from Miles to Ella and was also an in-demand session man.

Earl and Buddy came on stage to a round of applause. We started up a slow blues. Even back then, as a teenager, I had played a lot of rhythm & blues, but for some reason—perhaps because I was so influenced by John's jazz drumming—I must have sounded a little stiff.

"Hey, bass player," Earl hissed. "Shake your ass a little." I knew exactly what he meant.

Earl and I went on to work together on numerous occasions, while in the 80s he became the treasurer of my local musicians' union. One day I ran into him at the union and congratulated him.

"Yeah," he replied, grinning his cool grin. "Ain't that some shit."

At the time, back in 1959, John, Mike, Don, and I were 18, 19, 20 years old—we had no idea what kind of impact we might have on the music scene. As it happened, though, as well as having a profound impact on my musical development, these guys would also go on to have interesting careers in their own right.

During the 60s, John Guerin worked with jazz artists like Buddy DeFranco and Thelonious Monk before developing an interest in rock and touring with The Byrds and Joni Mitchell on the way to becoming one of the most recorded drummers of all time. He also founded the group LA Express and worked on film soundtracks, most notably Clint Eastwood's Charlie Parker biopic, *Bird*, for which he grafted new instrumental parts onto original recordings of Parker's sax.

Mike Wofford went on to work with everyone from Ella Fitzgerald and Sarah Vaughan to John Lennon and Quincy Jones. He has also recorded numerous albums of his own and was the staff pianist on *The Cosby Show*. He and I later worked together on an album by Howard Roberts called *Equinox Express Elevator* (which, coincidentally, John played on, too).

Don Sleet was the first of us to leave for the big time when he signed to the Jazzland label. He promptly went off to New York City to record his only solo album with Miles Davis's rhythm section: Jimmy Heath (sax), Wynton Kelly (piano), Ron Carter (bass), and Jimmy Cobb (drums). Sadly, however, Don did not have time to fulfill his genius. Like so many young jazz musicians of the time, he became addicted to heroin and was rumored to have been ordered by a judge, on his third conviction on drug-related charges, to give up playing jazz.

Several years later, I was playing at Shelly's Manhole in Los Angeles when someone came up and told me that Don was at the back door and couldn't come in. By the time I got there, however, he had gone. I never knew why he thought he couldn't come into the club, but maybe he was afraid he'd get busted. It's a heartbreaking story, and one that makes me think: it could have been me.

Back in the late 50s and early 60s, there weren't yet many freeways in Southern California, just a series of beach towns joined up by a two-lane highway. Every beach town seemed to have its own jazz club, and some of them opened out right onto the beach. If you, as a musician, could talk the talk, you would usually be allowed to sit in for a song or two—or more, if you could really play.

One night in 1961, I went with the Navy band to play a military function in Long Beach. It was only a two-hour drive, so we took our own cars up the beautiful coastline. I had just bought a sky-blue 1959 Pontiac convertible, so I put my sousaphone in the trunk and set out with a friend in the passenger seat.

On the way back to San Diego we passed through a little beach town called Mission Beach where I noticed a club with a sign that said Sunday Afternoon Jazz. I couldn't pass that up. We went in and listened to the band and were told that some Los Angeles session players were having fun on a sunny Sunday afternoon.

I was never too shy about asking to play, but this time the bass player said no. I was disappointed. I had been playing jazz on the tuba for a few months with a few of the guys from the Navy band so I asked if I could sit in on tuba. I saw their eyes dart around from one to the other until the trumpet player said: "Yeah, sure kid. Let's see what you can do."

The trumpet player, Jack Sheldon, was a member of Stan Kenton's band as well as a studio regular in LA. He was—and I presume still is—known for his jokes and monologues. I'm sure the only reason he agreed to let me play tuba with his band was because of the comedic possibilities on offer.

I ran outside to get my—or rather the Navy's—sousaphone. There was much laughter and eye-rolling as I came back in with such a huge horn. Jack called what I assume he thought would be a difficult, up-tempo song: 'Straight, No Chaser' by Thelonious Monk. Fortunately, it was one of my favorite jazz songs, and one I had been playing quite often on the tuba. After that, Jack asked me what other songs I knew, and I had a great time.

The crowd loved the novelty of jazz sousaphone. As I was leaving, the club's owner asked for my phone number. Sure enough, the following Wednesday, he called and offered me $50 to appear the next Sunday. That was a lot of money back then—$50 would cover my car payment for the month.

The next Sunday, I drove up the coast to Mission Beach to find a big paper banner that read: "Featuring Jerry Scheff On Jazz Tuba." I played two hour-long sets and had a great time, and the owner asked me to return the following week. Unbeknownst to me, however, Sid Zaramby drove through Mission Beach on his way home from Coronado to Long Beach at weekends. He'd spotted my name on the club as he drove by that second Sunday.

On Monday morning, Sid called me into his office and told me what he'd seen. I remember feeling quite proud until he asked me whose tuba I'd been using. That was the end of my jazz tuba stardom.

Fortunately, there were other jobs closer to home. Across the water from Coronado, the Black Elks Club in San Diego was what I would call a typical lodge hall with a nice-sized auditorium and a stage built into the wall. I got a job playing in the house band through Teddy Pico, a tenor sax player I met one Sunday afternoon at the house of legendary boxer Archie Moore.

Sunday afternoons at Archie's were heady times for a 20-year-old, but it was just one of many interesting places my bass-playing took me. Various luminaries of the San Diego scene would show up to enjoy the jam sessions, swim in the pool, and eat some great food, including several members of the Black Elks Club. One thing led to another and there I was playing in a kind of knock-off of the Ray Charles band: piano, bass, guitar, drums, three female backing singers, and four horns. It was a great band.

Every Saturday night we had a guest artist—usually someone from Los Angeles. When Ben Webster came to play with us —the same Ben Webster who had been a regular at my old haunt Jimbo's Bop City in San Francisco— he needed a place to stay, so some friends and I picked him up at the Greyhound station and took him to where we were living on Ocean Beach, San Diego. He had on a black suit, white shirt, and a hip-looking tie which was loose around his neck. He had his tenor sax with him and a small suitcase that we assumed was full of clothes and maybe a tooth brush.

When we got to the house, however, Ben opened up the case to reveal an assortment of carefully stacked half-pint bottles of Grand MacNish Scotch Whisky. He said that a distributor had given it to him by the case. We drank Scotch with Ben and picked his brain. Once we got him started he was a wonderful gossip, full of tales about people like Billie Holiday and Duke Ellington.

That Saturday night, when Ben played with us at the Black Elks Club, he asked Bob, the sax player, to pick a song. Bob suggested an uptempo number that Ben obviously didn't know too well. When the time came for the first solo, Bob ripped through the changes like a madman. He was obviously trying to make Ben Webster—arguably the greatest tenor sax player in the world at the time—look bad. Next, Bob asked Ben to pick a song, and Ben suggested a ballad, 'Body And Soul'—a beautiful song played in an awkward key and full of difficult chord changes. After Ben finished his solo, Bob decided he didn't want to follow him.

A week or two later, our guests were The Three Tons Of Joy: three black women who lived up to their name and who were most famous for singing on the Johnny Otis hit 'Willie & The Hand Jive.' That night I added some unexpected excitement to the proceedings. Before the show, one of the musicians invited me outside for a little of what he called mood stimulation. I had tried marijuana a few times by then but had never been too knocked out about it (no pun intended). He pulled a small pipe out of his pocket and lit up. I took a couple of hits and went back to work.

On my way out to the stage I remember thinking: God, this is starting to feel a little good. The dance floor was packed. We played a few instrumentals to warm up the audience and then the announcer introduced The Three Tons Of Joy.

All of a sudden everything went dark. The next thing I remember was opening my eyes and seeing three very large worried-looking African-American women peering down at me. I'd passed out and fallen flat on my back—luckily, somebody had caught my bass. The crowd had edged up to the front of the stage, and when a couple of guys carried me off there was a round of applause. I watched the world spin for a while and then went back out to play the rest of the show. Only later did I realize that what was in the pipe had probably been laced with heroin.

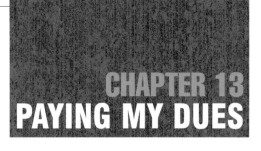

CHAPTER 13

PAYING MY DUES

U ntil now I had not really found myself out on my own in the world. I had the Navy to fall back on. As I got closer to my discharge date, then, I had some decisions to make. Sid, my bandmaster, was being transferred to Naples, Italy, where he would lead the NATO band. He wanted me to go with him. All I had to do was extend my enlistment by two years. By all accounts, there was no US Navy base in Naples, so the musicians in the NATO band lived in a hotel, ate pizza three times a day, rode around on motorcycles with beautiful Italian girls' arms wrapped around their waists, and drank Chianti on the beach with them until the sun came up.

It was all very tempting, and yet many of the musicians I had played with in San Diego had moved on to bigger things. John Guerin, Mike Wofford, and Don Sleet had all gone north to Los Angeles. Stan Bronstein had moved back to New York City. I called John and asked him if he knew of anybody needing a bass player in Los Angeles. He told me that things didn't work like that there—I would just have to come there and sit in at jam sessions until I developed a reputation. The thought of that scared the crap out of me. I envisioned hordes of monster bass-players fighting for every gig—and I was right about that. What I hadn't even started to think about was the electric bass and the potential for developing what was at the time a completely new concept in bass-playing.

In the end, the combination of a lack of self esteem and my not being able to make a decision caused me to embark on a two-year period of what I guess you'd call paying my dues. I was discharged from the US Navy on my 21st birthday and took a job in a San Diego jazz club. I got together with the singer there a few times and before you knew it I became a father to two sons, Jason and Darin.

My sons are now in their forties. After a few sputtering starts, Darin became an internet mogul while also dabbling in the real-estate business. He's a very talented musician and singer, too, but chooses just to enjoy his music, although he did work professionally for a while. (Once, in the early 90s, he surprised me at a music festival in Scandinavia, where I was playing with Elvis Costello, by showing up and revealing that his band was on the bill, too.) Darin and his wife Cindy have two daughters and a son: Lauren Eve, Rachel, and William 'Willie G.' Graham. He's a much better father than I have ever been, and I am very proud of him.

Jason is a professional bass player and pop singer. When he was in his early twenties, Jason's agent sent a tape of his songs to Warner Bros, where it wound up on the desk of top executive Michael Ostin. Sometimes timing is everything in music, and it certainly was then. The rock group Chicago had just lost their bass player and vocalist, Peter Cetera, who had left to begin a solo career. Michael called the other guys in the band: "You're not going to believe this … ." Twenty years later, Jason is still a member of Chicago. He and his wife Tracy have two sons, Jason Jerry and Connor, and Jason is also stepdad to Tracy's kids Clark James and Kayley Gable.

Back in 1963, I had some serious thinking to do about the future. I landed a job at a resort hotel six nights a week and enrolled at San Diego State College with hopes of becoming a teacher—a nice sensible career for a family man.

By now my political opinions had matured, but liberal and conservative agendas had not yet entered my realm of thought. As I look back on it, I had some pretty naïve opinions about America and the American people. I would never have believed that the average American would ever want to kill another person, and certainly not that anyone would—based on nothing more than a different political viewpoint—rejoice at the killing of the President of the United States of America. I was about to grow up fast.

I remember clearly standing outside San Diego State College at lunchtime on the afternoon of November 22 1963, when the public address announced that President John F. Kennedy had been shot in Dallas. A groan went up around me. I was shocked beyond imagination. This was not the kind of thing that happened in my country.

I was scheduled to play a formal ball that night at a Mission Valley country club but I was sure it would be cancelled. I repeatedly called the orchestra leader for updates, until I eventually learned that the show was to go on and that I was expected to show up in my tuxedo, bass in hand.

I parked in the back lot and entered through the kitchen. Many of the kitchen staff were crying or just standing around in shock. As I walked into the ballroom, however, I saw a group of rich white folk in gowns and tuxedos laughing and slapping each other on the back. I didn't understand what I was witnessing.

There were tables set up at one end of the ballroom with floral centerpieces, crystal wineglasses, and polished silver. We were expected to play quiet dinner music. After a few songs, a man stood up and gave a speech about business in the great country of America and the fact that nothing and no one could hold back those who truly understood the potential of this great land of opportunity. He then proposed a toast to the prosperity—which, it went without saying, would now surely bless those in attendance. Everybody stood to cheer and clink their glasses. Our president was dead, and these people were cheering.

My early career was awash with fits and starts. There are any number of reasons why I settled for whatever flotsam and jetsam floated up on my musical beach. I had already found myself working with great musicians, playing great music, but I lacked self esteem. I was not yet emotionally ready for the big time.

In the wake of Kennedy's assassination, I knew that I was on the wrong track. My plans for fitting into the 'straight' world were bullshit. After witnessing that night of revelry at the country club in Mission Valley, I didn't even know who was straight and who was really fucked up. What I did know was that I wasn't going to become one of those coldhearted people— not now and not ever.

It was also beginning to dawn on me that I couldn't carry on working until 2:00am and then going to school during the day. A few months earlier, I had met a trumpet-playing doctor back at Archie Moore's house who prescribed me Dexamyl spansules—or Christmas trees, as they became known. They kept me awake but my health soon started to slide.

I was looking for a way out of my six-nights-a-week hotel gig when I met a piano player and singer named Craig Evans. Craig sang standards and accompanied himself with a modern jazz-oriented style while his friend Gil Palacio sang and played congas and other Latin percussion. They asked me to join them for a regular gig at a place called the Club Marina in the San Diego seaside community of Point Loma.

Back in the early 60s there was still a big market at supper clubs and hotel lounges across the USA for show groups singing cornball songs mixed with stale humor. The audience was usually a mix of diffident diners, drunk businessmen, and tired hookers. The Club Marina catered to some of that crowd, but the club's mainstays were San Diego tuna fishermen, mostly of Portuguese decent. Craig and Gil were having a hard time keeping this crowd happy and were looking for a way to inject a little showbiz into the act.

It was around the same time that I heard about a musician in Las Vegas who played the electric bass by tapping the strings against the fingerboard with his left hand, leaving his right hand free to hold and play a valve trombone. I immediately went out and bought a Fender Precision Bass: my first electric instrument. I then got a valve trombone and a small drum set.

After a few rehearsals, the tapped bass part became automatic. It's like driving a car—after a while you don't really think about what you're doing with the pedals or the steering wheel. Once I'd mastered the bass part, I added a kick drum and a hi-hat, which I played with a drumstick in my right hand, hitting eighth notes with the tip and backbeats or bossa nova clicks with the butt. Once I had all of that down pat, I could put down the drumstick—still keeping the kick drum and hi-hat going with my feet—and pick up the valve trombone, or sing, depending on what the song needed. Craig, Gil, and I were fans of The Four Freshmen, so we worked up three-part harmonies in a similar jazz-vocal style, as well as playing bossa novas and rock songs like 'The Twist.'

What's wrong with that, you might ask? Well, suffice it to say that by the time we put our show together, it was filled with toilet humor, while at one point we all appeared in drag makeup and bras padded out with water balloons. (Needless to say, the grand finale revolved around bursting the balloons.) We kept the job for months. The fishermen and their dates loved us, but eventually we got stale and had to move on.

Our next job was at a club with a huge runway-style bar built in the shape of a piano. We were set up on the inside of the bar while the customers sat around the outside or at the tables and chairs that filled the rest of the room. Craig, Gil, and I were there to accompany the strippers who danced up on the bar above us. As the quasi-drummer, it was my job to follow the hip thrusts and shimmies of the girls as far as my neck would swivel and keep the music in time. One night an older couple came in and sat down at the bar opposite me. At the end of one of the songs, the woman said: "Isn't that disgusting! That filthy-minded drummer can't keep his eyes off those girls!" My neck ached for weeks after we left that job.

It was around this time that I was approached to go to Albuquerque, New Mexico, with a lounge act called The Chuck Steele Show Featuring Jeanie. Chuck was a guitar player, while his wife Jeanie was a beautiful girl with a jaw-dropping body and a voice like a dry axel. They had a pretty good drummer, at least, so all I had to do was play Fender bass and valve trombone and sing a few Dixieland songs like 'Bill Bailey, Won't You Please Come Home?' and 'St James' Infirmary.'

I also sang a comparatively recent song, '(Get Your Kicks On) Route 66' by Bobby Troup. As it happens, Route 66 was the road we took to Albuquerque. I rode out with the drummer. We were in the middle of the desert when we spotted Jeanie's car by the side of the road. We pulled over to see Jeanie, wearing a pair of tight shorts, standing by herself a few hundred yards out into the desert. This felt like a good opportunity to talk to her alone. She said she was just stretching her legs, and I scolded her protectively about being alone in the middle of nowhere.

A minute or two later, another car pulled up. It was Chuck's Cadillac. I didn't think too much about it but evidently he did. He stomped out to us, grabbed Jeanie by the arm, and told me he had something to show me back at the car.

Back at the cars, Chuck opened the trunk and there, beneath the guitars and amplifier, was a case full of guns and ammunition. He pulled out an enormous pistol and aimed it at a beer can down the road. When he fired, the can flew into the air, and as it landed he fired again and shot it back up—just like in the movies.

"Let's go, Chuck!" Jeanie said, grabbing him by the arm, but Chuck wasn't through yet.

"You ever shoot a gun, Jerry?" he asked.

"Yeah, I got my 'sharpshooter' badge in the Navy," I replied.

"Oh, a sharpshooter, eh? Let's see how sharp your shooting is."

With that Chuck handed me a .22 rifle and suggested we find something to shoot. We walked around a bit until Chuck flushed out a covey of quail and set the rules of the game: whoever hits a quail first is the winner. I had never even fired at a moving target before but I figured I might as well play along.

"You go first, Jerry."

Chuck threw a rock and a quail came running out from behind a bush. I fired a quick shot in the bird's general direction.

"Damn, Jerry, you hit one!"

We walked over and Chuck picked up the dead bird. I was devastated and ready to faint. I had never killed a living thing before and I would never do so again.

By the end of a month in Albuquerque I was sick of singing Bill Bailey songs and listening to Chuck butcher 'Malagueña,' so I quit The Chuck Steel Show and went back to San Diego to work with a deaf accordion player named Tony Lovello. Tony was and still is a star—the king of the bellows-shakers. If you've ever heard an accordionist play 'Lady Of Spain' while shaking the bellows of his instrument, you'll know what I am talking about. Tony had been a member of a group called The Three Suns, who'd had a big hit in 1944 with 'Twilight Time.' He wasn't the group's original accordionist, but he'd played with them enough times during the 50s that he was able to go on to become a showman on his own.

When I started playing with Tony I was told that he had lost his hearing—we had to play strictly with him because he couldn't hear us. I was also told that he knew every joke that could ever be played on a deaf accordion player—so don't even think about it. I never really knew the exact extent of Tony's hearing loss but I was amazed at how well he played. (I still think he must have been able to hear himself a little bit.)

While we played, Tony's wife and sister-in-law sang and danced in DayGlo costumes. We also had a trumpet player and song-and-dance man who played the bass while I did a soft-shoe routine with a cane and a hat. This was quite a challenge for me, so I wasn't exactly bored to death, but I knew this wasn't going to be the act that got me to the big time.

For this group, in fact, hitting the big time meant a booking in Nevada as a lounge act—and eventually we did make it, securing a slot opening for a guitar player named Nick Lucas at Harrah's in Reno. Nick was a white jazz guitar-player nicknamed The Crooning Troubadour. He'd recorded numerous hit records during the 20s and 30s, and there was even a special Nick Lucas model of guitar in the Gibson catalogue. One of his most famous songs was 'Tiptoe Through The Tulips,' which was later a hit for Tiny Tim in the 60s.

By the time I got to play with him, however, Nick's career was on the wane, and I couldn't help but laugh at the average age of the women standing at the edge of the stage, genuinely swooning as he sang. I was young, you see, and young musicians often don't realize that some day, if they're lucky, they'll be playing to *their* aged fans, too. (Believe me, I know, and I'm very grateful for it.)

Shortly after the Reno show I heard from my old pals Craig Evans and Gil Palacio again. They had a job lined up in a hotel in Palm Springs, California. There would be no comedy this time: all we had to do was play dinner music from 5:30 to 8:30pm every night except Sunday. The money was great and the hotel provided rooms and food.

I dusted off my drums and for a month or so we lived the sweet life: steaks for breakfast, lunch, and dinner; young women and older women; golf during the day; hanging out and sitting in with other musicians; all-night swim parties in the desert air with foot-long dead lizards floating in chlorine-soaked pools. Another bonus was that I was close to San Diego, which meant I could see my sons, Jason and Darin, more often.

I wasn't particularly happy with the music I'd been playing for the past two years but I figured that time was still on my side and I could move to Los Angeles as soon as I had worked up enough nerve. That came sooner than I expected.

In late 1963 I met an attractive woman named Vivian Varon in Palm Springs. Vivian was 34 at the time—about ten years older than me. She was a very diminutive four-foot eleven but her personality more than made up for the missing inches. If she was sitting down and someone asked her how tall she was, she always told them she was five-foot eight—and the other person would always believe her.

Vivian owned two shops in Palm Springs: a gift shop at the Spa Hotel and a flower shop on the Village Green. She also worked as an interior decorator, specializing in accessories. Her past clients include President Dwight Eisenhower and his wife Mamie, comedian Red Skelton, and singing cowboy turned hotel magnate Gene Autry. I went to the Eisenhowers' house with Vivian once to collect some money that Mamie owed. I heard Mamie complain that she had to pay Vivian out of her 'canasta money' because Dwight was too cheap to give it to her.

The first time Vivian and I went to dinner in a fancy restaurant was the first time I ordered a bottle of wine. I was pretending to read the wine list but I had no idea of what it all meant, so I put on my most sophisticated face and told Vivian I was sure she'd have a favorite.

"I would like pinot noir," she replied. I told her it was a good choice when in fact I couldn't even pronounce it. When the wine steward came back, I pointed to the name on the list and the steward complimented me on my choice. When the steward returned with the bottle, he held it out to show it to me and I jerked it out of his hands and asked him if he had a cork screw. We had a good laugh about that. I had a lot to learn.

On one of my Sundays off, Vivian and I hopped into my gold Ford Mustang Fastback and drove into Los Angeles for the day. When we returned to Palm Springs that evening, I pulled up to the hotel where I lived and worked, only to find that it was no longer there. My clothes, my instruments, and my job were all lost in piles of ashes, charred mattress springs, and other bits of debris. The hotel had burned down.

There was much speculation that the hotel owners had torched the place for the insurance money. Either way, I had nothing to lose now. No more excuses. Now was the time to move to Los Angeles and take on some of the best bass players in the world. The only problem was that, after the fire, I didn't have a bass any more.

CHAPTER 14
THE LA PLUNGE

spent the night after the fire at Vivian's house and drove into Los Angeles the next day. My sister Gloria and her husband Dick lived in Westminster, just south of LA, so I had a place to stay while I tried to find some work.

My only real lead was a saxophone player named Mike Henderson, who Craig, Gil, and I had played with a few times. I called him up immediately. Fortunately, Mike knew of a rock group who needed a bass player at a poker club in Gardena, California, just a few miles south of LA. I applied for the job and was accepted. It wasn't the most glamorous of jobs, however, and meant I'd be going from several hundreds dollars per week in Palm Springs to $90 per week in Gardena.

I had child support to pay for my two sons in San Diego, so now I was really in a bind. A few years earlier, when we'd first discussed the child support, I had agreed to pay more than the court had initially ordered. Now, I was struggling to make the payments. The boys' mother told the collection agency where I was living, and before long my beloved Mustang Fastback had been repossessed, and there I was, without wheels in a city with no public transportation to speak of.

I had lost my bass in Palm Springs, too, and had very little money to my name, so I had to settle for a borrowed Japanese bass for my first gig in LA. Today, Japanese instruments are very good. Back in 1963, they weren't so hot. Both the bass and the amp I borrowed sounded terrible to me. Nobody said anything negative, but there were no raves about my playing, either.

The leader of our group in Gardena was a drummer who also sang lead. As is so often the case, he was the worst player in the band—he would have struggled to find a groove in the Grand Canyon. (His vocals were passable.)

The guitar player in the band was a very likable guy from Texas named Billy Irwin. He and his wife, Shara, had a spare couch and let me move in with them and share the rent. All of a sudden I had a ride to work, decent food, and—most importantly—some companionship. Billy and Shara were the perfect couple. She had had surgery for a foot problem, and had to chose whether she wanted to wear flats or heels for the rest of her life. She chose high heels, and now when she tiptoed around the house she reminded me of a little girl trying to be taller than her brother.

Our piano player, who also doubled on saxophone, was Butch Parker. Butch knew Mike Henderson, who had helped get me the job in the band in the first place. Butch and Mike would continue to feature prominently in my early career—particularly when, a few weeks later, they introduced me to a guy from Arizona by the name of Gary Paxton.

Now, let me tell you about the vanilla pond that I, Jerry Scheff—a jazz and rhythm & blues junkie and one time would-be black person—was about to jump into. When I first met Gary Paxton, in 1964, he was living in an old two-story house on Argyle Avenue in Hollywood, California, with his wife Jan and their baby daughter. Jan called the place home; Gary called it his recording studio.

By the time I met him, Gary had already made and lost a couple of million dollars. I believe his first success came in the duo Skip & Flip—Skip being Gary's old buddy Clyde 'Skip' Battin, who would later play with The Byrds and The Flying Burrito Brothers. Skip and Flip went to Phoenix, Arizona, to cut the first song Gary ever wrote, 'It Was I.' It sold over a million copies. The follow-up, 'Cherry Pie,' sold 250,000 copies. After that, Gary and Skip went their separate ways.

Both of these records were produced by another friend of Gary's from Arizona, Kim Fowley. Gary and Kim went on to form a bogus group called

The Hollywood Argyles—named for the street Gary lived on—and had a huge hit single in 1960 with 'Alley Oop.' The drummer on the record was Sandy Nelson, who became the first successful instrumental rock drummer with his 1959 Number Four hit 'Teen Beat' and the album *Let There Be Drums*, a key influence on The Beach Boys and the surf boom. (A few years later, Sandy lost a leg in a motorcycle accident. I played some sessions with him after that and was amazed at how well he could still play.)

In 1962, Gary and Kim found an actor who could imitate horror-movie star Boris Karloff and made a record just in time for Halloween called 'Monster Mash,' which was billed as being by Bobby 'Boris' Pickett & The Crypt-Kickers. None of the big record companies were interested so Gary put it out on his own Garpax label. It was another million-selling smash hit (and indeed would re-enter the chart, twice, when it was re-released in 1970 and 1973).

Kim meanwhile went on to produce The Rivingtons' smash hit 'Papa-Oom-Mow-Mow.' I had the great pleasure of doing some recording with him later on. He would come into the studio and announce: "We're gonna cut some teenage Orange County dog-shit!" which meant it was time to record some bubblegum pop for the white teenagers of the OC, a Republican stronghold south of Hollywood.

If you have never heard of any of these people or songs, suffice it to say that I was not working my way into the Los Angeles Philharmonic. What I was doing, however, was picking up skills that would build into a lifelong career. Gary and Kim were the first people I had met who were grabbing the big bucks that were flying around the streets of Hollywood at that time— while I was still working nights at the poker club.

In the mid 60s, when I came to work with him, Gary was suffering from liver problems. I can remember times when he had to leave the studio between takes to vomit, and another occasion where he was rushed to hospital. As you'll see, however, he survived splendidly.

Gary had an Ampex four-track tape machine set up with his monitors and outboard gear in the upstairs bedroom of his house on Argyle Avenue. The musicians played in the living room downstairs. I had never been in a recording studio before, so none of this seemed unusual—not even the smell of dirty diapers in the hallways. Gary was always writing or producing demos, and I started working for him as the bass player on these demos. I would make $20 per song, but more importantly I was gaining experience and making contact with other musicians. My career was starting to get interesting, but although Gary was happy to let me use his Fender Precision Bass to begin with, I still needed a proper instrument of my own.

One day I was at my local musicians' union hall when I spotted a note on the bulletin board advertising a Fender Precision Bass for sale for $100. At that price I didn't even care what condition it was in. I grabbed the slip of paper and headed straight for the address listed, which was somewhere in the Hollywood Hills. It turned out to be a large, seedy-looking mansion. Most of the house was dark and there weren't any curtains or drapes on the windows. I tried ringing the doorbell but it didn't work. Finally, I banged on the door. When it opened, I found myself standing face-to-face with a filthy guy whose bare feet were the color of my dark-brown cowboy boots. He had stringy, shoulder-length hair and maraschino cherries where his eyes should have been. Remember, this was 1964—the music world would soon be full of guys like this, but at the time I had never seen anyone like it.

The man motioned for me to come in so I stepped into a large entrance hall, where it slowly dawned on me that there were no electric lights in the house, just a flickering from what I assumed must be a fireplace in the next room. When the guy went to get the bass, however, I walked over to the doorway and saw six or seven people sitting around a campfire in the middle of a marble floor. They had a skylight open but the room was still hazy with smoke. There was no furniture anywhere.

The whole thing reminded me of some surrealistic scene where the Cro-Magnon meet modern-day folk in a Hollywood B-movie. I took the bass, handed the guy my $100, and got the hell out of there as fast as I could. A few weeks later, I bought an Ampeg B-15 amplifier and I was back in business. That amp would get a lot of use over the years. I still have it, in fact, although it has since been retired to my son Darin's music room.

≡

In June 1965 my job at the poker club ended and my roommates Billy and Shera Irwin moved back to Texas. Around the same time, Vivian Varon moved from Palm Springs to a beachfront apartment in Malibu, so I became a beach bum for a few months. I was still working for Gary Paxton, but I was also starting to get a few outside sessions as well. I didn't know it, but I was in the midst of a year of great change—for the United States of America, and for me.

I'm not sure who recommended me, but one day I got a call to work three nights a week with the singer and keyboard player Billy Preston. Billy was a true child prodigy. He started playing professionally at the age of ten; by the time I came to work with him he was still only sixteen. In the meantime he had recorded and performed with Sam Cooke, Mahalia Jackson, and many others.

In 1965, Billy was the teenage star of The Billy Preston Review, with whom he held court in a large nightclub called the Sands in Watts, a predominantly black neighborhood of South Los Angeles. Billy's mother drove him to the club and home again each night—just like my mother had when I was his age. The Sands held about 500 people and Billy Preston filled it every Thursday, Friday, and Saturday night. Billy played the Hammond organ and the piano. He did James Brown imitations and had people on their feet, clapping on the offbeats and singing along—he was like a preacher with a rapt congregation.

I settled into the job right away. I had played black music in black clubs before, of course, but I was not aware of the charged atmosphere that was building at the time in neighborhoods like Watts. At the time, nobody even gave me a dirty look. I should have known something was up, however, when Billy sang the Sam Cooke song 'A Change Is Gonna Come.' The crowd at the Sands joined in and sang it over and over like they really meant it—and they did. The song was a beautiful anthem to the widespread social change that was just around the corner.

In the meantime, however, the shows went on and I was thrilled to be a part of them. We had a big-band with eight brass and woodwind players, a wonderful drummer nicknamed Torch, and a woman named Mildred who played the Hammond organ when Billy was playing piano or just singing. Then there was me. I played bass, of course, but I also played valve trombone when Mildred played the organ. She played the bass pedals on the organ—and she really cooked. I always felt a little inadequate when I switched back to my Fender bass.

Another of the stars of the show was a violinist named Don 'Sugarcane' Harris. Don was an LA native, and although he was a classically trained violinist he had skirted the edges of rhythm & blues stardom as part of a guitar-playing singing duo called Don & Dewey. Don and his musical partner Dewey Terry had made a number of records for the Specialty imprint in the late 50s, but they all seemed to be just ahead of their time: none were hits for Don & Dewey, but a number of them were later taken into the charts by acts such as The Righteous Brothers ('Koko Joe' and 'Justine') and The Premiers ('Farmer John').

By the time I met Don he was playing electrified violin—the first time I had ever seen such a thing. When the MC introduced him, it was touch and go as to whether he might show up or not. If he *was* there, he would walk out in one of his pastel-colored satin suits, plug his violin into his amp, and start playing whatever came to mind. He never knew whether the rest of us would know the song he was playing because we never rehearsed with him. He never even told us what key to play in. Furthermore, his repertoire was so extensive that he might start with a Hungarian gypsy-dance, segue into a Charlie Parker bebop riff, and then finish with one of the nastiest blues cuts you could imagine. We didn't mess with his classical numbers, but there were always a few of us who knew the bebop tunes, and of course we all jumped in on the blues. The audiences loved him.

One night I got talking to Don and he told me the reason he was absent or late so often was that he didn't have a car. I offered to give him a ride home that night, and so began my being his wheels. A few weeks later, on a warm August night, we got back from the club to find Don's windows were open, with smoke and rhythm & blues pouring out of them. There was a party going on.

Don invited me in for a drink. I didn't really want to go in—I had a bad feeling about the whole thing—but Don insisted. He told me he wanted to introduce me to his friends. Inside, there were six or seven guys sitting around. No women. Everybody's eyes were red. Two of the guys were sitting at a table cooking smack in a spoon, and there were bloody cotton balls on the floor. Don handed me a glass of wine. I chugged it and moved for the door.

When I got back outside I saw five or six guys standing around my car, a fire-engine-red Mercury Comet. My valve trombone and bass rig were still inside.

"Hey, you guys," I said. "Don't rip me off! I'm just giving Sugarcane a ride home from the gig."

They were not impressed. I just stood there; they just stood there. It seemed like we'd been standing there forever. Eventually, I turned around and ran up to the screen door, calling Don's name. I heard glass break. Don came to the door and yelled out at the guys who were pillaging my car. Finally, he told me to get in the car and get out of there.

None of the guys moved as I walked toward the car. I unlocked the driver's-side door and got in. The men just stared at me, anger contorting their faces. As I drove away, one of them kicked my car. Something was in the air. A change was gonna come.

At 2:00am on Saturday, August 7 1965, I packed my valve trombone and set off for Malibu, fully expecting to be back at the Sands the following Thursday. I even left my Fender bass and amp at the club. On Wednesday, August 12, I was having breakfast when the phone rang. It was Torch, the drummer. He told me that the Sands had been trashed and our instruments had been looted by rioters.

He told me that the owner of the club had said that if we brought him pre-dated bills of sales showing that we owned the instruments, he might be able to get his insurance company to pay for them. He gave me the owner's phone number and we said goodbye, not knowing if we would ever play together again. I called the owner and we set up a time to meet at the club that afternoon. I had no idea what was going on in South Central Los Angeles at that time. I didn't watch the news on television.

Vivian and I had a houseguest back then named Cal Cassidy. He was a flamboyant gay dress-designer: six-foot-four, willowy, and very effeminate. After I explained what had happened, I told Vivian and Cal that I had an appointment with the club owner at the club at 3:00pm. They hit the roof. We argued about it for a while until they realized I was set on going.

"You can't go by yourself!" Cal said. "I am going with you!" He was a stand-up guy.

At 2:00pm Cal and I left Malibu for South Central LA. We were driving Vivian's car, a blue 1964 Ford Mustang. I figured we'd be safe since the club was close to the Harbor Freeway, and the owner—and no doubt others— would be there to protect us. Boy was I wrong. It took us almost an hour to get to our turnoff at Manchester Boulevard. The club was just a few blocks away. As we came down the offramp we saw an armored military vehicle with a .50 caliber machine-gun mounted on it. The soldiers turned on their siren as we drove by, but I kept on going. I don't know how to explain how I felt. There was nobody on the street. Everything was quiet. As we pulled into the parking lot at the back of the club there were no other cars—no people, even—in sight.

Cal and I got out of the car and banged on the back door of the club. No response. We walked around the side of the building to the front where we were met with a shocking sight. The doors were wide open—the glass had been blown right out of them. Inside, we were hit by a blast of cold air from the air conditioners. All the lights were on. The place looked like a war zone but everything was eerily quiet. I called out a couple of hellos but nobody was there. Cal suggested we get the hell out of there. He didn't have to say it twice.

On our way back around the side of the building I heard someone yell "Hey, whitey!" I looked across the street and saw five black guys get up from a porch. They started to move faster; we started to move faster. They started running; we started running. They were pointing and laughing as we ran. I dread to think about how we must have looked: me with my long hair, red velvet bellbottoms, and sandals; six-foot-four-inch Cal in his brightly colored clothes and his signature satin cap with a ball on top. I can smile now, but I wasn't smiling then.

As we got to the car my legs grew colder and more buttery with every step. I couldn't remember if I had locked it. We had no time to spare. Fortunately, it was a hot day, so I had left the windows open. The five guys were at the back bumper as Cal and I jumped in through the windows, which we then frantically rolled up as I struggled to get the key in the ignition and the engine started. Luckily for us, these guys were unarmed, but they were hammering on the back of the car with their fists as I floored the accelerator.

The Mustang's tires were smoking as we made our getaway. The fastest way back to the freeway was down a blind alley that ran along the back of the parking lot. A couple of teenage kids jumped behind a dumpster for safety as we shot past. By the time we got back on the road, my legs were shaking so violently that I could feel the engine through the accelerator. Cal pointed at my lap, and I looked down to see a large wet patch forming. We started laughing hysterically, tears flowing from our eyes. The whole thing was like a scene from a Z-movie.

A month later, I got a call from Torch, the drummer. Like me, he hadn't been covered by the club's insurance, but he said the owner had called to say they'd rebuilt the club and wanted us to come back to work.

"Are you crazy?" I said. "I'm not going back there!"

Torch went on to say that he, Billy, and the owner had been discussing what to do with me, since I was the only white guy. There had been reports of white people being pulled out of their cars by rioters, but there was no record of any white person being pulled from a car being driven by a black person. Torch's plan was for me to drive my gear out to his house in Englewood and then ride with him to the club in his pickup truck in style and safety.

The plan worked. The only negative incident came during the first Thursday night back, when a big guy came over to the bar and started threatening me during the intermission. Out of nowhere, two even bigger bouncers grabbed the guy and took him out into the alley. I never heard what happened to him, but I felt a lot safer after that.

Two nights later, Torch and I were loading our gear into his pickup truck when he hit me with a request that sent me into a fit of terror. He said that B.B. King was playing at the 5/4 Ballroom, a short drive from the Sands, and would I like to go hang out with him?

"Are you fucking crazy?" I asked again.

Torch begged and promised that nothing would happen to me as long as I was with him. I didn't seem to have much choice in the matter, but I kept remembering peeing my pants in the car a month or so earlier.

We drove to the 5/4 Ballroom and parked across the way. The clubs were letting out and the streets were crowded with people. I balked and suggested to Torch that maybe it would be better if I climbed into the back of the pickup with the instruments and waited there. He wouldn't hear of it.

Finally, he lured me out of the truck and into the club. A few people seemed surprised to see me but nobody was threatening. We went down to a basement dressing room where Torch reminisced with B.B. King and his buddies. I remember being introduced to the band's bass player but I'm not sure what we talked about. Everybody was very polite, though. We left at about three in the morning. I was slightly drunk and trying desperately to melt into the pavement. Nobody on the street even looked at me twice.

CHAPTER 15
AND THEN ...

B y the time Billy Preston left the Sands, I was making enough money doing studio sessions that I no longer needed to work the clubs. One of the trumpet players from the Sands, whose name was Mel, started recommending me for recording sessions—not on bass but on valve trombone. The Sands had a jazz trio—piano, bass, and drums—that played during the intermissions. Mel and I used to play with them sometimes—me on valve trombone, him on trumpet—and we were pretty tight because of that.

So off I went to these recording sessions. My valve trombone was a student-model aluminum horn with lots of dents. I didn't have a case, or any mutes—I just showed up with my beat-up horn and borrowed someone's valve oil or whatever else I required. Most trombone music is written in the bass clef, same as with the tuba, so I did OK. One of the highlights of this period was playing on an album by one of my favorite vocal groups from the 50s, The Four Freshmen, who of course had such a huge influence on groups like The Beach Boys and The Mamas & The Papas.

Mel also recommended me for a live concert starring Della Reese—the same Della Reese I had heard at the Howard Theatre in Washington, DC, with Count Basie's band when I was 17 years old. As I arrived I looked over to the trombone section and recognized some of the most highly regarded session men in Los Angeles, not to mention one of the most famous conductors—a certain Quincy Jones. As soon as we started rehearsing the first song, however, I could tell that my valve trombone was not blending well with the other slide trombones. No one said anything about it, but I got up, walked over to Quincy, and said: "I would understand if you wanted to call another trombone player for the gig."

"That is very gracious of you," he replied. He smiled and gave me a hug. It ended up being my last ever outing with the valve trombone.

My last gasp playing the jazz string bass came around the same time when Gary Paxton called me about appearing on a live album by legendary guitarist Barney Kessel. I have no idea how Barney and Gary Paxton ever crossed paths, being that Gary was primarily a rock and country kind of guy. Barney had started playing jazz guitar in the 40s and since then had been the lead accompanist on almost every album Billie Holiday had ever recorded. He had played with Charlie Parker, Thelonious Monk, Benny Goodman, Lester Young, Ella Fitzgerald, Nat 'King' Cole, Sonny Rollins, and many more big names in the world of jazz. I was also well aware that he had spent a year playing with Oscar Peterson, whose band included my old bass-playing hero, Ray Brown.

I had not played the string bass much during the previous few years so my playing was not what it once was. In a way, however, I didn't feel like I had much to lose—after all, Barney would only be comparing my playing to one of the greatest bass players of the time.

OK, I'll admit it: I was scared shitless.

Fortunately, I had already met Barney at a few sessions and I liked him a lot. We'd worked together on a Hawaiian album for Capitol Records, where someone had gathered together a Hawaiian choir and recorded them a cappella, the only accompaniment being a count-off clinked on a Coca-Cola bottle before each song. We, the studio musicians, then had to tune to the choir at the beginning of a song, play until the choir went out of tune, retune, resume playing, and so on until the end of the song. Barney was a good source of laughs during those recordings. Being so green, I tended to keep my mouth shut.

This time, Gary Paxton had arranged for Barney and I to get together at his house to play through a few songs. I'm not sure what made Gary think I'd be a good enough jazz player to play with Barney—he'd never heard me play that kind of music. Come to think of it, I doubt Barney would have expected much from *any* jazz musician recommended to him by Gary. Maybe he was just placating Gary by listening to me.

Barney suggested we start with a 12-bar blues: the universal first song, because everybody knows the blues. I still had that old fire in my gut for playing bebop, so I hopped right on it. Barney smiled and we played for about 15 minutes, bouncing ideas off each other and swinging heavily. After that we tried a bossa nova and a ballad, and that was it: I was hired to make the album with Barney and drummer Frank Capp. My only problem was that, in my zeal to impress, I had played hard enough to work up a pair of blisters on my fingers—my old nemeses—but I was still confident that we would get a hot recording together.

The album we made together was called *The Fantastic Guitar Of Barney Kessel On Fire*, released on the now defunct Emerald label. A friend of mine recently gave me a copy of the album on CD, which he found in Japan. As it says in the liner notes, the first time Barney, Frank, and I played together as a trio was at the soundcheck at the club. I had no idea who Frank was at the time, but it turned out he was a fine big-band and West Coast-style jazz player.

Frank and I were like oil and water when we played behind Barney. I remembered the intensity and the swing that Barney and I had gotten when just the two of us played together at Gary Paxton's house, and I went for it. Frank had other ideas, however: he wanted to relax the feels to suit his West Coast style of playing. The resulting album reflects this conflict as well as my sore chops. I have always grieved over that album, wondering if it would have turned out better had I been more open to Frank's musicality. I wish I had something on record from my jazz days that shows my string-bass playing at its peak, but sadly I don't.

I went on to play with Barney and various other drummers for about a year and a half in the mid 60s. Then, having not heard from him for years, I got a call from him in the 90s. He had suffered a stroke and could not talk very well. He was unable to play guitar any more. Unbeknownst to me at the time, he had also been diagnosed with an inoperable tumor, which makes what he said to me after that even more poignant. He had been going over his albums and tapes, he told me, and he had come across recordings of some of our live concerts. He wanted me to know that I was "a really good jazz player." Those were his words. I was thrilled.

We talked for a while, filling each other in on where our careers had taken us in the years since we'd last spoken. I had to confess to Barney that I had eventually reached a point where I had to chose whether to be a jazz player or a studio player. I explained that I had heard the jazz virtuoso Scott LaFaro and realized that I would have to devote my whole life to playing if I was ever even to approach that level of talent—and even then I might not get close.

Barney said he had worked with Scott and would have liked to have seen how far I could have taken it. "And the money didn't even enter your decision?" he asked.

"Well, maybe," I laughed. Then, as now, jazz players were not known for becoming rich. I never quite became rich either, but I would come close on several occasions.

If you were to ask me to name one breakout year in my career it would be 1966. Before then, few outside the studio business would have known who I was, unless they happened to have heard one of my valve trombone sessions or one of the demos I recorded for Gary Paxton. That was about to change.

Coincidentally, this was also the year I had my first contact with Elvis Presley. I am listed as having played bass on a song called 'City By Night' from the movie *Double Trouble*. I don't remember that session, but I do remember getting a call from Red West, one of Elvis's bodyguards, who wanted to know if I was Jerry Scheff the trumpet player. I assured him that I was, even though I had never played the trumpet in my life. Red asked me to play trumpet on the soundtrack of the movie *Easy Come, Easy Go*.

"Sure," I said—if I was terrible, I reasoned, the worst they could do was send me home. I would still get paid.

I called Gary Paxton and asked to borrow his old silver trumpet. Then I went straight over to the MGM soundstage, where we spent two days sweetening songs that Elvis had already recorded. He wasn't present, so it would be a while yet before I got to meet him. Over the course of those two days I never played anything higher than a middle C, but by the time we finished my lips were like lunchmeat. Nobody complained about my playing, however, and I made $900 for two days' work—a huge windfall in those days. Of course, nobody ever called me to play the trumpet again.

As important as the Elvis connection would become later on, the real change in my life came later in the year when I got another call from Gary Paxton. He wanted to book me for a week to do an actual full-paying record album—my first for him. I showed up one morning at his Argyle Avenue home studio and met a group of people who called themselves The Association. They seemed a little strange to me at the time because the idea of hippies had not yet entered the US mainstream.

Anyway, Gary was due to engineer the album. A small but talented man named Curt Boettcher was the producer. Curt looked like he had just stepped out of the Scottish Highlands—the way he wore his hair, the tight loose-fitting blouse, and the leather sandals he had on were highly unusual for the time, even in California. The Association were similarly dressed. I guess you could say they had a medieval aura with a 60s bent.

To be honest, I don't remember how many days we spent working on those songs for the album, which ended up being called *And Then … Along Comes The Association*, but five sounds about right. We were using Gary's Ampex four-track tape recorder, which was state of the art at the time. As before, he sat in a bedroom upstairs and we set up in the living room downstairs. If we needed to talk to him we had to get close to one of the microphones. If he wanted to talk to us he had a mic patched through to a speaker in the living room. If he forgot to turn our mics off before he turned his on, we were subjected to feedback that sounded like an alien mating ritual.

Nowadays, with digital recording technology, each instrument is recorded on its own separate track. Back then, with only four tracks at our disposal, we had to double up. If one player made a mistake, the whole track containing however many other instruments would have to be erased. I don't remember the exact configuration, but I know the bass and drums were on the same track, and as it happens I made a few minor mistakes on a song we were working on called 'Along Comes Mary.' Unfortunately, my bass playing was locked in with the drums—to erase the bass mistakes, we would have had to wipe the drums, too. Everybody loved the take, and nobody was too concerned by my playing, so I was stuck with the mistakes.

I have always been a very self-critical musician, to the point where I often don't like to listen to any of the music in which I have been involved. (I am a bit neurotic, I know, but I am who I am.) When I listened to 'Along Comes Mary' in Hollywood in 1966, the whole record felt wonderful to me—until my mistake thundered through my brain, every single time I listened to it.

A year or two later, I was in my local supermarket, minding my own business, when a muzak version of 'Along Comes Mary' came through on the speaker system. I had played on muzak recordings myself and knew how they worked: somebody would transcribe the parts of a song and hand them out to musicians who would barely get one take to record them, regardless of whether they were ready or not. Listening in the supermarket, I was intrigued as to whether either the transcriber or the bass player on the muzak version would have corrected my mistake, but of course they hadn't. I couldn't get away from it. That mistake would haunt me for years. On a more positive note, however, the next single to be drawn from *Along Comes The Association* was a ballad called 'Cherish,' which was perfect, and which went all the way to Number One on the national charts.

As soon as 'Cherish' hit the charts, I started to get more calls for record sessions. There were a few bumps in the road, however. In 1966, the two predominant electric bass players in Los Angeles were a guy named Joe Osborn and a woman named Carol Kaye. They both played with a pick, whereas I had developed my sound using my bare fingers. Many engineers and record producers had gotten used to hearing Joe or Carol's 'pick attack,' however, especially in combination with the heavy kick-drum sound originated by Carol's Wrecking Crew cohort, Hal Blaine. I had to decide whether to adjust my style or stand my ground and make my sound acceptable on its own. I chose to stand my ground.

I remember being called for a record date by one of the premier bubblegum-pop producers in LA, Mike Post. We started to rehearse the first song when Mike stopped us.

"Jerry, do you play with a pick?" he asked.

I assured him that I did.

"OK," he said, "let's run it down again."

About ten seconds later, Mike stopped us again.

"Jerry!" he said. "I thought you said you could play with a pick?"

"I *can*," I told him.

"Jerry, *will* you play with a pick?"

"No," I said.

I never worked for Mike Post again. He went on to be a prolific writer of music for television, but I never missed playing his kind of music.

This story might make me sound like a smart-ass, but I was *good* at being a smart-ass. Besides, I found his attitude condescending. The pick-or-no-pick controversy was something I would have to get used to, however. In 1971, for example, I was invited by producer Tom Catalano to appear on a Neil Diamond album. The engineer insisted on trying to make me sound like I was playing with a pick. The bass sounded terrible—so terrible that at one point I suggested he bring in Joe Osborn instead.

That's not to say that I would just stubbornly refuse to play with a pick on principle. During those same sessions, Tom came to me with a song that he said could really do with a picked-bass sound. "Of course," I said. The resulting track, 'Song Sung Blue,' ended up becoming a Number One hit.

Back in 1966, I found myself getting busier and busier. I would sometimes find myself booked for three or even four sessions per day: 10:00am to 1:00pm; 2:00pm to 5:00pm; 6:00pm to 9:00pm; and then 10:00pm to 1:00am. This would invariably mean driving to a studio, lugging my bass and amp from the car, setting up, playing, packing my equipment away, and then moving on to the next session. It was just too much work.

Fortunately, I then learned about cartage services, whereby the record companies would pay for my gear to be hauled from studio to studio. I could just walk away and it would be there waiting for me at the next job. I also started to consider commissioning someone to build me a six-foot-tall Plexiglas box on wheels with its own air supply, a comfortable upholstered chair, an ashtray, a wine cooler, and built-in phono jacks to connect me and my instrument to the mixing board. That way, I thought, I could just drive to the cartage company's warehouse in the morning, get settled into my own little environment, and then be driven around all day, freeing me up to play music, drink coffee and wine, and smoke my brains out. I'm sure it would have made me an instant legend on the Los Angeles studio scene, but it never quite came to fruition.

More seriously, I found out that you could pay an answering service to maintain your schedule for a monthly fee. I decided to sign up with a company called Arlyn's. They would take my calls from music producers or labels who wanted to hire me, run my diary, and on occasion refer me to someone who was desperate for a last-minute bass player.

As a gimmick, Arlyn's female operators were instructed to speak in a sexually provocative manner to their male customers.

"Hi, this is Jerry Scheff," I'd say.

"Hi sweetheart," a soft voice would reply. "You have three sessions today. Wanna have a drink after your 10:00pm?"

I never took any of this too seriously, but I did soon learn that some of these young women had their favorites, and that sending them flowers periodically was much appreciated. In return, if a client called for a bass player who was already booked, the operator might say: "He's fully booked, but Jerry Scheff is available. You don't know who Jerry is? Oh, he works for so and so, he's played on this and that ... ." On more than one occasion, after I had broken down on one of the LA freeways, one of the Arlyn's girls came to pick me up and arranged for my car to be towed and repaired.

(Even after I moved to Canada in 1971, I still booked wakeup calls through Arlyn's.)

I often didn't know who the artist was until I showed up for work. One morning, I walked into the studio and was greeted by a group of musicians I knew well: teenage drummer Jim Gordon, who would go on to play with Eric Clapton in Derek & The Dominos; guitar legend Ry Cooder; and Clarence White, one of the originators of country-rock and a latter-day member of The Byrds.

Today, many musicians and producers would drool at the thought of having these musicians in the same room together. At the time, however, we were all a little scruffy looking. I had long hair and a mustache and tended to wear cut-off jeans and sandals. I was no longer smoking marijuana, following the incident at the Black Elks club, but I carried around with me a half-gallon bottle of cheap California wine (a cool rebuff, I thought, to the champagne set).

So there we were, the four of us, jamming a little bit, when the door opened and Pat Boone walked in. He looked at us and his mouth dropped open. It was like he had seen the devil. Without even so much as a nod he walked stone-faced over to the glass-enclosed vocal booth and shut the door. We all just stared at him. After a moment, Pat realized that in order to get to the control room, where the producer was waiting for him, he had to come out of the booth and run the gauntlet past us again. We all had big grins on our faces. And Pat? Let's just say he was very uptight.

CHAPTER 16
ANOTHER DIMENSION

f I could have picked a group to start my touring career, I don't think that I would have done better than The 5th Dimension. As it was, they picked me. The 5th Dimension consisted of three guys from Detroit and two beauty-contest winners from Los Angeles. They were all African-American, they all sang their asses off, and they were all wonderful to me. I had some of the best times of my life on the road with them.

I first met the group in 1966, around the time they were working on their debut album for Johnny Rivers's new label, Soul City. They had yet to have a hit record but their magical conglomeration of backgrounds and musical styles would soon serve them well. The three male members of the group all grew up in St Louis, Missouri. Lamonte McLemore came from a jazz background and worked as a professional photographer; his cousin, Billy Davis Jr, had grown up in an African-American neighborhood with a deep passion for soul music; Ron Townson was a trained opera singer who had played a small role in the 1959 film of *Porgy & Bess*.

The group's female members both hailed from New Jersey. Lamonte first encountered the tall, beautiful Marilyn McCoo while photographing the Miss Bronze talent pageant during the early 60s. Marilyn was a college graduate with physicians for parents—not the background you would expect of someone about to join a would-be soul group. (She and Lamonte were dating when I first met them, but she ended up marrying Billy.)

Lamonte discovered Florence LaRue in exactly the same place a few years later, while she was vying to become Miss Bronze 1966. Florence is as petite as Marilyn is tall. Both have incredible voices.

I played a few local club gigs with the group, and then all of a sudden— *wham!*—they had a hit record called 'Up, Up, And Away,' which went on to win five Grammys. Touring with The 5th Dimension was a barrel of laughs. They were all funny people. The guys in the band had a signal for alerting the others whenever an attractive woman came into sight. If one of us saw a foxy lady, we would say "spoop" in a high, falsetto voice. Sometimes, in Los Angeles or New York, spoops would be flying all over the place.

Before long, The 5th Dimension felt like family. In fact, soon after I started working with them, we had a week to kill between concerts, and they asked if I would mind staying with Billy and his family in St Louis. I knew they were trying to save money, but I didn't mind.

Billy's family wouldn't let me go out by myself because tensions were still high after the riots in St Louis, but we had a great time anyway. They treated me like gold. His grandmother even taught me how to make greens and ham hocks. "You gotta get them cooked down until the pot liquor tastes just right," she told me. I never forgot.

I'm not certain about the timing, but I believe we went straight from St Louis to London, England, to appear on the pilot for a new Tom Jones television series, and then on to Las Vegas to play the lounge at Caesars Palace. The show was recorded, but I don't remember the tapes ever being released— possibly because of an incident that happened during the first night.

We had a brass section on stage with us, and the lead trumpet player was a guy named Al Longo, who later became part of the Elvis Presley touring group. Al came from the Italian community in South Philadelphia. That evening, we had started a beautiful ballad with Marilyn McCoo singing lead, the tape was rolling, and then right at the most tender part of the song came a voice from the audience, yelling: "Hey! It's Al Longo! Al Longo from South Philly! How youse doin', Al?" ... and stop the tape. One more time, take two.

Around the same time, the members of The 5th Dimension had a potluck soul-food party. Except for me and a few of the other musicians, everybody present was African-American. Sammy Davis Jr came along and brought with him listeners, walkers, and waggers—that is, pigs' ears, feet, and tails, all cooked in a spicy tomato sauce. In 1972, when Sammy switched sides politically and embraced Richard Nixon on stage, the members of The 5th Dimension considered him to be a traitor. I don't suppose he ever made listeners, walkers, and waggers for Tricky Dicky, though.

A few years later, I did some benefits with Sammy, as well as a recording session, for which I was called to a Vegas studio right next to the railroad tracks. Every so often, a train would come by and we'd have to stop, but we did manage to cut a version of 'Mr Bojangles.' Sammy was a star—and he knew it. He showed up smiling and laughing, dripping with jewelry, a beautiful woman on each arm. He was very gracious and friendly, but I later came to the same conclusion as the members of The 5th Dimension: he'd sold out to the establishment. The horror!

Another memorable trip with The 5th Dimension was to a theater in the round out in the countryside just outside Springfield, Massachusetts, where we were to open for film star and singer-comedian Martha Raye. I believe we played there for a week. We had a great four-piece band at the time: drummer Toxie French, who I knew from my old Gary Paxton days; guitar player Larry Carlton, who was just starting a decades-long career on stage and in the studio; and piano player Rene DeKnight, the 5th's musical director, who had also been a member of The Delta Rhythm Boys.

Martha Raye never quite got the credit for being as brilliant as she really was. She was in her early fifties when we played with her, but her voice was still as great as ever. Meeting her was like contacting a long-lost relative. She sang jazz and was a big fan of Ella Fitzgerald and Sarah Vaughan, as well as being close to Anita O'Day, perhaps the first white jazz singer to phrase with a sideways, wiggle-your-ass feel.

The first time I saw them both was in a jazz club in Hollywood around 1966. Martha was sitting in the audience in a sleeveless summer dress, and when Anita introduced her from the stage, Martha stood up to receive a round of applause, placed her hand over her bare armpit, and flapped her arm, thereby sending out a blast of fart sounds. The audience howled; here, I thought, was a woman after my own heart. When I finally met her in Springfield, I reminded her of that night. She told me she was right on the edge of being able to play Sousa marches on her armpit, although sadly I never did get a demonstration.

The theater in Springfield was like a miniature Roman coliseum with aisles like wheel spokes radiating upward from the stage. During the show the stage revolved so that everyone in the audience had a chance to see the faces of the performers. There was room for a small orchestra in the pit. The plan was that each of us would be assigned our own aisle, and would gather at the tops of them, in the dark, when Martha started to sing 'San Francisco.' Then, as she took her bow, stagehands would move the drums, amps, and electric piano onto the stage while our four-piece band rushed down the aisles, ready to plug in and start playing 'Up, Up, And Away.' That would be the cue for the 5th, who would run down and start singing.

Once we had rehearsed our part of the show we packed up our gear and went back to the hotel. I had a rental car so I drove back on my own to have dinner and get myself ready. When I got back to the theater, there was a surprise waiting for me: somebody had decided to change the set around— only they forgot to tell me.

Midway through the show I left the dressing room, smiled knowingly to my bandmates, and climbed to the top of my aisle, ready for 'San Francisco.' The lights were down low, which meant that nobody could see me—but also that I couldn't see anyone else. I wasn't worried, though, and as Martha finished the song I ran down the aisle ready to plug in my bass. When I got there, however, there was no amplifier on the stage. In fact, the stage was empty except for Martha, her microphone, and me, standing there with my cord in my hand.

Martha had a huge ear-to-ear grin. Without missing a beat, she said: "Ladies and gentlemen, I would like to introduce you to a very fine bass player, Jerry Scheff. Jerry is going to accompany me on this next song— aren't you, Jerry."

I bobbed my head up and down with a sick expression on my face as a stagehand lifted my amp onto the stage. Martha announced the next song: a ballad, 'All The Things You Are.' She raised her eyebrows as if to say: "Do you know this?" I smiled. Fortunately, I had played it many times.

After we finished the song, and once the applause had died down, Martha looked over to me. "Thank you, Jerry," she said. "I'm surprised you knew that song. We will see you again when The 5th Dimension comes out."

It was around this time that I started to experiment with hallucinogens. One day, Vivian's son Marlo showed up at the house scared out of his wits. A friend of his had scored a bag of hundreds of mescaline tabs and in the process had drawn the attention of a narc from the Los Angeles Police Department. When the police showed up at his friend's crash pad in Venice Beach, Marlo ran out the back door with the baggie and came straight to us. He was shaking as he handed me the stash.

"What am I going to do with this?" he asked, terrified that the cops were right on his tail.

"Don't worry," I said. "I know just what to do with it." Thus began my four years of on-and-off experimentation with mescaline and LSD.

Listening to music under the influence of hallucinogens was, for me, like using a kind of truth serum. If I listened to, say, The Mamas & The Papas (or something similarly lightweight) they would sound like cartoon characters. Lawrence Welk would put me on the floor laughing—everything sounded like it was playing at the wrong speed. Listening to Ray Charles or Otis Redding or Prokofiev, however, would send me to music heaven. It was the same with sex—hallucinogens could turn making love into a much more animalistic rite. All my senses were wide open.

Playing music while stoned on hallucinogens took some getting used to. The experience of going into a record studio under the influence of hallucinogens for the first remains as clear as a DVD in my brain, except that I can't remember who was there—not the singer, not the producer, not any of the other players.

Darkness had just begun to fall that night. I remember Vivian driving me to a studio in Hollywood—I was already stoned on mescaline before we left the house. (As a matter of fact, I had come to the place where I would nibble on mescaline tabs all day so that I could maintain a certain level of high without becoming unable to function.) As we entered the studio, Vivian went into the control room while I plugged in my amp, tuned up, and, as it so happened, tuned out. When the producer played the demo tape of the song we were due to record, I remember thinking: this is the biggest piece of shit I have ever heard. I actually started laughing until I looked around and everybody was staring at me like I was insane.

I tried to stop smiling but I couldn't always hold it in. I smirked a lot. We finished listening to the demo and then recorded the first take. I played what I thought should be the bass part and we went into the control room to listen. As I listened back, I realized that I hated everything I'd played—it was too busy, too contrived—but everyone else seemed to be happy.

We went back to do a few more takes. After the second take we went back in to have another listen, and even though I had taken a hatchet to the bass part, it still sounded too busy and contrived to me. This process went on for about five takes, until the producer came over to speak to me.

"Jerry," he began, "do you realize you are only playing one note to the bar?"

"Yeah," I replied, "but aren't they beautiful?"

The producer made me go listen to what I had played on the first take and overdub it onto the third take, which was the overall best take. When I later listened to the song in question it sounded great. What I learned from that day, and from many other later experiences, was that I was able to function *fairly* realistically when I was high on hallucinogens. It was like pretending to play what I thought I would play if I wasn't stoned. (Wait: what?)

A few years later, I played five or six Elvis Presley shows stoned on mescaline. I was shell-shocked the first time the curtain opened: I couldn't look at Elvis or the other band-members without grinning. The whole visual theatricality of the scene, with the jump suits and the lighting, was just too much for me. I tried to look at the audience and felt like I was on another planet. (The bar scenes in *Star Wars* come to mind.) I finally found that if I looked at the floor and concentrated on the parts of the music that pleased me—Elvis's voice, The Sweet Inspirations, James Burton—I could really enjoy myself. Later, Vivian told me that the people sitting in the booth next to hers were worried I might freak out: "He's been staring at the floor for the whole show!"

During the 60s, record companies started to make big money, which led to increasingly big budgets for record-making. Some of that money eventually found its way into the pockets of the people making the records—and into our noses, too. By the end of the decade, cocaine had become a popular 'amusement' drug in the studio. I would regularly be booked in for two or three weeks of tracking songs for an album, where the following scenario would invariably play out.

> *1:00pm: We arrive at the studio, where the producer (or someone close to him) immediately lays out several lines of cocaine on the speaker cabinet of a Hammond B3. The producer and engineer then decide that they want to get an organ sound. The organist starts playing, the cabinet vibrates, and the cocaine gets blasted onto the carpet. Everybody gets out a straw and starts vacuuming it up.*
>
> *1:30pm: The engineer, producer, and drummer work on a kick sound for two hours while the rest of us try to find a way to talk with our lips stuck to our teeth.*
>
> *3:30pm: The producer lays out some more lines along the top of the recording console.*
>
> *4:00pm: The engineer, producer, and drummer work on the snare sound for two hours.*
>
> *6:00pm: A dinner break is called, even though no one is really hungry. We snort a few more lines of cocaine and head for a club*

called the Bat Cave on Sunset Boulevard. (The Bat Cave, incidentally, did not serve food: it was a bar where you rented flashlights at the door and sat in the dark. Once you had ordered your drinks, nude women would pose on the bar; flashlight in hand, you became your own personal lighting director.)

8:00pm: Back to the studio. Finally, after several more grams of cocaine and three or four martinis, we're ready to play some music. For the next seven or eight hours we play through different songs, listen, play again, snort some more cocaine, and carry on until around 4:00am, when we all trudge home like zombies ready for the next day—which invariably begins with listening back to the previous day's work and finding out that the drum sounds suck and the tempos are all too fast.

Back then, I would make around $50 to $100 per hour for this kind of work, but if it all sounds like fun and games, the dark side of the 'high' life would soon follow. On a positive note, however, one experiment worth mentioning is the one that took place in the garage of my friend Jim Gordon.

Jim is certainly one of the greatest rock drummers of all time. He started playing with The Everly Brothers at 17 and by the time of our garage session a few years later he was in great demand both in the studio and on the road. He was tall, blond, and very attractive. He was married to a beautiful woman named Jill with whom he had a young daughter and owned a house—hence the garage in which this experiment took place.

The other participant was a studio guitar player named Mike Deasy. Mike was a bit eccentric, shall we say—we all were, back then, but Mike more so than the rest of us. Jim, Mike, and I worked together a lot (you'll remember Jim from the Pat Boone session earlier). Mike was married, too: to Cathy, his high-school sweetheart, with whom he had three children.

While Jim gave the impression, outwardly, of being a clean-cut college boy, Mike had long hair and dressed in heavy, gray monk's robes and lace-up leather sandals. He was known as Friar Tuck. Mike and Cathy had a great-horned owl living on the mantle in the living room—something I only discovered when we were playing poker one night and all of a sudden this huge bird came swooping through the kitchen doorway.

On this particular evening, Vivian, Cathy, and Jill set up shop in the kitchen—not knowing quite how deep into the night our antics would take us—while Jim, Mike, and I took LSD and hauled a case of Château Margaux out to the garage, where our gear was set up. The original plan was that we would write some songs, but we soon went off track into something that, at the time, seemed much more important: pushing our psychic boundaries to see whether, in a pitch-black room, we could play single notes together. The idea was that we would start with a fast, soft tempo and gradually slow down, playing harder as we went, until what felt to us like vast amounts of time passed between the notes—and at that point we would see if we could still feel what each of us intended and stay together.

We finished a bottle of Margaux each and started to play. After what seemed like an age, we got to the point where the gap between the notes felt like it was around five minutes long. We stopped, laughing and shouting, and then Mike suggested we start again, so off we went. We were sure at the time that there was some kind of psychic communication at work, but whether this ever had any bearing on the quality of our playing, then or later, I just don't know.

Our jam session finally came to an end when Jill Gordon came out to the garage and told us that the police were at the house. Mike didn't want to stop playing, and was ready for a fight. Fortunately, calmer minds prevailed. We decided to call it a night when one of the officers told us that they would put us in cuffs and haul us off to jail if they had to come back.

On the way home I asked Vivian to pull over so that I could open the door and vomit several hundred dollars worth of Château Margaux onto the pavement. The curious thing was that I had absolutely no sense of nausea—I could feel the individual stomach muscles working.

"Far out," I said to Vivian. "You gotta see this stuff—it's a work of art."

"Close the door, Jerry," she replied.

Our tastes in art were always different.

Some time later, I played on a few records by the bubblegum-pop singer Tommy Roe with Mike and Toxie French. One day, Tommy asked us if we'd like to go to Disneyland with him. When we showed up, however—Mike in his monk's robes and me with my long hair and sandals—they turned us over to some security guards, who promptly escorted us out of the park, lest we contaminate their clean-cut patrons.

CHAPTER 17
GREEN IN THE
BIG APPLE

I n the summer of 1968 I traveled with The 5th Dimension to New York City to do *The Tonight Show Starring Johnny Carson*. It was a great show, but the real action didn't take place until the next day, when I met up with an old friend from the Naval Amphibious Base in Coronado, California, Stan Bronstein. It was my first trip to NYC and I was as green as a sour apple. I called Stan and he gave me his address.

After a short cab ride across the city, I started to make my way up the first of five flights of stairs when I looked up and saw this madman peering down at me from the top. He had long black hair and a goatee—picture Rasputin and you're halfway there. It was Stan. I hadn't seen him in about five years.

We had a few beers and bullshitted for a while, after which Stan asked if I wanted to drop some acid with him. Wow, I thought. LSD in New York City.

"Are we just going to sit here with our eyes spinning all night?" I asked.

"No," Stan replied. "I gotta go play a gig in Queens with Tito Puente's band. We'll drop the acid, go down to the pizza parlor, eat, and come back here. You can listen to some music while I change, and then we'll hop the subway to Queens."

Tito Puente was king of what would later be known as salsa. At the time we called it Afro-Cuban music. Stan had toured all over Central and South

America with him. All in all, then, it sounded like a pretty good night to me.

By the time we got back from the Italian restaurant we were flying all over the place. I could see every pore in the plaster on the walls. Stan went over to the record player and put on some music. As soon as it started I forgot all about the plaster. I knew I was hearing something monumental. It was *Sgt Pepper's Lonely Hearts Club Band*. I was stunned. I had never been too sold on The Beatles' early stuff, 'Love Me Do' and that kind of thing, and I liked *Revolver* but it wasn't earth-shattering. This, however—this was something else.

Stan laughed when he saw the effect the music was having on me. We listened to some more and then he grabbed his alto sax and we headed for the subway. As we sat there on our way to Queens, Stan had to keep telling me not to stare at people. All of a sudden I was discovering the beauty in older, beat-up-looking people. There was this big 50-something longshoreman sitting across from us, and I was just knocked out by the scars and ridges on his face. Stan told me later that he was afraid this big bruiser would take my attentions the wrong way and beat the crap out of me. For now, however, I was possessed with the ultimate flower-power and convinced that I knew some spiritual way to convey to this guy the true meaning of universal love. I sat there with a big grin on my face, watching his facial muscles squirm and his complexion turn scarlet. Finally, he spoke to me in a hushed, hissing voice.

"What the hell's wrong with you? You on acid or something?"

"Yeah," I said.

The longshoreman smiled. "Oh, that's OK then."

I was leading a charmed life.

We got off the subway and found our way to the club. Stan knew all of the band-members' wives and girlfriends, so he took me over to sit at a big table full of Latinas who immediately started teasing me in Spanish. A few minutes later the band started up and I was in heaven. What a great band.

People were up dancing immediately, and to me, in my condition, the energy being produced by this band—and these dancers—was almost unbearable. Before long a very beautiful blonde woman with a heavy

Brooklyn accent came and sat down at our table. We'll call her Barbara. The other women seemed to know her, and she cleared the air by telling me in English that she was a friend of Stan's. I introduced myself. One of the other women said something in Spanish and the whole table started shaking with laughter. Barbara told me the ladies wanted to dance with me. I must have looked horrified because the laughter doubled in intensity.

I demurred for a little while until the women got up and pulled me to my feet, and there I was: on a crowded dance floor, stoned on acid, making an ass of myself, and enjoying every minute of it. The rhythms were infectious and the air was full of smoke, sweat, and perfume. In my enhanced hallucinatory state, the dance floor was full of diamond-and-fishnet pantyhose covering a forest of legs protruding downward from various colored miniskirts. It was like having 20 talking vaginas whispering in my ear at once.

By the time the night ended, I was still stoned, drunk on rum and Cokes, and covered with sweat after running the dancing gauntlet with 14 or 15 women—not counting Barbara, with whom I had enjoyed countless slow-dances.

At closing time, Stan packed away his sax and the three of us left Queens in Barbara's car—she was the only one in any condition to drive. Stan pulled me to one side as we walked to the car and told me that he and Barbara were just friends; if I wanted to try my luck, I could. I was elated … until he added that Barbara was the girlfriend of a well-known mobster. I needed to play it cool.

Barbara drove us down to Greenwich Village. It was almost four in the morning and she wanted some breakfast, so we stopped at an all-night diner. Stan and I were still flying around the room, grinning and smirking to each other. I remember ordering sausage and eggs but I couldn't eat anything—it all looked like it was made of plastic.

We made our way back to the car through several blocks of empty streets still wet from a sudden shower. I heard laughter and footsteps behind us and turned around to see three guys and a girl running with boxes and suitcases under their arms.

"Hey man," one of them said, "give us a hand."

Without thinking, we took some of the load and ran behind them along the street, up a stoop, and into a hallway, where we put the boxes down. When they started opening the boxes we realized these four people had just burglarized a store—and we three had just unwittingly helped them on their getaway. The boxes were full of loose currency, cigarettes, and booze. We left laughing our asses off and stumbled back down the street. Stan and Barbara were embarrassed—they were New York natives and felt they should have known better.

We dropped Stan off at his apartment and I gave Barbara the name of my hotel. She had a better idea, however, so we drove over to the East River to watch the sun come up. I was never the greatest of philanderers, but I probably would have given in to her charms right there—except that I was scared shitless. I could see the headlines: 'California Bass Player Found Cemented In East River.'

Six months later, back in Los Angeles, I answered the phone to a woman with a heavy Brooklyn accent.

"How youse doin', Jerry?"

I knew right away that it was Barbara. She told me that she and her hit-man boyfriend were staying at the Beverly Hilton and wondered if I'd like to have a drink with them. I was nervous but curious—and in any case, surely he couldn't rub me out by the pool? I drove over to the hotel and spotted them immediately. Barbara was wearing a killer bathing suit, if you'll pardon the pun; her killer boyfriend was a short, dark-haired Italian guy. He looked at me the way a mongoose looks at a cobra: a hairy mongoose with a tan, a big smile, and ten pounds of gold chains tangled up in his sweaty chest hair.

My hair was standing on end. I could tell that Barbara was tickled by my discomfort—she pushed the situation as far as she could to see how much she count flaunt me in front of her boyfriend. I excused myself as soon as I could and heard them laughing on my way out. Various scenarios went through my mind. Was she pissed at me for not hitting on her in New York? Did she tell her boyfriend I *had* hit on her?

"This asshole came on to me in the city," I imagined her telling him. "Why don't we wind him up a little?"

The day after the *Tonight Show* appearance, I headed with The 5th Dimension to Chicago, Illinois, where we were slated to play a concert at the Playboy Club, sharing the bill with a very young Richard Pryor. Our drummer at the time was a hotshot Canadian jazz player named Terry Clark. Terry had heard that Buddy Rich and his big-band were playing in town at Mister Kelly's, so he and I greased the palms of the maître d' and got a table close to the band.

A couple of songs into the set, Buddy stopped right in the middle of a song and threw his drum sticks at the bass player before firing him right there and then. I was appalled. The guitar player took over on bass for the rest of the show, but we decided to leave. We went next door to a small neighborhood bar where we found the bass player. He told us this was the fourth time he'd been fired by Buddy, but he kept getting called back because there no other bass player in Buddy's price-range wanted to work with him. As far as the bassist was concerned, however, he was through with the bullshit. Terry and I felt very sad for the guy. We agreed that we had it pretty good with the 5th.

The next day we left Chicago for Minneapolis, Minnesota. It was an election year, and we were due to perform at a Democratic fundraiser for Vice President Hubert Humphrey, who was running against Richard Nixon. We were sharing the bill with Frank Sinatra, Dean Martin, and a host of other big stars. And who was to accompany them? None other than The Buddy Rich Big Band. I couldn't believe it.

Coincidentally, Buddy Rich's agent also handled some of the people I had recorded with in Los Angeles, and he had heard me play jazz with Barney Kessel. He saw me from across the room and came over to say hello. "Don't move," he said. "I'll be right back."

Ten minutes later, the agent came back and told me that Buddy wanted to know if I would play the show with them—apparently his bass player hadn't shown up. I was dumbfounded: first because I knew he was lying about the bass player not showing up, and second because I had witnessed the very same guy being violently ejected from the stage the night before in Chicago.

"Listen," I said. "I have to talk to The 5th Dimension and find out if they want me to do this." I begged and pleaded with them to say no. Fortunately, they did.

As is probably apparent, my way of playing—and my way of dress—did not please everyone, nor did it fit some of the things I was hired for. One weekend in the late 60s, I got a call from an old friend from my Navy School of Music days, Sal Nistico, who had gone on to play tenor sax with Count Basie and Bill Holman. He was considered a musician's musician. At the time, he was playing a prominent weekly gig at the Hong Kong Bar in Century City, California, with The Woody Herman Orchestra.

Sal told me that Woody had lost it during the second show the night before. He had gone up to the band, picked up a huge folder of music, and thrown it at the bass player. The band was about to travel to Japan, but before that they needed a new bass player for two Saturday shows.

The whole thing reminded me of Buddy Rich throwing his drumsticks at his bass player in Chicago, but I couldn't resist. I called up my cartage service and had them deliver my bass and amp to the Hong Kong Bar. At the time I was doing a lot of sight-reading for my studio work and felt I could play the shows without rehearsals—of which it turned out there would be none. No matter, whatever; I was ready for it.

I had never been to the Hong Kong Bar before and wasn't aware of the dress code, so I decided to split the difference and wear jeans with a long-sleeved silk shirt and cowboy boots. My amp looked huge sitting there in the middle of the orchestra, but I thought hey, I'm just sitting in temporarily.

I didn't meet Woody Herman himself until the start of the first show. I knew by his demeanor that he was not happy with how I was dressed, but as we started the first song I felt like I was nailing it. The other guys in the band were nodding and smiling at me.

In most of the big-bands I had played in over the years, the bandleader would call up the songs in sets of three. Woody, however, called the songs one at a time. They were supposed to have been arranged in numerical order, but many of the sheets were out of order following the incident with my predecessor.

The songs proceeded in fits and starts as I searched for the out-of-order sheets. Woody was glaring at me like it was all my fault. Finally, he stomped up to where I was sitting and spent about two or three pregnant minutes riffling through the music, after which he slammed it down in front of me. I was not happy. As far as I was concerned, I was sight-reading his music, and the band was kicking ass. The crowd loved it.

Sitting in the front row that night was the jazz vocal group The Four Freshmen. I knew them well, and we had already exchanged nodded hellos. Then, midway through the show, Woody called a slow blues number. I looked at the chart and saw that it had a bass solo. When I started my solo, however, Woody grabbed the mic and started talking to different people in the audience—effectively ruining my moment. I reached back and spun the volume control on my amp to the maximum. Every face in the crowd jerked up and looked at me with horror. The Four Freshmen were laughing, however, because they knew what was happening.

After the show, Woody came over to me. "You think you can find the music now?" he asked.

"I'm sorry," I replied, "but I won't be playing the show again." And that was that.

CHAPTER 18
THE SUNN AMP

After the tour with The 5th Dimension, I headed back to Los Angeles to think about what to do next. It had been a troubling year. I remember watching TV on April 4 1968 when the news came through that Martin Luther King had been assassinated. By then, of course, I had worked with and been exposed to many different races and felt strongly that people were people—period. I knew the ramifications of what had happened in Tennessee, however, and I was heartsick.

Two months later, on June 6, Bobby Kennedy was killed at the Ambassador hotel in Los Angeles. I was booked to play a banquet for an African-American women's club at the Ambassador the following night with some of my friends from the Billy Preston days, but I assumed—just as I had when John F. Kennedy was shot—that it would be canceled, especially since the food was to be cooked in the very room where Bobby had been murdered. Wrong again.

Fortunately, this time around I was surrounded not by cheering and gloating but by a group of decent, honest people who had in mind the idea of giving a suitable sendoff to two fallen pathfinders who stood for the good of humanity: Bobby Kennedy and Martin Luther King. In the end I was pleased to have been there that night, even as I was beginning to learn more than I might have cared to know about some other pockets of American society. In Chicago with The 5th Dimension that summer, I had felt the rumblings of what would turn into a bloodbath as the city police, armed with truncheons, dogs, and water cannons, clashed with anti-war protestors outside the Democratic National Convention. I felt like I lost all of the rest of my innocence about American life during those months.

Not long after that, I was reunited with my old friend Jim Gordon when we worked together on an album by The Ventures. Jim had just returned from touring with a group called Delaney & Bonnie & Friends, featuring Eric Clapton on guitar. I had watched them play in Hollywood a few weeks earlier, marveling as Jim and bass player Carl Radle laid down a groove that was so infectious I couldn't stand still. I was learning new things just by listening to them.

At the Ventures sessions I tried to listen harder to Jim's feel, and I must have communicated my trust in his playing because we soon fell into that sweet place where mutual agreement leads to magic. After the morning session I invited Jim over to my place for lunch. As we ate he told me that Eric Clapton had asked him to move to England to start a new group. The only problem was that Jim's wife Jill had threatened to divorce him if he left. I'm not sure how much weight my opinion carried, but I remember saying something along the lines of: "You gotta do what you gotta do."

Jim duly left for England, where he was folded into a shortlived group with Clapton on guitar, Carl Radle on bass, and Bobby Whitlock on keyboards. Derek & The Dominos recorded one album, *Layla And Other Assorted Love Songs*, from which the title track became a huge hit. Unfortunately, Clapton had a heroin problem at the time, and his addiction eventually caught on with Jim and Carl.

When the group broke up, Jim had to come back to the USA to deal with his addiction and other problems. He and I worked together again in the 70s, with the Capitol Records cajun artist Doug Kershaw, by which time this once rock-solid drummer had lost his self-confidence. The rest of the band must have been on coke or speed because they were speeding up horribly. I remember finding Jim in the men's room during a break. He was upset—he asked if he was playing behind the rest of the band, and I had to reassure him that his playing was great. He really didn't know.

Back in late-60s LA, the mood of peace and love and optimism was waning. Another musician who left the music scene around the same time as Jim Gordon was Mike Deasy, aka Friar Tuck. Mike had worked with a producer named Terry Melcher, who was the son of actress Doris Day and lived in an ill-fated house on Cielo Drive with the actress Candice Bergen. At some point, Beach Boy Dennis Wilson introduced Terry and Candice to Charles Manson. Manson auditioned for Terry but Terry turned him down. A few months later, Roman Polanski and Sharon Tate moved into the house on Cielo Drive. Shortly after that, Tate and the house's other inhabitants were slaughtered by members of Manson's 'Family.'

All of this is well known, of course, but what is not so well known is that just before the murders, Terry Melcher took Mike Deasy to Manson's Spahn ranch with another friend, Skip Carmel. Mike and Skip spent some time with the Manson Family, taking with them a trailer with a remote recording setup. Mike took acid with some of the members. Skip told me that Mike became belligerent after taking the LSD, and that Manson came after him with an axe.

In Mike's words, the Manson Family stole his soul and played 'keep away' with it. Mike ran into the hills and hid—he was missing for around three days. The next time I saw him, he looked like a vampire had taken hold of him. He was white as a sheet and still shaking. After he recovered, Mike became a born-again Christian, and has been a music minister ever since. It makes me sweat to think about just how close I was to all of this at the time.

Somebody else who pulled up stakes and moved out of Los Angeles, albeit sooner than most, was my friend and sometime employer Gary Paxton. Gary resettled in Bakersfield, which had become the country-music mecca of California, in part because of its cotton farms and oilfields, which had been attracting migrants from Texas and Oklahoma since the 20s. Country stars Buck Owens and Merle Travis had honed their songwriting and instrumental skills in Bakersfield. There were honky-tonks galore in the town during the 30s, 40s, and 50s, offering plenty of places for young pickers and singers to get heard.

I never did ask Gary Paxton why he moved to Bakersfield, but I suspect that he thought he might better expand his empire there than in the more expensive fast lane of Hollywood. I was impressed the first time he called me out there to see his new studio setup. He had bought an old bank building downtown with a big open area that now housed the bulk of his equipment: tape recorders, playback speakers, and various mysterious little boxes for manipulating sound. There was a separate carpeted soundproofed room for the musicians to play in with a black grand piano in the center. Gary had also opened up a music store on the adjoining corner, so in effect he owned (or leased) the entire block. He called his complex Nashville West.

Gary also owned a resort up in the mountains above the town called Democrat Hot Springs. The long winding road up from Bakersfield follows the route of the Kern River and is covered with live oaks and chaparral. At one point you come to an old bridge out to the left; crossing it would take you to a parking area next to a fairly modern restaurant overlooking the river. Part of the resort had been an old hotel that served as a stop on the Butterfield Stagecoach route during the late 18th and early 19th centuries. It was not a resort hotel in the true sense of the word—the floors were uneven and the walls were paper thin. Nonetheless, we musicians were each allowed to chose and decorate a room, and we felt like we were living in the Old West.

To complete the picture, water from the hot springs was pumped into the swimming pool. We spent our days recording in the downtown bank recording studio and then soaked in the mineral water at night under the stars, high on the drink or drug of our choice. Guitarist Clarence White was there, and Gary had hired Clarence's dad as a caretaker. I believe Mr White Sr was originally from Quebec—he had tapes of wonderful Acadian music, which he played softly through the outside speakers so that we could still hear the river rapids bouncing over boulders below us and the owls and coyotes singing in the distance.

Gary had a girlfriend at the time named Brandy, a beautiful girl who could cook her ass off. She made us steak and eggs in the morning, and off we went down the mountain to play some music. If this sounds wonderful to you, you're damn right it was. I hated having to go back home to LA. Sadly, everything about Bakersfield and Gary Paxton came to an end in the late 60s. I had carried on working for him from time to time but on one occasion he was late paying me. I called him and he told me that he was going bankrupt. He suggested I come up to Bakersfield and pick out something of equal value from his music store, which was included in the bankruptcy.

I called an old Navy friend in Bakersfield, Randy Fendrick, who was keen to come with me to the store. We parked on a side street by the bank building and went in. Gary seemed a bit hyper when we arrived but otherwise I didn't feel any hostility from him. He owed me around $700, so I walked around the store and eventually settled on a big Sunn tube amp. I asked Gary if he thought that would be a fair trade; he agreed, so we shook hands and I told him I was sorry about his troubles. The amp, meanwhile, was fairly heavy, so Randy and I rolled it through the store into a big room with a cement floor, where Gary's bus was parked. The bus was up against the wall, so there was a lot of open, empty space.

We had made it halfway to the door when we heard someone growling behind us and running footsteps on the concrete floor. I turned to see Gary running at us with an old Civil War sword that he kept laying around. Suddenly, he stopped and turned around with his ass sticking out toward us. "Here, why don't you just go ahead and screw me right here!" he yelled.

Randy shoved the amplifier at Gary and we both flew out of the door toward my car. I took one last look behind me and saw the amplifier fly out and crash into the gutter. The door slammed, we picked up the amp, and that was the last time I saw Gary Paxton.

Gary's story doesn't end there, however. He moved to Nashville in 1970 and took a job as a songwriter for $100 a week. It did not take him long before he had built another empire. He became a born-again Christian and proceeded to write about 150 gospel songs, most of which have been recorded by a range of gospel artists. He also wrote the Number One country hit 'Woman (Sensuous Woman)' for Don Gibson and the Grammy-winning 'L-O-V-E Love' for The Blackwood Brothers. When you consider everything about Gary during the time I knew him—including the fact that he was almost dead from liver failure when we first met—the fact that he is still healthy and successful as I write this makes me think he is probably a walking miracle. A very talented walking miracle.

Speaking of Nashville, I always used to feel as though I never played country music until I worked with Elvis Presley, but in fact that's not quite true. Back in the 60s, I didn't think much about musical genres: I just played music. In 1967, however—back when Gary was still based in Hollywood—I had played on an album by some musicians who would later form the nucleus of his Bakersfield studio group. The album was *Sounds Of Goodbye* by The Gosdin Brothers, and by virtue of my appearance on it, according to modern reviews, I was a pioneer of country-rock. I just didn't know what it was at the time.

That Sunn amp, meanwhile, would serve me well, over the years, as I used it for good jobs and bad.

From 1969 until the mid-to-late 70s, much of my working life was devoted to playing with Elvis Presley, as detailed earlier in this book. But I still found time to fit in various sessions with a wide range of musicians, from Johnny Rivers to Todd Rundgren. Perhaps the most famous of these sessions—for me and for my Sunn tube amp—was *LA Woman* by The Doors, which I spent six weeks working on, either side of Christmas 1970.

Until then, I had not paid a lot of attention to The Doors. 'Light My Fire' was on the radio constantly, of course, but at the time I was more interested in jazz and Jimi Hendrix. Now, with the benefit of hindsight, I realize what was going on at the time: those four guys were introducing the love-child generation to what they thought was a more mystical and intellectual type of music and poetry. They certainly had a point, when you consider that the charts at the time were full of records by The Mamas & The Papas and The Monkees.

Up until now, each of The Doors' records had been produced by Paul Rothschild. The chief engineer on those records was Bruce Botnick. In late

1970, The Doors had a meeting with Bruce and Paul, during which Paul announced that he did not like the group's new songs. Fortunately, the others disagreed and called in session-guitarist Marc Benno and I to begin work on the album.

We recorded *LA Woman* at The Doors' offices, which were housed in a two-story corner building on Santa Monica Boulevard in West Hollywood. When I first arrived to set up and get a sound I was confronted by six people—the four Doors plus Marc Benno and Bruce Botnick—who were all serious about making music. Marc and I were the newcomers but we felt a part of things from the beginning. Most of the songs had already been written but a few were finished right there in the office. The 16-track board and all the outboard equipment was set up in the second-story room, while the microphones and amplifiers were arranged on the first floor along with a pinball machine and a refrigerator full of beer.

Paul Rothschild later claimed that he bowed out of working with the band because he thought they'd become The Drunken Doors and because their new songs sounded like lounge music. I knew Paul vaguely—in fact, for a very short time I had lived with a girl I met at his house—but he was wrong about the *LA Woman* material. Similarly, I have read a lot since about how Jim Morrison drank so much that he had to record his vocals in the restroom because he needed to be close to the toilet so that he could relieve himself at any point.

That's not how I remember it at all. Jim may have recorded one or two songs in there, but only because Bruce Botnick liked the echo it produced. Beyond that, I think Jim could have drunk or taken whatever he wanted and still fulfilled any musical expectations made of him. Nothing got in the way of the music. There are plenty of photographs of Jim in the recording room with us during the sessions, but I'm not aware of any of him in the toilet. In any case, if you've not heard the album, give it a spin and see if it sounds like the work of a bunch of out-of-control drug addicts and alcoholics.

≡

In 1971, Vivian's son Marlo was approaching the age where the military draft might grab him. The war in Vietnam was in full force and we were very worried. One day, Vivian showed me a classified ad in the *Los Angeles Times* offering for sale a small farm on an island in Western British Columbia: Salt Spring Island.

As it happened, the 80-year-old man who owned the farm had lost his wife and was in LA looking for a new one. He had long grey hair and spoke with a German accent. The main thing that stood out about him was his lack of footwear: he didn't own any. His farm sounded wonderful, though, and within a few days we were on an airplane with him—bare feet and all—headed for Salt Spring Island.

I didn't like the farm but I loved the island. We flew back to Los Angeles, where we learned that Marlo had drawn a very high number in the draft lottery and wouldn't be enlisted. I was happy about that but I couldn't get the island off my mind. Even though I was at the height of my musical career, I decided to leave the whole recording-studio life behind. We hopped in the Blazer and off we went.

In the meantime, my accountant—who later wound up in jail on tax evasion charges—advised me that I could save money if Vivian and I got married. Now, she and I had already made a pact—her idea—that if one of us wanted our freedom, we could leave, and the other would not make a fuss. With that in mind we decided to get married in Las Vegas the next time we were there. In fact, we decided to see exactly how quickly we could do it. We parked illegally in front of the courthouse door, started a timer, and ran for the door. The civil servant was alone, but a janitor was there to act as a witness, so we pleaded with them to hurry because we had an important meeting. We took the vows, signed papers on the run, and were out of there in less than 15 minutes.

Living on Salt Spring Island was wonderful. I had bought an old farmhouse with five acres of land: two acres of pasture and three acres of forest full of huge fir and cedar trees. The house had been built around 1900 by a remittance man from England—that is, a black sheep who had been sent to one of the colonies and would receive money from home each month on the proviso that he never came back. The house was large and was built from redwood logs which had been towed all the way from California.

After a while I had a boat built: a small *African Queen*-style lap-strake construction. It was slow, but I was never in a hurry on the island. I used the boat to collect dinner. I would typically make a late-afternoon run to a rocky point where an old boatman told me I could depend on catching lingcod as long as my arm. I didn't need a fishing pole: I would just throw line with a jig attached, let it touch the bottom, jiggle it up and down a few times, and haul in a fish big enough to feed four. Then I would head for Ganges harbor, where I had four Dungeness crab traps. My floats were bright yellow so they were easy to see. Most times I pulled up the traps there would be two or three crabs in each. I measured the crabs, threw the undersized ones back, and put the remainder in a box. Back then, there were beaches where I could stop and fill a gunnysack with oysters. The sack would stay on my kitchen porch—if I kept it wet, the oysters would usually keep until they were eaten.

I was heavily into my mountain-macho stage by this time—the hippie lifestyle had grown stale for me. Charles Manson, Vietnam, the National guard shootings at Kent state, and all the rest had pretty much killed the peace and love movement that had been so close to my heart. Work replaced all of that for me. I dug a large garden and built a seven-foot-high fence around it to keep out the island deer.

At the bottom of my property was a stream with large cedar logs laying across it. They were covered in thick moss, like huge pick-up sticks—they had obviously been felled years before, but being cedar there was very little rot. I needed fence posts, so I drove my four-wheel-drive Chevy Blazer through the forest to pick them up. I then cut the logs with a chainsaw into ten-foot lengths before splitting them into fence posts with steel wedges and a sledgehammer, and into the back of the Blazer they went.

With my mountain-macho mindset, I was not happy when the teepee-dwelling hippies in the surrounding forest started playing 'Big Yellow Taxi' by Joni Mitchell over and over on their battery-powered cassette players. I love Joni Mitchell, and I love that song, but it got to be torture. I had two huge Voice Of The Theater speaker cabinets that I had liberated from the main show room of the International Hotel in Las Vegas while I was playing there with Elvis. I brought them out onto my porch and started playing Otis Redding, Ray Charles, Prokofiev, Miles Davis, Alban Berg's *Lulu Suite*, Italian operas—anything to relieve the monotony. The music echoed and cascaded up and down the hills and through the trees and ferns while I worked.

In the meantime, I started getting calls to do studio work in Vancouver, so we rented an apartment overlooking English Bay. The lease was mostly tax-deductible because of my work. We also bought the main corner of Ganges, one of three villages on Salt Spring Island, and opened a small store to sell bric-a-brac to the tourists. Because they are protected from the open ocean, the gulf islands are heaven for sailboating in the summer. The yachting crowd would pull into Ganges and tie up at the marina, which was fairly close to our store filled with candy and expensive German wooden toys, perfect for keeping the yachters' children quiet while they were at sea. We also sold small Victorian antiques such as picnic baskets with Sterling cutlery.

We still had Otis the parrot with us on Salt Spring Island. During the Summer, Vivian took him to the store every day. Unfortunately, Otis had a foul beak on him, and some of our regular customers came from the more staid island families. We had a bell on the door, which Otis would imitate whenever it rang, and then he might follow that with "You little shit!" ad nauseam at inopportune times, or sometimes "Get back in your goddamned cage you little fucker!"

The island ladies would gasp and sputter, but usually they were drawn over to Otis's cage, where he usually fluffed his feathers out, lowered his head like he wanted to be scratched, and said in his/my sweetest tone of voice something like: "Hi baby, give me a kiss." He always followed that with a wet kissing sound. If any customer was foolish enough to try to put his or her fingers in the cage to pet him, Otis bit the hell out of them.

There were musicians on Salt Spring Island, some of whom were very good. One of them, Valdy, was known as the Canadian Troubadour and is now considered a national treasure in his home country. He was one of a group of people who used to wind up on my kitchen porch, drinking Wee Heavy (strong Scottish ale) and eating crabs and oysters on the half-shell. The Canadian band Chilliwack, led by singer-songwriter Bill Henderson, also came by.

Back then the island had a year-round population of about 2,000 people, including several hundred teens who were bored to death because there was very little for them to do. To help remedy this, every once in a while we would throw dances in an old community hall out in the woods off the main road. I had my various colored rhinestone bop-suits from the Elvis show— we would wear those and call ourselves Sticky Lifter & The Sharks. The hippies would come out of the woods, see the jumpsuits, and say: "Aww, man! What a bummer." They had no sense of irony.

The construction of the community hall was so poor that we had to put tables and chairs in the middle of the floor so that people couldn't dance there. Had they done so, the floor might have collapsed, and we would all have ended up in the basement.

A lot of young would-be musicians would come along to hear us play, and I got to know some of them. I had stopped using my Sunn amp by then, so I gave it to one of these kids.

I left Salt Spring Island in 1975 and didn't think about the amp again until years later, by which time my son Jason had taken Peter Cetera's place in the group Chicago. One day, after arriving home from a tour, Jason told me a story. He had received an email from a bass-playing Chicago fan in Cleveland, Ohio, who wanted to know whether Jason was Jerry Scheff's son. When Jason replied to say yes, he was, the man told him that he had my old Sunn amp. He knew it was mine, he said, because both the top and the speaker cabinet had had my name stenciled onto them by the Elvis Presley show's stagehands. The guy said he had only paid a few hundred dollars for the amp and would gladly send it to Los Angeles if Jason agreed to reimburse him and pay for the shipping.

By now the amp was worth quite a lot of money—there are numerous pictures of Elvis and I standing in front of it, as well as photos of Jim Morrison and I sitting on the amp head during the *LA Woman* sessions.

Jason and I talked it over and decided to reward this kindly bass player from Ohio. Jason donated a vintage Fender Precision Bass, worth several thousand dollars then and no doubt more now, which we both signed. Jason has the Sunn amp stored away for my grandchildren. You see: good deeds do get rewarded on occasion.

In the meantime, back in the early to mid 70s, the money was still pouring into the coffers of Los Angeles recording studios—and hence into recording budgets—and I started getting calls for work. A typical trip to LA started at eight in the morning, when I would be at the dock in Ganges to be picked up by the Victoria Flying Services. The airplane was a single-engine de Havilland Beaver floatplane—the plane that's remembered for opening up the Pacific North West and the arctic. We flew low over the Georgia Strait and landed in downtown Vancouver at the Bayshore Inn, where I grabbed a taxi to Vancouver airport. Once the plane landed in Los Angeles, I took another taxi to whatever recording studio I was booked into, and I was ready to rock.

One of the projects that I flew to Los Angeles for was an album by singer Hoyt Axton on A&M Records. It was not one of Hoyt's best albums, but there were a couple of interesting things at play that show how small the music business was at that time. Hoyt's mother Mae wrote 'Heartbreak Hotel,' and Hoyt himself later wrote the Elvis blues song 'Never Been To Spain.'

When I arrived at A&M to start the sessions, the drummer, Jim Keltner, was nowhere to be found. After we'd waited for a while and Jim still hadn't arrived, Hoyt said he had a song that needed no drums or bass, just cello, ocarina, and guitar. Fortunately, the cello player was there already, and sax player Jim Horn played the ocarina. I on the other hand hadn't played a note yet and probably wouldn't do so for at least another hour or two.

I had just settled down into the recording booth to listen to the song when Jim Keltner showed up with the singer Harry Nilsson, whose hit records included 'Everybody's Talkin'' and who a few years earlier had been described by John Lennon and Paul McCartney as their favorite American singer. This might well have been around the time Lennon was staying in Los Angeles while separated from Yoko Ono, and it could even have been that he, Harry, and Jim had hung out the night before. Certainly, when Jim and Harry got to the studio they looked really fuzzy around the edges.

In any case, Hoyt and the producer decided to go ahead and do the quiet song because the cellist and ocarina player were already setup with microphones in place. Jim Keltner went off to get some coffee and Harry Nilsson sat down on the couch in front of the recording console. Hoyt started the song with a soft fingerpicking pattern before the cello and ocarina joined in with a beautiful theme the players had just come up with. Then, in the middle of all this, came a buzzing sound.

Zzzzzzzzzzzzzzzzzzzzzzzzzzzzzz.

"What the hell is that?" the engineer asked.

I followed the sound and it led me to Harry Nilsson on the couch— sound asleep, snoring up a tempest.

Jim Keltner and I would end up working together quite a lot in the ensuing years. He and I eventually toured together with Elvis Costello in the 90s. Before that, we did a live *Rolling Stone* TV special in 1977 with Bette Midler at the Roxy club in Los Angeles. Jerry Lee Lewis was on the show, too, and asked Jim and me to accompany him; we both said: "Shit yeah!" We loved Jerry Lee.

Following on from the *Rolling Stone* special, we worked with Bette on an album called *Broken Blossom*, which in turn led to our being hired to play a concert with Bette at the Hollywood Bowl: A Star Spangled Night For Gay Rights.

The weather was beautiful that night: soft air and soft seats, because everyone who comes to the Hollywood Bowl knows that you bring your own cushions as well as your own food and drink. There were about 20,000 people in the audience: movie stars, singers, you name them and they were there, providing they were against certain legislation that was being drawn up in Sacramento to the detriment of the California gay community.

Johnny Mathis, with whom I had once recorded a Christmas album, was sitting in a cream-colored summer-suit at one of the hundreds of table-clothed tables with silver champagne buckets that wrapped around the stage. Catered gourmet dinners gave way to brown baggers in the back, but everyone was there for the same reason: good feelings and camaraderie with a purpose. All of this was to be topped off by a huge fireworks display at the end.

Besides Bette Midler, the entertainers for that night included comedians Lily Tomlin and Richard Pryor. At the start of the show, Jim Keltner and I were in our dressing room loading our noses. We had the intercom on and could hear Lily Tomlin introduce Richard Pryor. Pryor said a few things using the word faggots and queers as punctuation, which drew some catcalls and whistles. Then he said: "Now, I understand that this show is about the right of one man to suck another man's dick ..."

Whoosh!

Jim and I were up the stairs and backstage in a second.

"I sucked a dick one time," Pyror continued. "Some big motherfucker comes up to you in the ghetto and says 'suck my dick,' you suck his dick."

There was a little nervous laughter from the audience, but I could feel the anger start to rise. Then Pryor said: "When the niggers was burning down Watts, you motherfuckers was doin' what you wanted to do, mincin' up and down Hollywood Boulevard ... didn't give a shit about us ... You Hollywood faggots can kiss my happy, rich, black ass."

With that, Pryor left the stage, climbed into his limo, and got out of there. The party was in a shambles: cushions were being thrown, people were on their feet booing, and 20,000 people were deteriorating into a mob. Lily Tomlin came out and tried to calm them down. I thought we might have a riot on our hands.

After a half hour or so things calmed down a bit, but the mood seemed forever lost. Maybe if an upbeat act had come on stage exhorting the audience to boogie a little the mood might have changed as well, but the next scheduled performer was Tom Waits. Now I love Tom Waits, but with his growly voice and laid-back attitude, maybe he wasn't the one to try and pull this show out of the fire.

We were set to go on last, to close the show. We, the band, and Bette's backing singers, The Harlettes, were on stage ready to go when Bette came out in a flamboyant outfit with a skirt slit up to her waist. She walked up to the microphone, chewing gum, pulled the dress open, and said: "How'd you like to kiss this rich white ass?"

The laughter exploded into the night, and even though Bette pared our part of the show down a bit, the tension never dissipated completely, so you might say that Bette and the fireworks were the best that were available.

CHAPTER 19
CHANGING OF
THE GUARD

I n 1977, after Elvis Presley's death, I moved into a beachfront apartment in Malibu, California. It was time for me to get back to business in Los Angeles: to carve out a niche again. I did jingles, motion-picture soundtracks, television work, albums, and assorted live performances. Little by little, I was building my career back up.

I first met country singer Tanya Tucker in Las Vegas after an Elvis show. She was just a baby then, but had already started a promising career with 'Delta Dawn,' released when she was just 13 years old. She adored Elvis. We all did. Suddenly, Elvis was gone.

Now, in 1977, Tanya was 19 years old. She had just signed a management deal with Far Out Productions in Los Angeles, which consisted of producer Jerry Goldstein and manager Steve Gold, who had previously worked with the rock group War and promised Tanya crossover pop fame. I don't know how I became involved with all this, but I was asked by Jerry Goldstein to put a band together, and I did it. I got what I considered to be the cream of the crop of young country-rock musicians based in LA at the time: drummer Paul Leim, piano player John Hobbs, and guitarist Billy Walker—all of whom now live in Nashville, and have their initials carved in the modern history of the city's music business.

The album we made with Tanya was called *TNT*. There was nothing earth-shattering about it, but it duly became her first Gold album. And we had a good time making it. Before the first session, John Hobbs and I went off to get a gram of cocaine, figuring we could do with some mood enhancement. The cocaine came wrapped in a folded paper envelope. John took charge and put it in his shirt pocket. We set to work on a very strenuous song, and when we finally finished it a very sweaty John and I slipped off to the restroom for a quick pick-me-up. John pulled the paper packet out of his shirt—it was soaked. The contents looked like they were to be used to build the foundations of a brick wall in miniature. Not to worry, though: John got a paper cup and diluted the coke with water. We snorted the sweaty, watery cocaine and got on with the next song.

After we finished Tanya's album, we went with her to Texas to play a few songs at a Willie Nelson concert. I have always loved Willie, and his bass player at the time was an old acquaintance of mine, Chris Ethridge, who had co-founded The Flying Burrito Brothers. After I'd finished playing some songs with Tanya, I sat backstage with Chris and shot the shit. Chris started complaining about the bass player in the opening act—a young guy with ideas above his station. Chris never said a bad word about anyone, so when he started on this bass player, I knew the guy must be leaning into his own wind.

Chris had worked out a scenario where he and I would come out and play bass together for a few songs with Willie: I would play a high guitar-like part and Chris would play the low, bottom grooves for which he was justifiably famous. After a few songs, Willie called out the other bass player, from the opening act, who came strutting out to take my place. Unbeknownst to him, however, his bass was never patched into the system—I was waiting behind the curtains with my bass, which was what everyone would hear. Of course, Willie was in on the whole scheme.

As the next song started up, I watched the other bass player carefully. When his fingers touched the strings, I played something that would fit the song, but I added a wrong note or two. The bass player looked, in shock, at his hands; Willie, who knew what was going on, started giving the kid dirty looks. Everyone backstage was cracking up. Finally, the poor guy just put down his bass and walked off.

Soon after that I started to get phone calls from an old friend of mine, saxophone player Steve Douglas, who like me had served in the Navy for a while before going on to play with everyone from Duane Eddy to The Beach Boys. Steve had just returned from a tour of Japan, New Zealand, and Australia with Bob Dylan. The bassist and bandleader on that tour was Rob Stoner, a veteran of Dylan's Rolling Thunder Review, but for some reason I never really understood he left or was asked to leave once they got back to Los Angeles.

The reason for Steve's call was that they were rehearsing in Santa Monica with a new bass player who nobody liked very much. Maybe I could take his place? Now, I had worked hard to rebuild my career in the time since Elvis's death, and I knew that if I went out on the road I would have to go through the same paces once again when I got back. I was working on the Tanya Tucker project at the time, plus I had various jingles and soundtrack sessions booked, so I told Steve I didn't have time to come down to rehearsals.

A week or so went by before Steve called again. "Jerry!" he said. "Get your ass down here!" I told him I'd come down the next morning before my 1:00pm recording date. They had an Ampeg tube amp set up when I got there, so I introduced myself to everyone—Steve was the only person I knew—and plugged straight in.

Bob came in after a while and we played a few songs. He looked at the rest of the band and they all nodded their heads in affirmation. Bob and I went into his office and he offered me a deal. The money was right, as far as I was concerned, so that was that: I was Bob Dylan's new bass player.

I'd been told to come back to the rehearsal studio the following day, so I called my answering service and had them cancel any work I had scheduled. I then called Jerry Goldstein to tell him I'd be leaving the Tanya Tucker project. *TNT* was done by that point, so I wasn't leaving a very big hole in the project. There was only one small hitch: when I arrived at Dylan's studio the following morning, somebody else's bass was standing in front of the amp. Steve came into the room with a guy I'd not yet met, who he introduced as another bass player they'd been rehearsing with. I went straight into Bob's office and told him I felt like he'd been wasting my time and that I was out of there.

"No, no, no," Bob said, following me out of the room. "You got the gig." We shook hands and started rehearsing that afternoon. I never saw the other bass player again.

We were already well into May 1978 by this point, and the tour was due to start on June 1 with a week-long run of shows at the Universal Amphitheater, Los Angeles. That left very little time for me to learn the songs for the show—in fact, I didn't even get a chance to learn the whole thing.

We had rehearsed about half of the set when Bob made an announcement. "OK," he said. "I have some new songs and we are going to record a new album." He had arranged for a remote recording truck to come to the rehearsal studio. All work on the live set stopped and we were off into new territory, learning the songs that would eventually make up the album *Street-Legal*.

Imagine you were due to arrive on stage with Bob Dylan at the Universal Amphitheater in front of thousands of people—in your own town, no less—and you have never played a third of the songs in the show. That's what happened to me. I had at least been given a tape of the songs, but I knew it wouldn't do to be seen reading chord charts on stage with a rock band like this, so I wrote myself some notes on small pieces of paper and laid them out behind me on the drum riser.

The drummer in Dylan's group was Ian Wallace, best known at the time for his work with Robert Fripp in King Crimson. We hit it off straight away. I later heard that Rob Stoner had called Ian a 'mechanical' drummer, but I never thought that about him. I felt that he played grooves that allowed Bob and the rest of the musicians to express themselves.

The first show went better than expected. I played almost flawlessly. The second night ... well, let's just say my concentration slipped due to overconfidence. We played seven shows over seven nights at the Universal

Amphitheater, which back then was an outdoor venue with a capacity of around 6,000. One night after the show, Bob introduced me to the actor-singer Connie Stevens. I had had a huge crush on her during my teens, even though I never cared much for her movies. Meeting her in person almost floored me. The following morning, I was taking a shower when the phone rang. My then-wife Diane answered. It was Connie, who wondered if I could come to Lake Tahoe for a month to work with her. Without asking me, Diane told Connie that I was fully booked. Oh well.

We had a few days off between the LA shows and the start of a month-long tour of Europe. I had been warned that Bob didn't like small talk, so during the Universal Amphitheater shows I spoke to him only about the music. It seemed like we had a good understanding. When we set off for Europe, however, I was surprised to find that Bob was seated next to me on the plane. After takeoff, Bob started talking about broken marriages and how his was affecting his relationship with his children. It seemed someone had mentioned to Bob that I had two sons from a failed marriage, and he now wanted to know how I had dealt with the situation as a father. I told him I hadn't dealt with it very well at all. We discussed various other things during that flight to London. This certainly wasn't small talk.

I never really felt that Bob and I were friends, but we did have some great times together. Arriving in London, the show group checked in to a beautiful hotel right on Hyde Park. There were antique shops right on our doorstep and we had all the usual rock-tour accouterments at our disposal. We had a few days to recover from jet lag, and on one of those days my phone rang. It was Bob. He asked me if I liked reggae music, and I told him I loved it. He said to meet him in the hotel garage at a certain time and not to mention it to anyone else. As it turned out, Bob had a Mercedes stashed there. He was going to give his security team the slip and we were going to a club in a West Indian neighborhood to hear some live reggae.

When I got to the garage, Bob had with him his beautiful background singer, Helena Springs, and the group's female percussionist, Bobbye Hall. Bob drove us across town and found a parking space about a block away from the club. It was then that it hit me: here we were, two very white guys in a Mercedes with two attractive black ladies in a predominantly black area of London with no bodyguards. What kind of statement were we making?

We could hear the music from outside—it was almost as if the outer walls of the club were throbbing. We stepped into a room where a few people were sitting around in folding chairs against bare walls; the music, already very loud, was coming from the other side of a closed door. In front of us was a ticket booth made out of raw plywood. Bob stepped forward and asked for four tickets. A guy in dreadlocks told him that you needed to be a member to gain entry, and that membership was £100 apiece. The band sounded great, though, and we were all getting turned on to whatever was happening on the other side of the door. Bob handed over £400 (around $750 at the time). We had our hands stamped and in we went.

There were no chairs or tables in the main room of the club. The walls were lined with speakers pumping out recorded music. There was one couple swaying in the middle of the room and a bottle of wine on the floor but no glasses. We looked at one another and started laughing.

Fortunately, Bob had another plan for the night and drove us to an old Victorian theater where the guitarist Link Wray was just finishing up his set. The place had seen better days and people were standing wall-to-wall on the inclined main floor. The only seats that hadn't been ripped out were in the balconies, so we headed up there to watch the end of the show.

After the show we were escorted down to the basement dressing rooms, where tables were set up and everyone was toasting the end of a successful engagement with glasses of champagne. A couple of members of our band were already there: rhythm guitarist and background vocalist Steven Soles and guitar and violin player David Mansfield. Steven set the champagne on the table where we were sitting and a surly young guy reached over, glared at him, and snatched the glass away. He took a sip, smiling through the corners of his mouth, and then put the glass back down. Steven reached over to take the glass back and wound up with a switchblade in his face. We decided to change tables. And that was our introduction to Sid Vicious from the Sex Pistols.

A few nights later, we finally got down to business: six shows at Earls

Court, playing to 19,000 people a night. That's a lot of people. It was way beyond anything I had ever experienced. I remember thinking: Elvis could have done something like this. (In fact, Elvis had bought the jet we used from 1975 to 1977, the Lisa Marie, in order to tour Europe and Asia.)

At one of the Earls Court concerts, the actor Jack Nicholson came backstage and told Bob that he had been invited to a housewarming party after the show. Some of his friends had evidently just come back from South America, where they had bought rugs for their new house. Jack suggested that we all show up at his friend's door: "Surprise!"

The house was sparsely furnished, and there weren't many places to sit, but there was plenty to drink and some interesting characters to chat with, including Bianca Jagger, who was dressed in a frilly white frock. We were introduced but I didn't feel much kinship with her, so I sat on the floor with my drink in hand and introduced myself to the gentleman sitting next to me. He said his name was Roddy Llewellyn. We talked about music and his big interest, horticulture, and we laughed at Bianca Jagger's little-girl outfit and Jack Nicholson's bad-boy antics. Only later did I realize that this Roddy Llewellyn was in fact the Roderick Llewellyn who at that very time was in the middle of an eight-year affair with Princess Margaret.

After the Earls Court run we had two days off before our next concert, at the Feijenoord Stadion in Rotterdam, The Netherlands—a soccer stadium that held around 60,000 people at the time. It was around this point that we hooked up with a private train that included what we were told was Hermann Göring's private railway car. Bob spent a lot of time in that car. I never asked why, but I imagine it had a lot to do with his Jewish ancestry, although he never mentioned that, either. We just never discussed it.

The train had two baggage cars and a posh dining car with tablecloths, fine wines, a great German chef, two waiters, and the best beer money could buy. I think I only left the dining car a few times that month. We never slept on the train, however: we would pull into the next city on the tour, get on a bus, and check in to a hotel. Our luggage would join us an hour or two later.

After Rotterdam, we crossed into Germany for two shows in Dortmund and then one night at the Deutschlandhalle in Berlin. To get to Berlin we had to go through the East German checkpoints. The border guards came out with dogs and machine guns, and they had trolleys with mirrors on them to check underneath the train. The guards boarded the train and checked our passports in the dining car. It was my then-wife Diane's birthday, and the guard—with machine gun in one hand and her passport in the other—looked over to her and with a small crack of a smile, said: "Happy birthday."

On the day of the concert we rode out by bus to the Deutschlandhalle with the German journalist Günter Amendt, who was covering the tour for *Der Spiegel*. I liked him a lot. We did the soundcheck, ate dinner ... and then went out on stage to loud booing and a hail of articles of all kinds: cigarette lighters, coins, oil-based paint-bombs, and various items of food.

The majority of the audience of 8,500 people was interested in the music, but there was a sizable faction hell-bent on disruption. I was scared! Who knew what else they'd throw? One of the paint-bombs landed between Ian Wallace and me. Grey paint splattered all over Ian's drums and up the front of my custom-made black suit, leaving just a small area of untouched black fabric where my bass was in the way.

I kept waiting for Bob to say "guten nacht" to the audience but he was not going to let these people run him off the stage. We stood there and took it until the last song, when we filed off the stage with dignity. Some people were still booing but most of them were applauding. We went to the dressing rooms where the support act, Elvis Costello & The Attractions, were waiting, half laughing at us and half cheering us on. I had never met them before.

We all got towels and wiped food, paint, and, in a couple of cases, even blood off clothes and bodies. All of a sudden, Bob yelled: "Come on!" We were going to do an encore! I couldn't believe it. Most of the audience was on their feet and heading for the exits. When they heard us start playing, the cigarette lighters came out. If I remember correctly, people were swaying their lighters to the song 'Forever Young.' Günter Amendt told me that the troublemakers were young neo-Nazis who had decided to use our concert for a political statement.

The following morning we boarded our train and headed for Nuremberg. I fell in love with the city, with its big medieval walls and the square with its charcoal burners in front of the cathedral, where people were grilling Nuremberg bratwurst on a roll with mustard. I must have eaten 20 of them on my first day there.

We were scheduled to play the next day for 80,000 people at the Zeppelin Field, which was where the Nazis had staged their big rallies during the 1930s and 40s. Albert Speer, the Third Reich architect (and later Minister For Armaments And War Production), had designed the marble viewing platforms and the speaker's stand where Hitler stood as he delivered his speeches. The famous searchlight displays and the giant eagle behind were also Speer's ideas. Much of my family came from Germany, of course, and this first trip to the country was a very moving experience for me. I soon learned that most Germans were just like us in their thinking, but just like at home there would always be people like those who tried to disrupt the Berlin concert.

After our experience at the Deutschlandhalle, I wasn't quite sure what to expect at the Nuremberg show. In the end, however, we left our hotel under beautiful sunny blue skies to find a huge crowd of warm, appreciative people awaiting us. It was one of the most enjoyable concert experiences of my career, bathing in a sea of positive emotions.

The next day we were back in the dining car and off to Paris. From there we were bussed to our hotel, Le Meurice, a luxury establishment right on the Rue de Rivoli. It was where Pablo Picasso and his wife Olga Koklova had hosted their wedding dinner in 1918, and where Salvador Dali still liked to spend at least one month per year. Bob was treating us right.

As it happened, Dali and his wife were staying at Le Meurice while we were there. We used to hang out at what was then the Copper Bar in the hotel, where we became friends with a Moroccan barman named Talal Lamrani who had been given an autographed lithograph by Dali.

It was during this part of the tour that drummer Ian Wallace and I decided that we should take our wives to dinner at a Michelin three-star restaurant. I don't remember the name of the place, but it was not far from the hotel in the middle of a park.

Ian's wife Sandy was tall and very attractive. She had on an above-the-knee dress and very high heels, topped off with a mink bowler-style hat. Ian had very long hair and looked every bit the English rocker. I guess I was slightly less conspicuous with my medium-length hair and sunglasses.

We started off with two or three martinis each and then two or three bottles of champagne. We ordered Chablis with our starters, vintage Bordeaux with our main courses, and Sauternes with our dessert. After that, we had Napoleonic Cognac. We were shellacked by the main course, and of course the drunker we got the louder we got. The diners at the other tables were giving us unfriendly looks at first, until they realized that we had become the floor show. It all started with Sandy's mink hat, which was already a little too big for her head. As the dinner wore on, it gradually slipped down—by the time we were having our dessert, her ears were sticking straight out.

Don't get me wrong: we all contributed to the spectacle. We were laughing and having a great time and didn't notice people pointing and smirking. Every once in a while, Sandy would push back her chair and swing one of her long legs out toward another table and smooth her nylons halfway up her thighs. I don't know if you have ever seen grown men drool caviar, but a man at the next table showed us that it is not a pretty sight.

Finally, it was time to pay the bill. We all pulled out our credit cards and the waiter informed us that *this* restaurant did not accept them. We owed a lot of money. Ian and I dug in our pockets, Diane and Sandy dug around in their purses, and in the end we came up with a pile of bills and coins in French francs, UK sterling, and US dollars, with a few German marks to top it off. We had just about enough cash but nothing left for the gratuity. I think it's safe to say that we were not very popular with the staff.

We had no money for the cab back to the hotel, either, so Ian and I had to leave our ladies waiting in the car while we went upstairs to refill our wallets. Then we got Bob's limo driver to take us back to the restaurant, at which point we instructed him to go inside, tip the staff, and point to us so that we could wave. We thought we had done everything we could to save whatever honor we had left.

During that week in Paris we did six shows at the Pavillon, a very undistinguished venue located in a neighborhood full of slaughterhouses and thus nicknamed Les Abattoirs. Even so, we played six successful shows there to approximately 60,000 people before climbing back onto the train for the last few shows of the European tour.

Our next stop was Gothenburg, Sweden, where we played two shows before heading back to the UK to play an outdoor concert at an abandoned Air Force base, Blackbushe. As far as I knew this was going to be just another concert. I was wrong. Estimates vary, but some reports indicate that as many as 300,000 people were in attendance. The event was billed as The 'Picnic' At Blackbushe Aerodrome. Also on the bill were Graham Parker & The Rumour, Joan Armatrading, and Eric Clapton. Still playing bass with Eric was my old friend Carl Radle, who I'd first seen playing with Delaney & Bonnie & Friends a decade earlier. We had a great time laughing and catching up before and after the show, but sadly this was the last time I would ever see him. Shortly after that, he was fired from the band and headed back to the USA. According to his sister, he spent some time in Los Angeles, strung out on drugs, before heading home to Tulsa, Oklahoma, where he was found dead in his bathtub, having succumbed to kidney poisoning following years of drug and alcohol abuse. He was a great man and a great bass player.

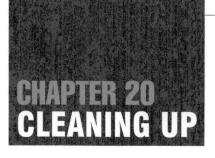

CHAPTER 20
CLEANING UP

After a three-week break, we were back on the road again with Dylan for a three-month tour of the USA. I had thoroughly enjoyed the European concerts and was looking forward to getting back out there. As far as I was concerned, the rhythm section was very tight and the grooves were falling right where they should be. That would not last for long, however. According to Ian Wallace, percussionist Bobbye Hall had complained to Bob about Ian's playing, saying he was dragging the beat. After that, the whole show never felt the same. It was a sad thing to happen.

I didn't hang out with Bob very often during the US tour. He seemed to have become very reclusive. I remember being in his hotel one night after a show. He had sent his valet out in the limo to pick up some soul food. The valet was wearing a nice leather jacket which, under duress, he ended up having to give to a tough-looking guy standing in the doorway of the restaurant.

On another occasion, I remember Bob wanting a bunch of us to go to a movie with him. We all found our seats, but soon after the movie started Bob walked out. When it was over we found him over at the popcorn kiosk having what looked like a deep conversation with the lady who worked there.

Another time, Bob took the whole cast and crew to dinner in a huge, famous steakhouse in Chicago called the Stock Yards. Once again, Bob disappeared soon after the rest of us sat down. After we'd finished eating, Bob's road manager went to look for him and eventually found him talking to locals in a little bar that catered to the stock yard workers. I remember thinking he must probably be a master at extracting feelings and essences from life in general. Where else would be find those dead-on lyrics and melodies?

As we approached the end of the tour, Ian told me that he had spoken to Bob, and that Bob had said that he planned to keep the same band together for the next year. "Great," I said. "See you then." Ian laughed and carried on past me to the back of the bus.

A few minutes later, Bob got on and sat down next to me. "Jerry," he asked, "what drummers do you liked to play with?"

I was dumbfounded. I told Bob I was very happy with Ian, but at that moment alarm bells started to ricochet around my brain. I thought back to that time we had shaken hands in his office, and then I'd come in the next day to find some other poor bassist about to be sent packing. If he was stringing Ian along now, would I be next?

That night, before the final show of the tour, I went to Bob's dressing room and told him that I couldn't commit to being there for him next year without a guaranteed contract—that I couldn't leave my studio scene hanging unless I had a secure job. I asked him for a $100,000 guarantee for 1979, with a minimum of two weeks' notice before any gigs or rehearsals. Any amount left over would be paid to me at the end of the year. Bob seemed to be in agreement, but as I headed home to California I knew that I wouldn't feel comfortable until I got that contract.

A week or two later, I was in the bathtub when the phone rang. My wife brought me the phone. It was Bob's manager, Jerry Weintraub. I knew him from the Elvis Presley tours. Jerry said that he was working on my contract and wanted to know exactly what I wanted. He also informed me that Bob had made up his mind to change drummers, so I suggested I bring Ronnie Tutt down to Bob's rehearsal studio.

It was just the three of us that day: Ronnie, Bob, and me. Unfortunately, it had not occurred to me to play or tell Ronnie about any of the music we had been playing on tour during the previous year. Looking back, I think Ronnie may have assumed that Bob was back to playing folk arrangements. He played very light drum parts with nowhere near the energy required. It wasn't long before Bob called us to a halt and said he would be in touch.

That was also the last I heard of my deal. For a few years, every six months or so, I would get a call from Bob's office, enquiring as to my schedule. That was it.

A couple of years later, I heard from Ian Wallace. He had been playing with Bob again for a while, but once again things were not quite as they seemed. "You're not going to believe this," he told me. "I had just shipped my drums to London to start rehearsals for an upcoming tour when my phone rang. It was Bob's manager, telling me that he was hiring another drummer." What could I say? I just commiserated with Ian the best I could.

On another occasion, I was in the studio one day with my old friend Jim Keltner when the conversation turned to Dylan. Jim had recently been playing in Bob's live band. He said that at the end of rehearsals one day, Bob had asked: "Jim, what guitar players do you like? I'm not digging the guitar players." Sound familiar?

Jim said that he loved the players they had already. "By the way," Bob replied, "I'm not digging the drums either." What a way to get fired. Fortunately, Jim and I were able to laugh about this in the way successful old band-mates can.

In 1979 I was invited by my friend Steve Douglas, the saxophone player, to go to Paris to make an album with Mink DeVille. Steve was co-producing the album and had invited Ronnie Tutt to play drums. I don't know how Steve came to the impression that Ronnie and I would fit in this scenario, but I have to say that the end result, *Le Chat Bleu*, is one of my favorite rock albums of all time.

Mink DeVille was a group fronted by a New York punk named Willy DeVille, about whom it was once memorably said that you never knew "whether he was going to croon to you or pull a knife." Willy's songs had a heavy Hispanic influence as well as a hint of cajun music. Put all of that together with street-corner doo-wop, accordion playing, and Willy's wonderful velvet voice and what you get, in my opinion, is great rock'n'roll.

While we were in Paris we stayed at our old Dylan haunt, Le Meurice. The night we finished the last track for *Le Chat Bleu* I returned to my fifth-floor room with a gram of cocaine and half a bottle of Courvoisier—the remnants of the mood enhancements I had taken with me to session. I was still high from the other gram and the missing half of the bottle of cognac.

I walked over and opened the french doors that led out onto a small balcony. I looked down at the street below and wondered—in a cold, calm manner—what difference it would make if I took a nosedive off the balcony. I was not depressed, but nonetheless the answer seemed to be: no real difference that I could see at the time.

I eventually went back inside to the bed and swallowed as much of the cognac as I could. I awoke several hours later, draped over the side of the bed, the morning traffic buzzing through the open french doors. I remembered everything from the night before, but now I was horrified at how close I had come to jumping. I made up my mind that my days of playing around with drugs were over. Alcohol aside, they were.

Back in California, I began to slip deep into the born-again Christian trip—and 'trip' was the word. Bob Dylan and several members of his touring band had joined a church in Malibu called the Vineyard. I was baptized in the surf there in 1979, and I was on fire with what I was experiencing. We sang simple songs (not hymns) and I felt a real sense of community. The pastor there knew that what we needed wasn't a big church; we were a homeless congregation, and we spent our Sunday afternoons together in school auditoriums and derelict movie theaters. What we needed—what the pastor knew we needed—was an outlet for our need to help others. It was a time of innocent space in my life, one that I desperately needed.

Although I had not played with Bob since the end of the 1978 US tour, I saw him several times at the church. His lady friend at the time, Mary Alice Artes, was a fervent member of the congregation. One night Bob and Mary

Alice came to my house for dinner, along with some other members of the 1978 band. We didn't talk business, but after dinner Bob asked if I had a stereo. "Of course," I said. He put a cassette in the player and announced that it was his next record. It was the final mix of *Slow Train Coming*. None of us had played (or been asked to play) on the album. Bob sat by himself in the corner of the room while we listened to a couple of cuts, and then he got up and said goodnight. That was the last time I ever saw him.

About a year later I moved from Malibu to Simi Valley, California. I left the Vineyard behind and joined a Foursquare church. I hadn't been aware of any political involvement at the Vineyard, yet now at my new church I began to get a sense of what was to become a huge, nationwide right-wing Christian movement.

I also started to think more about the claim that every word in The Bible was the inerrant word of God. I was reading Leviticus one day when I came upon chapter 18, verse 22: "Thou shalt not lie with mankind, as with womankind: it is abomination." Of course, I had—and still have—friends who are bisexual or homosexual. I wondered whether this meant they were doomed.

I read on to Leviticus 25:44–46, which seemed to be telling me that I could acquire slaves from the nations around me (Canada and Mexico?) and that, if I wished, I could will them to my children as "inherited property." Then, in Exodus, I read passages about selling one's daughter and beating slaves. I was astounded. I have discussed these passages with various pastors and Christian people in general, who tend to say something like: "We look to the Holy Spirit when it comes to interpreting The Bible." But to which Holy Spirit should one listen, I wonder? There seem to be about as many Holy Spirits as there are Christian churches.

After much thought and study, I arrived at the point where I found a way I could reconcile all of these different opinions and cherry-pick the scriptures that teach love for my fellow human beings. With that, surely, I can't go wrong. This way, I cannot use the scriptures to condemn others for not being Christian, or for being homosexual, or for anything else The Bible may not approve of. Quite where I ended up in my spiritual quest is another long story—too long for this book. Suffice it to say that I now have one great belief: that anything that can be done to alleviate the suffering of others should be done. Period. That is the message of the Holy Spirit that speaks to *me*.

You may wonder what any of this has to do with my musical memories. Well, I have only included this topic because religion really did have an effect on my music, if only for a year or so. After I stopped working with Bob Dylan, I took time out from the secular music world and worked for a minimum wage at a Christian music warehouse at Word Records in Los Angeles, where I packed records for shipment. I was truly at a crossroads: should I continue to play secular music, or only ever play in church?

Around 1980, I joined a Christian music tour that covered the whole length of the West Coast of North America, from California up to Vancouver, Canada. Also on the tour were Barry McGuire, best known for 'Eve Of Destruction'; guitarist Mike Deasy, who you'll remember as Friar Tuck; and my old Elvis sidekick, Ronnie Tutt.

We called ourselves The Sanctified Boogie Band. We traveled around in a truck and were our own roadies and drivers, so there were no salaries to pay. We stayed in friends' homes along the way, so there were no hotel bills, either. We carried and set up our own equipment inside maximum security, medium security, and juvenile facilities. (My mother, Lois, was the head official at one of them.)

From my perspective, the main emphasis of the tour was to speak out about drug use. Exactly when I became drug free, however, is another story. I don't want this to turn into one of those confessional autobiographies where I point out how cool I am for cleaning up. Besides, back then I still had my drug: alcohol. But I stand by my feelings, and in particular I stand by the words of that great song by Nick Lowe: '(What's So Funny 'Bout) Peace, Love, And Understanding.'

CHAPTER 21
COUNTRY ROADS

I n 1981, around the time I was playing with The Sanctified Boogie Band, I got a call from John Denver's office wanting to know whether I would be interested in joining The John Denver Band. I had never met John, but I had played on the soundtrack to his film *John Denver & The Muppets: A Christmas Together* a year or so earlier—and, as he later explained, this was not the first time I had been considered for the band. When my name first came up, however, it had been vetoed by two existing members of the band, drummer Hal Blaine and my old pal Glen D. Hardin, who had refused to work with me because of my close relationship with the born-again Christian movement in LA. Perhaps they were worried I might get too sanctimonious about their rock'n'roll behavior.

Ironically, it was through Hal Blaine that I had first heard about the John Denver tours. He first mentioned them while we were working together on a jingle for McDonalds in the late 70s, and since then had continued to brag about what a wonderful gig it was. In fact, the tours had become legendary. John had limos pick up the musicians and singers at their homes and drive them to the airport, and then after the tour the limos would be there at the airport to ferry them home.

Several bass players came and went during the late 70s, including Emory Gordy, the guy who had taken my place in the Elvis Presley band in 1973. When John decided to let Hal Blaine go too, it opened the doors for drummer Jerry Carrigan and me to become the band's new rhythm section.

Playing in The John Denver Band was a wonderful job, even if his was not always my type of music. John could still draw crowds around 20,000, the money was great, and good food and drink was never more than an arm's length away. John paid for everything: I just had to sign the hotel bill or produce the receipt and it was a done deal.

I first joined up with the band at a studio in the Rocky Mountains. Glen D. Hardin was still part of the band, his opinion of me evidently having softened over the past year. Also present was another of my cohorts from the TCB days, James Burton, as well as various other guitarists, banjo players, mandolin players, assorted singers, and my old sax-playing buddy Jim Horn.

Jim was a great guy. He was about six-foot four with long hair at the sides but not much on top, which gave the effect of a lop-eared rabbit (hence the nickname Big Bunny). He was always good fun—things always used to happen to him. I remember one time, when the John Denver tour hit the UK, our bus pulled up outside a hotel at four in the morning. Jim, in his Italian shoes and expensive-looking slacks, was the first to get off the bus in the dark. He stepped down straight into an artificial pond. Another time, in Berlin, we were in a taxi crawling down the middle lane of one of the city's wide boulevards. At one point, when the cab had slowed almost to a stop, Jim jumped out to take off his coat. Just then, the traffic surged forward, leaving Jim stranded between hundreds of cars. I still remember looking out of the rear window at Big Bunny, pumping away like a marathon runner. Eventually, the driver realized what had happened, and a very sweaty Jim Horn climbed back into the cab.

Perhaps my favorite Jim story comes from the time we were playing somewhere in Southern Florida. During one of John's slower songs, Jim would come out to the front to play a beautiful flute solo. It was on the loveliest moments in the show. On this particular tropical night, however, Jim started to squirm as he walked out and before long was doing the full-on hootchy-kootchy dance. Only at the interval did we discover that something had crawled up his leg, and that he had been squirming around because he was not wearing any underwear. At the end of the solo he ran off stage, dropped his pants, and a two-inch cockroach fell out onto the floor.

Back in the Rockies, where rehearsals were continuing for the upcoming tour, we were bunking in a huge log house with dead animals in the hallways. Aside from having to confront stuffed grizzly bears when I went to pee during the middle of the night, however, it was all very comfortable. The first night of the tour was at the Red Rocks Amphitheatre just outside Morrison, Colorado. As with any first show with a new band, I was on my toes. After the show, however, John came over and told me he was glad I was working with him, and so began a new multi-year phase of my career.

John was like a host to us all when we were with him. He arranged things to do on the days off. We had a softball team, for example, and played local police and sheriff's-department teams. I played a little but I wasn't very good. We took over movie theaters and raced go-carts, and we played golf, too, but I wasn't very good at that either. In later years, John seemed to arrange his tours around the various venues' proximity to golf courses—in the UK, for example, we would stay near to St Andrews— although the non-golfers among us weren't always happy to be stuck in country clubs out in the middle of nowhere.

John would also set up skeet-shooting, skiing, and gliding expeditions. On one occasion, after we had played a magical show on the beach in front of local tribespeople in Darwin, Australia, John invited me to join him and his soon-to-be second wife Cassandra on a trip into the outback on a two-engine plane. We boated down a river full of crocodiles and waterlilies and enjoyed the aboriginal art that had been painted on the cliff-faces as long ago as 8,000 BC.

John was still drawing big audiences when I first joined the band but his album sales were falling. He was writing love ballads, and we were recording them, but not very many people were buying them. Over the course of the next couple of years, his live audiences began to dwindle, too, to approximately half of what they had been when I first came onboard.

As the audiences began to shrink, so too did the whole enterprise. To begin with, we had traveled with a large cast in a jet stocked with catered food and a full bar. We would land in the next city and be bussed to the venue, where our dressing rooms would be stocked with fruit trays, sandwiches, fresh shrimp cocktails, and of course all manner of beer, wine, and soft drinks. After the soundcheck we would sit down to a dinner of steak, seafood, and vegetarian entrees, plus three or four desserts. Then, after the show, we would be bussed back to the plane, where we would devour trays of fresh sushi, washing it down with vintage champagne. And then the whole cycle would begin again the following day.

All of this was great, of course, except that the amount of food we wasted. We eventually asked John to cut back by doing away with the hospitality suite. We really didn't need it—we could order what we wanted from room service, which John paid for anyway. We didn't need the dressing rooms to be stocked with table upon table of food, either. Some fruit and raw vegetables would be fine.

The cast of musicians started to shrink, too. I had some soundboard tapes of some of our earlier shows, and listening back I could hear so many people singing and playing that the shows were starting to sound like a giant Dixieland ensemble. John listened to some of the tapes at my suggestion and the whole show was scaled back.

Every year we played in the show room at Harrah's Lake Tahoe Hotel & Casino for The John Denver Celebrity Ski Tournament. The group for these shows became smaller and smaller with each passing year until John eventually decided to cut us all loose and play with just his original string-bass player, Dick Kniss from Peter Paul & Mary, and guitar player Steve Weisberg.

John still invited the rest of us to the show, however, and at the end of the ski tournament he re-hired James Burton and me for his next tour. This opened up a lot of space in his music. James, John, and I were like a small orchestra: I could play open basslines and not clash with the lower octaves of the piano or the three rhythm guitars all playing the root notes of the chords.

I enjoyed this period with John Denver more than any other. We added a series of Latin percussionists to the band for some of the shows and would bring together the whole ensemble for recordings and other special events. It was during this period that my hearing began to fail, however, and I was constantly saying things that could be construed as being derogatory without realizing John was in earshot.

Shortly after returning from a trip to China, John wrote a ballad called 'Shanghai Breezes.' Later, when we performed the song, John would do a monologue about how he had been inspired to write the song while standing on a bridge in Shanghai. He had then gone back to his hotel room, he told the audience, and called his ex-wife, Annie. He had told her that the moon on the river had brought her to mind, and she, he said, had responded by asking him if it was the same moon she saw in Aspen, Colorado.

I always winced when John said this. I thought it was condescending toward Annie, who I gather was a university graduate and surely well aware of how many moons there are orbiting the Earth. Six months later, a few of us in the band were playing cards on the back of the bus as it traveled across the New Mexico desert at night when we came to a sudden halt. Somebody asked why we had stopped and word came back that there was a full moon and John had wanted to get out and look at it.

I looked across the table to Glen D. Hardin and said: "I wonder if that's the same moon Annie sees?" Glen's eyes got huge and he looked over my shoulder. I turned to see John right behind me.

"Jerry Scheff, are you making fun of my music?" he asked.

What could I say? John was not a man capable of laughing at himself.

On another occasion we were playing a song that I had played hundreds of times—'Country Roads,' I think—when I stopped concentrating momentarily and played a wrong note. John turned around, shook his head, and frowned at me. During our mid-show break I told John's road manager, Kris O'Connor, how pissed off I was, and that I would have a few words for him at the end of the show.

Kris brought John straight to my dressing room, where John asked what was bothering me.

"You never give dirty looks to someone during the show!" I told him. "It's unprofessional!"

"Jerry, I thought I was the one who played the wrong note," he replied with a smile. "I was frowning at myself."

Later in the 80s, John went to Russia to record an anti-war song called 'Let Us Begin (What Are We Making Weapons For?)' with a huge Soviet orchestra and a singer named Alexander Gradsky. He also put together a powerful video showing the effects of nuclear weapons, which he would play during his live shows while he sang the song. I was, and still am, sympathetic to the views in this song, but as ever I couldn't help but open my big mouth when I was around John. One night, as we were boarding the bus, our Latin drummer, Richie Garcia, decided to put on the movie *Lethal Weapon III*. Not knowing John was right behind me, I said: "Oh look— what are we making *Lethal Weapon III* for?"

"Jerry Scheff!" came the familiar voice. "Are you making fun of my music?"

Once again, I was fortunate that John was a forgiving man. I never quite felt that we were friends, however. He never asked me how I felt about the world, or indeed about anything else except for his music. That was the hole in his personality as far as I was concerned. He would speak at length about world hunger, weapons of mass destruction, and the environment. I never doubted his sincerity about these issues, but he never knew I felt the same way because he neither asked nor listened when I tried to discuss these things with him.

In January 1985, a group of artists and producers got together to write and record the song 'We Are The World.' John, who at the time had probably put more effort into trying to solve world hunger than any other artist, and who had previously been awarded the Presidential 'World Without Hunger' Award, was not asked to attend the session. I later learned from some of the musicians who had been there that John had been left out because of his tendency to try to take control of projects in which he was involved. To some, it seemed, he had messianic tendencies. Either way, John said it broke his heart when he was not invited to take part.

■■

During the 80s, John Denver was busted in Colorado a few times for driving under the influence. In restitution for one of these charges, he agreed to donate the proceeds from a concert that was set to take place in Aspen. Glen D. Hardin, James Burton, Jim Horn, and the rest of the band flew in to perform. In the dressing room afterward, John informed us that he had lined up a tour of the Far East and Europe. He asked us to enter the dates into our schedules. Those of us who had worked with John for years left Aspen in a hopeful mood. Maybe things were going to turn for the better.

A month later, however, John called me to ask me how I would feel if he replaced Glen and James with two younger, less expensive musicians from Nashville. I reminded John that he had already hired James and Glen for the two upcoming tours.

"Oh," he replied, "I hadn't thought about that."

After the phone call I began to think that if he was going to do this to two of his oldest comrades, who else might be in danger? I was also expensive. How long would it be before it was my turn to go?

John called again a few days later. He could not afford to pay Glen and James, he said, and that was the end of it. I knew that Kris O'Connor had been thinking about downsizing for a while—it seemed to me that this had Kris's name written all over it. It also transpired that, even though John had worked with Glen and James for years, neither he nor Kris had called to give them the news. (Delivering bad news was just not part of John's makeup— he hadn't called Hal Blaine when it was his turn to be let go, either.)

I felt conflicted about the whole thing, but I decided to complete the tour before I made any decisions about my future. The new players were very good, and they were all very nice to me, but John was becoming one with the faceless. He was writing nothing but mundane love songs, and the band had become the equivalent of your average country road-band. In my opinion, Kris O'Connor was responsible for that, too, but maybe it was unavoidable.

The UK leg of the tour was largely uneventful. Most of the fans I talked to asked about James Burton. They missed him. I had a hard time dealing with Kris and the rest of John's business people. I thought that after all the years they worked with James and Glen, they could have handled things a lot better.

The audience reception for these UK shows was pretty good, even though John had loaded the middle of the second half of the show with his new, slow ballads. The response was less good in Asia, however. For 30 minutes or so, the audiences would have to endure a sequence of slow songs in a foreign language that you couldn't even tap your toes to.

I pointed this out to John but he didn't want to hear it. It all came to a head when we arrived in Hanoi, Vietnam, where John was to be the first American to perform in the country since the war. The day of the concert was meltingly hot. We rode to the venue in an air-conditioned van, but after we climbed outside we were soaking. Moving into the backstage area of the venue was no different.

As we staggered out onto the stage to do the soundcheck, I noticed that all of the people around us were waving fans in front of their faces. John was standing next to the grand piano, looking through the setlist. I was about to suggest that he move things around when he said: "I think these people are going to like my love songs!" What could I say? During the second half of the show, the only people not still waving their fans were the ones who had fallen asleep. I gave up.

When I eventually left The John Denver Band, I got a note from John in which he wrote: "Jerry, I neither understood nor appreciated you leaving me like you did." Fortunately, just a few months before he died in a plane crash in 1997, we had a chance to speak again. I had been going through some rough times and he must have heard about it. He called to ask if I needed anything. I told him no.

"I thought we were friends," he said.

I told him that he had always been good to me, but that I had never really felt we were friends. Nevertheless, of all the musicians with whom I have been acquainted who have since died, John is the one I miss the most.

CHAPTER 22
CONVICTS AND
CONFEDERATES

During the mid 80s, I started to suffer from cluster headaches. I would get them every spring, from April to June, sometimes as often as three times a day. The pain was incredible, and back then there was no treatment for it—my doctor gave me morphine but it did nothing to stop them.

If you mention headaches to almost anyone, chances are they'll immediately think of migraines. Well, cluster headaches are a different thing. In 1999, Dr Peter Goadsby, Professor of Clinical Neurology at University College London, described them as "probably the worst pain that humans experience ... if you ask a cluster headache patient if they've had a worse experience, they'll usually say they haven't. Women with cluster headaches will tell you that an attack is worse than giving birth."

So what does this have to do with music? Well, imagine coping with these headaches in the recording studio or on the road. Just the mere thought of these headaches had a profound effect on my personality and my interaction with other people. Fortunately, except for a brief relapse during the early 90s, my cluster headaches only lasted for a few years.

I think of my career in terms of three phases, and the third started in 1986 when I got a call from record producer T-Bone Burnett, asking me if I was available to record with Elvis Costello. I said yes, of course, and headed out to Ocean Way Recording in Los Angeles to begin work on *King Of America*.

Costello (or E.C. as I tended to call him) had hired me and two other members of the Elvis Presley band, Ronnie Tutt and James Burton, to play on the record. The original plan was for us to appear on three tracks, but I eventually wound up playing on most of the album.

One day, after we had finished running through a very energetic song, I walked over to a sweaty Elvis and jokingly said: "That's the way we did ballads with Presley." He had a wary smile on his face—either he thought I was being serious or he thought I was messing with him. We later found out that he had been a bit apprehensive about working with us for fear that we might not like the fact that he had taken Elvis as his stage name. He needn't have worried, though—we didn't care.

At the end of the day, Elvis's manager, Jake Riviera, walked around and tossed a stack of greenbacks into each of our laps. It was quite a bit more money than I would have asked for. The same thing happened whenever I recorded or toured with Elvis during the 80s and 90s—I would never ask how much I was going to be paid, but it would always be more than I had anticipated.

I went on to play on three more Elvis Costello albums: *Spike*, *Mighty Like A Rose*, and *Kojak Variety*. Before that, however, I was invited to join the *King Of America* tour. Elvis had two bands at this point: his longstanding cohorts The Attractions, and The Confederates, which consisted of me, James Burton, drummer Jim Keltner, and keyboard player Mitchell Froom.

We spent the month of October playing theaters across America before heading out to Europe, Australia, and Japan in the new year. One show that comes to mind is the one at the National Stadium in Dublin, Ireland. That particular venue is known more for boxing than music, and our dressing room smelled of liniment. Later, in Japan, Jim Keltner and I agreed to try fugu sashimi. Fugu is a poisonous type of blowfish, and people have died from eating it—but only after eating the meat from the liver. When Jim and I ordered the dish, Elvis's then-wife, Cait, announced that she wanted to try it as well. Elvis was not too pleased, but eventually he nervously tried a piece, too. As for me: my mouth got a little numb, and I thought the fish was lacking in taste, but we all lived.

After the tour ended, things went quiet on the E.C. front and I resumed touring with John Denver. (I had had to pull out of a few gigs with John earlier in the year due to a clash with the *King Of America* tour.) Then, in 1988, I got the call to play on a number of tracks for Elvis's next album, *Spike*. Paul McCartney plays bass on the album, too, but sadly I never got to meet him. In August 1989, I went back out on tour with E.C. and his band, which was now known as The Rude 5 and comprised Marc Ribot on guitar, Larry Knechtel on piano, Pete Thomas on drums, Michael Blair on percussion, and me on bass and tuba. (Evidently Paul McCartney wasn't rude enough to join us.)

In 1991, I recorded another album with Elvis, *Mighty Like A Rose*, before going out on tour again with The Rude 5. I flew to Dublin for rehearsals before heading off on a four-month semi-world tour—the longest tour of my career. It was a spectacular time, marred only by my cluster headaches, which fortunately came to an end with the passing of the seasons midway through the run. We played the Montreux Jazz Festival in July, and I got to see Miles Davis perform a selection of Gil Evans arrangements with a large band led by Quincy Jones. It was only the second time I had been able to see Davis live, the first having been all the way back in 1958. He died a few months later.

Elvis Costello and the people who planned his tours went out of their way to make us comfortable. We stayed in great hotels and flew business class—in fact we even traveled by Concorde from New York to London. In Madrid, where we were due to play a bullring just outside the city, we stayed at the Hotel Ritz, right across the street from the Prado Museum, where I saw *The Garden Of Earthly Delights*. I swear Hieronymus Bosch must have been on acid when he painted it.

The music business is a small community, and that really hit home when I was walking in the park beside the Prado. It was a sparkling day, and as I walked past various mothers and nannies with their chicos and chiquitas in brightly colored prams, I kept thinking I was hearing a jazz saxophone in the distance, but with hearing like mine—and the ringing in my ears and the other strange sounds that come with it—I didn't trust myself. As I rounded the corner, however, I saw a black tenor-sax player standing by a tree with a vinyl record album propped up against it. He was playing a beautiful jazz ballad. I shook his hand and asked where he was from. It turned out he was from Sacramento, California. We were about the same age and it transpired that, although we didn't remember each other, we knew some of the same people and had frequented many of the same jam sessions back in the 50s. He told me he would soon be heading to Stockholm, where he now lived, and where we had played just a week earlier. I tightened him up with a $20 bill and carried on my way.

After Madrid, we moved on to Barcelona and then to Gijón, where I visited the international bagpipe museum, and finally to beautiful San Sebastián, where I ate tapas until I was sick. When we arrived at the venue, however, all of the windows overlooking the parking lot had been blown out. The Basque separatist group ETA had got there before us.

The last Elvis Costello album I worked on was his covers record, *Kojak Variety*. We went to Barbados to record it in a converted sugar plantation owned by the singer Eddy Grant. E.C. himself wrote extensively about the sessions in the liner notes to the Rhino reissue of the album, so I think it would be better if I let him describe it.

> *The simple idea of going to a Caribbean island to record "some of my favourite songs with some of my favourite musicians"—as the original sleeve note defined the record—seemed like an inviting prospect.*
>
> *The sessions for King Of America in 1985 had been my first experience of recording original material with musicians other than The Attractions since 1977. The lineup of Elvis Costello and His Confederates changed during three subsequent tours, but guitarist James Burton, bassist Jerry Scheff, and drummer Jim Keltner were common to all of them.*
>
> *Jerry and Jim were among the many players involved in the 1988 sessions for Spike, which also heavily featured the guitar playing of Marc Ribot and included a small cameo appearance by*

Pete Thomas. When it came time to tour, I invited Jerry and Pete to be the rhythm section and asked Marc to play guitar and E-flat horn. Mitchell Froom, who had played keyboards on both albums and toured in the original Confederate lineup, was now so involved in production that he was unable to join the Spike tour. At Jerry Scheff's suggestion we enlisted Larry Knechtel, who probably has some of the heaviest session credits in popular music. Having left behind both the security and creative impasse of a permanent group, I thought myself lucky to be able to call on such a rich group of players in both the studio and during live adventures.

Thank you, E.C.

It was during the *King Of America* sessions that I got to know the record producer and singer-songwriter T-Bone Burnett. T-Bone is a tall, lanky Texan with a well thought-out aura of rock'n'roll hipness about him.

I worked intermittently with T-Bone from the late 80s through to the mid 90s, mostly in the studio. My name appears on three of his solo albums: *T-Bone Burnett*, *The Talking Animals*, and *The Criminal Under My Own Hat*.

We appeared on stage together occasionally, as well, although usually that tended to be when he happened to be sitting in with somebody else I was playing with. The only other show that he and I played together was at an outdoor concert for the inmates of San Quentin State Prison.

The 'yard' at San Quentin is a very large lawned area with a pronounced slope. It can probably hold around a thousand prisoners—maybe more. The prison laundry is down at the bottom of the slope, and is a paradigm of every prison laundry you have ever seen in the movies. I expected Burt Lancaster to walk in at any moment.

That day, the laundry doubled as our dressing room. The stage was set up just in front of it. I have no recollection of what songs we played, but the inmates' reaction ... well, put it this way: we weren't quite at the level of

Johnny Cash, but we certainly got a better response than the local church choir would have received.

After we'd finished performing and changed out of our stage clothes, T-Bone and I strolled through the densely packed crowd of convicts. We smiled and nodded as they complimented us on the show. Then, all of a sudden, we heard a rumbling, bullhorn-powered voice from above.

"You! Men! Get back to the laundry!"

I looked up and saw several guards on top of the wall, looking down at us through the sights on their rifles.

Perhaps the most notable project I was involved in with T-Bone as producer was Roy Orbison's *A Black & White Night*, a live show I mentioned earlier that was subsequently released on home video. As well as Roy, the show featured Bruce Springsteen, Bonnie Raitt, Elvis Costello, Tom Waits, and kd lang.

Unfortunately, the show's producer had some fairly serious financing problems. She waited until the day of the show and then reneged on her deal with the background singers—and then had the nerve to insist that we all give up the rights to future royalties. Several of us thought about walking out, but we stayed out of love for Roy and took our place on the bandstand.

Around the same time, T-Bone started producing the pop singer Sam Phillips, first for the Christian label Myrrh, for whom she recorded as Leslie Phillips, and then for Virgin Records. Sam was a critical darling, as they say: she received rave reviews and was admired by music-business insiders, but she seemed to be stuck behind a smokescreen as far as the general public went.

I played on five of Sam's albums between 1987 and 1996: *The Turning* (her fourth and final album as Leslie Phillips), *The Indescribable Wow* (her first as Sam), *Cruel Inventions*, *Martinis & Bikinis*, and *Omnipop*. I tended to overdub my bass parts after the fact rather than playing live in the studio with a band, and I came to enjoy working in this manner. I had started to lose my hearing, but this way I could sit in the control room and get a better perspective of how what I was playing matched up with what was already on tape. Quite often, the parts that had already been recorded were drum machine, rhythm guitar, and lead vocals. This simplistic setup allowed me to run barefoot through the bass space that was left for me in the arrangement. After that, T-Bone would have the other musicians (including a real drummer) add their parts.

Shortly after we made *Martinis & Bikinis*, I was invited to go out on tour. This was 1994: I was still playing with John Denver from time to time, and in fact had just finished a tour of Asia with him. By then, however, he had let go of James Burton and Glen D. Hardin, and I figured it could easily be me next.

When the offer came in to join Sam's touring band, I took it. John had been good to me, but I was ready to play a little frisky pop music. Also, at the age I was then, I knew this kind of gift might never come my way again. It didn't hurt, either, that all sorts of hints were being dropped about getting "a piece of the action" and this being "retirement time." Of course, I never even got a whiff of any action.

T-Bone Burnett was not the only useful contact I made during the *King Of America* sessions. One of the other musicians on that album was Mitchell Froom, an excellent keyboard player with an exploratory mind whose career as a record producer was about to take off.

I was fortunate to be on hand for Mitchell's first production effort, *Amnesia*, by the singer-songwriter and guitarist Richard Thompson, with whom I wound up joyfully recording three more albums, *Rumor And Sigh*, *Mirror Blue*, and *you? me? us?*, as well as appearing on the compilation *Watching The Dark*.

Richard is always included on lists of the greatest guitar players of all time, and he is definitely at the top of mine. He is a very bright man, and even though he is a much honored musician with a steady following, he deserves much more recognition than he gets from the general public.

Meanwhile, I ended up playing bass on a number of projects that Mitchell Froom was involved in over the next decade or so, including albums by Crowded House, Suzanne Vega, Ron Sexsmith, and Lisa Germano. I guess I have a lot to thank him for.

CHAPTER 23
THE TRAP

The entertainment business has a nasty habit of chewing up and spitting out certain kinds of performers, including some of the people I performed with over the years. Of course, the 'business' is only partly to blame. These performers have their own expectations—the same expectations that helped them climb to the top and, in some of the worst cases, pushed them back down into the dark alley of despair.

Management, musicians, gophers, even friends and family exert a certain amount of pressure. I have even been part of that background pressure at times, although in my defense I have never depended on anyone for my whole livelihood. I enjoyed working with Elvis Presley, Jim Morrison, Bob Dylan, and the rest, but for me life would have gone on the same with or without them.

A few of the performers I have worked with seemed to have had that innate ability to continue their careers in a series of progressions, or gradual re-inventions of themselves, allowing themselves to stay alive physically, mentally, and creatively. Bob Dylan and Elvis Costello come to mind. Although I never quite got to play with him, Miles Davis belongs in this category, too, for making it through intact, never resting on his laurels, and never looking back. (The closest I got to sharing the stage with Miles was when Marc Benno and I opened for him at Harvard University.)

On the other hand, we have Elvis Presley, Jim Morrison, and John

Denver, and of course people like Jimi Hendrix. They all died young—much too young. I don't claim to know all the answers to their problems, but I can tell you what I observed at the time.

I didn't spend much time with Jim Morrison—just the six weeks we spent working on *LA Woman*. Looking back, though, I see him at the Doors office with his face full of hair, his posture slumped. To me, he looked like he was hiding himself: hiding from his leather-panted stage persona. Maybe he was caught with no way out that he could see; maybe he couldn't get on stage, or into his 'pop' persona, without getting high first?

Hendrix, too, seems to have been under considerable pressure. I don't know any more than anyone else does about his mental state, but I have seen and heard and read enough to know that he was being told by some very tough people to go out and burn up his guitar on stage at the end of every show. The audience would be disappointed, they told him, without a free fire show.

I don't claim to have been under anything like the level of pressure these two were under at the time, but I have enough of a sense of what it was like to go through that kind of thing—what it's like to fall into The Trap.

It seems strange to think that, during my career, some of my best and worst times were with John Denver. By the time I came to work with him, John was at the peak of his career. He was 'Country Boy'-ing to audiences of up to 20,000 people. And yet, maybe like Elvis Presley before him, John felt that he needed to reinvent himself, particularly when the attendance levels at his shows started to recede. He got contact lenses, he changed his clothes and his hairstyle, he even changed his onstage personality. He started writing slow love ballads and big, bombastic songs with Wagnerian orchestral arrangements.

Like Elvis, John seemed to be struggling with where to go with his music. Early on, he allowed people to discover him and decide what to make of him. I believe he started to slip when he started to tell people what to think—what *he* wanted them to think.

One night, we were playing in a huge arena. The curtains were slowing moving back. John was standing next to me.

"I used to be a star," he whispered.

I wasn't sure whether to hit him or hug him. In the end I did neither. What could I do? He was wandering in his own wilderness, unable to listen to any of the people around him because he knew we were all full of shit. He was stuck, and maybe he knew it.

As I have said elsewhere in this book, I am sure Elvis Presley was going through an artistic change when he returned to the stage in 1969. He might not have known it at first. I have read that, initially, the plan was for him to go back to his old band and The Jordanaires, but for whatever reason they never even got to the rehearsal stage. Sam Phillips told him that he needed a kick-ass band for his new show.

I would love to know what Elvis really thought about going back to his old band, sound, and material from the 50s. He had played Las Vegas in that configuration at the time with little success. When you think about Colonel Tom Parker's ideas about Broadway-style singers and dancers, however ... well, it's clear that Elvis was under pressure from at least a few sides.

Enter the TCB Band. Elvis was thrilled during our first night of rehearsal, and we, like him, were relieved that the music was not just a rehash of 50s rockabilly. The next clue to his musical state of mind was the way he asked us to turn most of his oldest songs into medleys, which we would play as fast as we could. He knew he had to do those songs, but we got them out of the way quickly as one might an old worn-out pair of ice skates. He had newer fish to fry: modern rockers and ballads that went with his new costumes and choreography.

We played these shows for two years, and during that time he started to drop some of the rockers and replace them with more traditional Vegas-type shows songs: 'My Way,' 'What Now My Love,' and so on. What was he trying to do? Did he feel that he wasn't getting enough praise for singing rock numbers, and that he should try presenting a more mature, dignified image as he aged? Did he think it was time to show people how *he* could sing those songs? I think so—and to be fair, he did sing most of them as well as anyone else.

In any case, I don't believe any of this worked. No matter how well he sang the songs, he was very often panned by the reviewers, especially when he went out on the road. *Aloha From Hawaii* was his last big triumph. I took a two-year break shortly after that—not because I disapproved of what he was doing, but because I just needed to take a break. I told Elvis that I needed to get my head together. The truth is that I was sick of the Elvis circus—not him, but everything around him.

By the time I came back to the show, in 1975, Elvis had gained weight, but I didn't care about that and nor did most of his audiences. Sometimes he was high on stage—but then, hell, so was I. More than that, however, there were signs of depression. It had become very difficult for the rest of us to get close to him. Bodyguards would turn us away from his dressing room like they were Howard Hughes's Mormons.

One night, just before a show in Las Vegas, Charlie Hodge came down to our dressing room and told Ronnie Tutt and I that Elvis was upset because we didn't come to see him before the shows any more. Ronnie and I got dressed and went down to see him. When we reached the bodyguards, we had to insist that Charlie had sent for us. The Elvis I saw that night was extremely depressed. When we explained what was going on with the Memphis Mafia, Elvis hit the ceiling. He already knew: people were running his life. "Don't let them kill you, boy!" Frank Sinatra once told him. Frank knew all about The Trap.

Maybe Elvis didn't know where to go any more. He was taking painkillers and sleep aids, but back then there was no real acknowledgement of what would now be called clinical depression. All he had were his uppers and downers, his ill-fitting jumpsuits, his huge entourage exuding waves of pressure over him like a buttermilk bath, all sour and cold.

Elvis loved singing gospel music. Perhaps, if he had been left to do what made him happy—and if he no longer had to consider what the Colonel or anyone else thought—he would still be here with us singing 'How Great

Thou Art.' Maybe all he was trying to do was say to his mother, Gladys: "It's OK, mom, I am still a good boy." RIP E.P.

What about me, Jerry Scheff? I certainly don't equate myself with the level of importance of the many stars I have worked with, but I have had an amazing ride. Several times I have thought I had escaped, only to end up in the jaws once more.

I wound up at 70 years old, playing a European tour with the TCB Band and a conductor in my face. It felt OK, as a bit of showbiz, until we did 'An American Trilogy.' When we got to the most poignant part of the song—"Hush little baby, don't you cry"—the conductor started moving his body and arms like a vulture fighting over its spoils, three feet away from my face. I asked him at rehearsals to cut back the intensity. He yelled back at me, and that was the end of these kinds of shows for me. I just wanted to play music.

My wife Natalie saw all of this coming and finally gave me permission to play coyote and gnaw off my own leg in order to escape The Trap. Surprisingly, I felt no pain. I will go on playing behind people I love—even if it means playing alongside some people I don't. But I don't think I will dance on Elvis's grave again.

SELECTED DISCOGRAPHY

Jerry Scheff has played on hundreds of recordings over the years. What follows is a list of just some of them. Some of his earliest session work features on compilation volumes such as *Hollywood Magic: The Gary Paxton Story* (Ace 2004) and *Where The Action Is: Los Angeles Nuggets 1965–1968* (Rhino 2009), as well as on retrospective compilations such as *The Drugstore's Rockin'* by Pat Boone and *Heartaches And Harmonies* by The Everly Brothers.

The Daily Trip, Your Gang (Mercury 1964)
The New Mustang & Other Hot Rod Hits, Road Runners (London 1964)
The Fantastic Guitar Of Barney Kessel On Fire, Barney Kessel (Emerald 1965)
And Then … Along Comes The Association, The Association (Valiant 1966)
It's Now Winter's Day, Tommy Roe (Fallout 1967)
Here's To You, Hamilton Camp (Warner Bros 1967)
Friar Tuck & His Psychedelic Guitar, Friar Tuck & His Psychedelic Guitar (Fallout 1967)
Phantasy, Tommy Roe (Fallout 1967)
Double Trouble, Elvis Presley (RCA 1967)
The Holy Mackerel, The Holy Mackerel (Reprise 1968)
Sounds Of Goodbye, The Gosdin Brothers (Capitol 1968)
Misty Mirage, Curt Boettcher (Together 1968)
Sandy, Sandy Salisbury (Together 1968)
Head, The Monkees (Colgem 1968)
Goodnight Everybody, Mary McCaslin (Barnaby 1969)
The Moonstone, Tommy Flanders (Verve 1969)
Nancy, Nancy Sinatra (Reprise 1969)

Running Down The Road, Arlo Guthrie (Rising Son/Koch 1969)
Slim So Slider, Johnny Rivers (Imperial 1969)
Working!, Bobby Jameson (GRT 1969)
Freeway Gypsy, Lynne Hughes (Fontana 1969)
Ananda Shankar, Ananda Shankar (Reprise 1970)
Marc Benno, Marc Benno (A&M 1970)
To Bonnie From Delaney, Delaney & Bonnie (Atco 1970)
Elvis In Person At The International Hotel, Las Vegas, Nevada, Elvis Presley (RCA 1970)
On Stage, Elvis Presley (RCA 1970)
That's The Way It Is, Elvis Presley (RCA 1970)
America's Sweetheart, Sandy Szigeti (Decca 1971)
Helen Reddy, Helen Reddy (Capitol 1971)
Minnows, Marc Benno (Atco 1971)
Home Grown, Johnny Rivers (International Artistsi 1971)
Sunstorm, John Stewart (Warner Bros 1971)
LA Woman, The Doors (Elektra 1971)
Runt: The Ballad Of Todd Rundgren, Todd Rundgren (Ampex 1971)
Other Voices, The Doors (Elektra 1971)
Great Scott, Tom Scott (A&M 1971)

John Hurley Delivers One More Hallelujah, John Hurley (Bell 1971)

Benny, Benny Hester (VMI 1972)

Gladstone, Gladstone (ABC 1972)

Through The Eyes Of A Horn, Jim Horn (Shelter 1972)

Weird Scenes Inside The Goldmine, The Doors (Elektra 1972)

Elvis As Recorded At Madison Square Garden, Elvis Presley (RCA 1972)

Buckingham Nicks, Buckingham Nicks (Polydor 1973)

Letters To My Head, Mike Deasy Sr (Capitol 1973)

Lookin' For A Smile, Gladstone (ABC 1973)

Aloha From Hawaii Via Satellite, Elvis Presley (RCA 1973)

Dylan, Bob Dylan (Columbia 1973)

The Golden Scarab, Ray Manzarek (Mercury 1974)

Equinox Express Elevator, Howard Roberts (Impulse! 1975)

Ain't It Good To Have It All, Jim & Ginger (ABC 1975)

A Cowboy Afraid Of Horses, Lobo (Big Tree 1975)

The Paxton Brothers, The Paxton Brothers (Anchor 1975)

Valdy, Valdy (A&M 1975)

Fearless, Hoyt Axton (A&M 1976)

Photograph, Melanie (Atlantic 1976)

Broken Blossom, Bette Midler (Atlantic 1977)

The Other Side, Tufano & Giammarese Band (Epic 1977)

Road Songs, Hoyt Axton (A&M 1977)

Moody Blue, Elvis Presley (RCA 1977)

Spirit Of A Woman, American Flyer (United Artists 1977)

Oh! Brother, Larry Gatlin & The Gatlin Brothers Band (Monument 1978)

Randy Richards, Randy Richards (A&M 1978)

Handcuffed To A Heartache, Mary K. Miller (Inergi 1978)

TNT, Tanya Tucker (MCA 1978)

Well Kept Secret, Juice Newton (Capitol 1978)

Street-Legal, Bob Dylan (Columbia 1978)

An American Prayer, Jim Morrison (Elektra 1978)

Le Chat Bleu, Mink DeVille (Capitol 1980)

Seasons Of The Heart, John Denver (RCA 1982)

It's About Time, John Denver (RCA 1983)

Johnny 99, Johnny Cash (Columbia 1983)

Alive, She Cried, The Doors (Elektra 1983)

Desert Rose, Chris Hillman (Sugar Hill 1984)

Ever Call Ready, Every Call Ready (Maranatha! Music 1985)

Dreamland Express, John Denver (RCA 1985)

Southern Pacific, Southern Pacific (Warner Bros 1985)

One World, John Denver (RCA 1986)

Peter Case, Peter Case (Geffen 1986)

King Of America, Elvis Costello (Columbia 1986)

T-Bone Burnett, T-Bone Burnett (Dot Records 1986)

Wild Dogs, Dwight Twilley (CBS 1986)

Daring Adventures, Richard Thompson (Polydor 1986)

Stand Up, The Del Fuegos (Slash 1986)

Crowded House, Crowded House (Capitol 1986)

Slam Dance (Original Motion Picture Soundtrack), Mitchell Froom (Island 1987)

The Delgado Brothers, The Delgado Brothers (Hightone 1987)

The High Lonesome Sound, Tim Scott (DGC 1987)

Out Of Our Idiot, Elvis Costello (Demon 1987)

The Turning, Leslie Phillips (Myrrh 1987)

Amnesia, Richard Thompson (Capitol 1988)

The Indescribable Wow, Sam Phillips (Virgin 1988)

Pat McLaughlin, Pat McLaughlin (Capitol 1988)

Salty Tears, Semi-Twang (Warner Bros 1988)

The Talking Animals, T-Bone Burnett (Acadia 1988)

Gagged But Not Bound, Albert Lee (MCA 1988)

Black And White Night, Roy Orbison (Virgin 1989)

Great Balls Of Fire (Original Motion Picture Soundtrack), Various Artists (Polydor 1989)

Mystery Girl, Roy Orbison (Virgin 1989)

Spike, Elvis Costello (Warner Bros 1989)

The Man With The Blue Post-Modern Fragmented Neo-Traditionalist Guitar, Peter Case (Geffen 1989)

Maria McKee, Maria McKee (Geffen 1989)

The Flower That Shattered The Stone, John Denver (American Gramophone 1990)

Christmas Like A Lullaby, John Denver (Windstar 1990)

Deadicated: A Tribute To The Grateful Dead, Various Artists (Arista 1990)

Mighty Like A Rose, Elvis Costello (Warner Bros 1991)

Cruel Intentions, Sam Phillips (Virgin 1991)

Rumor And Sigh, Richard Thompson (Capitol 1991)

Arkansas Traveler, Michelle Shocked (Mercury 1991)

Radical Light, Vonda Shepard (VRA 1992)

The Criminal Under My Own Hat, T-Bone Burnett (Columbia 1992)

Strange Weather, Glenn Frey (MCA 1992)

99.9 F°, Suzanne Vega (A&M 1992)

Through The Looking Glass, Eliza Gilkyson (Private Music 1993)

Watching The Dark, Richard Thompson (Hannibal 1993)

Take A Step Over, Dan Crary (Sugar Hill 1993)

Weapons Of The Spirit, Marvin (Restless 1994)

Mirror Blue, Richard Thompson (Capitol 1994)

Dart To The Heart, Bruce Cockburn (Columbia 1994)

Martinis & Bikinis, Sam Phillips (Virgin 1994)

Bring On The Weather, Jackopierce (A&M 1994)

Earth Songs, John Denver (Windstar 1995)

Torn Again, Peter Case (Vanguard 1995)

Kojak Variety, Elvis Costello (Warner Bros 1995)

Ron Sexsmith, Ron Sexsmith (Interscope 1995)

XXI, Dwight Twilley (The Right Stuff 1996)

you? me? us?, Richard Thompson (Capitol 1996)

Braver New World, Jimmie Dale Gilmore (Elektra 1996)

Omnipop (It's Only A Flesh Wound Lambchop), Sam Phillips (Virgin 1996)

An Afternoon In The Garden, Elvis Presley (RCA 1997)

Lay Me Down, Nancy Bryan (APO 1997)

Somewhere In The Middle, Eric Martin (Elektra 1998)

Like A Hurricane, Chris Hillman (Sugar Hill 1998)

Slide, Lisa Germano (4AD 1998)

Elvis: The Concert: 1999 World Tour (BMG 1999)

A Hundred Lies, Malcolm Holcombe (Hip-O 1999)

Loose Ends, Larry John McNally (Leni Stern Recordings 2000)

Live In Las Vegas (boxed set), Elvis Presley (BMG 2001)

Louisiana Rain, Gib Guilbeau (Big Beat 2002)

Elvis At The International, Elvis Presley (BMG 2003)

Olympia 2003, Frank Michael (Up 2003)

Who's Gonna Go Your Crooked Mile?, Peter Case (Vanguard 2004)

Live In Los Angeles At PJ's Club, Barney Kessel Trio (Empire 2006)

Pilgrim's Progress, Mark Levine (Dynamic 2007)

Stone Of Sisyphus: XXXII, Chicago (Rhino 2008)

The End: A New Beginning, John Krondes (Funky Sound 2009)

I Believe: The Gospel Masters (boxed set), Elvis Presley (RCA 2009)

INDEX

Words in *italics* indicate album titles unless otherwise stated. Words in 'quotes' indicate song titles. Page numbers in **bold** refer to illustrations.

Adventures Of Ozzie & Harriet, The (TV show), 12
'Alley Oop,' 148
Aloha From Hawaii, 48–9, **114–15**, 232
'Along Comes Mary,' 161
Amendt, Günter, 204
Amnesia, 228
And Then ... Along Comes The Association, 160–1
Anderson, Max, 103, 108–10
Ann-Margret, 9, 25
Artes, Mary Alice, 211–12
Association, The, 160–1
Axton, Hoyt, 193–4

Ballard, Hank, & The Midnighters, 83, 96
Bardwell, Duke, 28
Basie, Count, 100–1
Battin, Clyde 'Skip,' 147
Beach Boys, The, 148, 156, 199
Beardsley, John, 85–7
Beatles, The, 176
Benno, Marc, **118**, 188, 229
Bergen, Candice, 184
'Big Yellow Taxi,' 190
Billy Preston Revue, The, *see* Billy Preston
Bird (movie), 132
Black & White Night, A, 33, **123**, 227
Black Elks Club, the, 134–5, 164
Black Hawk, the (club), 85–6
Blaine, Hal, 43, 162, 214, 220
Blair, Michael, 224
'Blue Suede Shoes,' 27, 60
'Body And Soul,' 135
Boettcher, Curt, 160
Boone, Pat, 164, 172
Bosch, Hieronymous, 224
Botnick, Bruce, 187, 188
Briggs, David, 62
Broken Blossom, 194

Bronstein, Stan, 41–2, 137, 175–8
Brown, Ray, 75, 80, 106, 157
Browne, Jackson, 33
Buie, Cynthia (aka Little Sister), 99–101
Buie, Florence, 98–9, 101
Buie, Les, 92–101, 111, **113**
Burnett, T-Bone, 222, 226–8
'Burning Love,' 60–1
Burton, James, 12, 13, 14, 32–4, 49, **116**, **124**, 171, 215, 217, 220–1, 223, 225, 228
Byrds, The, 132, 147, 164

Cady, Bill, 130
Capp, Frank, 158
Carlton, Larry, 167
Carmel, Skip, 184
Carrigan, Jerry, 215
Cassidy, Cal, 153–4
Catalano, Tom, 162
Cetera, Peter, 138, 192
'Change Is Gonna Come, A,' 150
'Cherish,' 161
'Cherry Pie,' 147
Chicago (band), 138, 192
Chilliwack, 192
Chuck Steele Show Featuring Jeanie, The, 141–2
'City By Night,' 159
Clapton, Eric, 164, 183, 207
Club Marina, the, 140
Collette, Buddy, 131–2
Coltrane, John, 23, 85, 107
Confederates, The, **124**, 223, 225
Cooder, Ry, 164
Copeland, Gene, 86
Costello, Elvis, **124**, 138, 194, 204, 222–6, 229
'Country Roads,' 218
Criminal Under My Own Hat, The, 226
Cross, Billy, **120**, **122**
Cunningham, Jerry 'Toad,' 69, 70

Dali, Salvador, 205
Davis Jr, Billy, 165–6
Davis Jr, Sammy, 25, 167
Davis, Miles, 85, 106, 131, 133, 224, 229
Deasy, Cathy, 172–3
Deasy, Mike, 172–4, 184, 213
DeFranco, Buddy, 132

DeKnight, Rene, 167
Delaney & Bonnie (& Friends), 48, 169, 207
'Delta Dawn,' 197
Denver, John, 66, **122**, 214–21, 224, 228, 230
Derek & The Dominos, 164, 183
DeVille, Willy, 210–11
Diamond, Neil, 34, 162
DiMaggio, Joe, 40
Diskin, Tom, 21, 22
Don & Dewey, 151
Doors, The, **118**, 187–8, 230
Double Trouble (movie soundtrack), 159
Douglas, Steve, 199, 210
Dunn, Duck, **127**
Dylan, Bob, **119**, **121**, **122**, 199–207, 208–10, 211–12, 229

Easy Come, Easy Go (movie soundtrack), 159–60
Eddy, Duane, 199
Edwards, John 'Jimbo,' 86
Eisenhower, Dwight, and Mamie, 144
Elephant's Memory, 42
Ellington, Duke, 135
Elvis Day By Day (book), 28
Elvis: The Concert, 34, 233
Equinox Express Elevator, 132
Esposito, Joe, 13
Ethridge, Chris, 198
Evans, Bill, 106–7
Evans, Craig, 140–1, 144, 146
Evans, Gil, 224
Everly Brothers, The, 172, 234

Fantastic Guitar Sound Of Barney Kessel On Fire, The, 158
Federal Terrace Elementary School, 65, 67
Fehler, Douglas, 65, 67, 73
Fendrick, Randy, 92, 186
Ferry, Rom, 106–7, 109
5th Dimension, The, 165–9, 175, 179–82
Fike, Lamar, 13
'Fire Down Below,' 60, 61, 62–3
Fitzgerald, Ella, 75, 157, 167
5/4 Ballroom, the (club), 155
Flying Burrito Brothers, The, 147, 198

Four Freshmen, The, 141, 156, 181
Fowley, Kim, 147–8
Franklin, Aretha, 7, 15
French, Toxie, 167, 174
Friar Tuck, *see* Mike Deasy
Fripp, Robert, 200
Froom, Mitchell, 223, 226, 228
Frost, Richie, 13

Garcia, Jerry, 28–9
Garcia, Richie, 219
Garrett, Snuff, 31
'(Get Your Kicks On) Route 66,' 141
Glaub, Bob, **127**
Goadsby, Peter, Dr, 222
Goldstein, Jerry, 197, 199
Gordon, Jill, 172–3, 183
Gordon, Jim, 164, 172–3, 183–4
Gordy, Emory, 214
Gosdin Brothers, The, 187
Grant, Eddy, 225
Grateful Dead, 28–9
Guercio, Joe, 9, 26, 53
Guerin, John, 131–2, 137
Guralnick, Peter, 17, 21, 28

Haley, Bill, 83
Hall, Bobbye, 201–2, 208
Hampton, Lionel, 75
Hardin, Betty, 29–30, 31, 32, 42
Hardin, Glen D., 29–32, 33, 42, 49, 66–7, **116**, 214–15, 218, 220–1, 228
Harrell, Marty, 9, 10
Harris, Don 'Sugarcane,' 151–2
Harris, Emmylou, 49
Henderson, Mike, 146–7
Herman, Woody, 29, 180–1
Hobbs, John, 197–8
Hodge, Charlie, 13, 35–7, 50, 63–4, 232
Holiday, Billie, 135, 157
Hollywood Argyles, The, 147–8
Holman, Bill, 180
Horn, Jim, 215, 220
'Hound Dog,' 19, 60, 87
Houston, Cissy, 7
Hughes, Howard, 40, 232
Humphrey, Hubert (Vice President), 179

ILWU Labor Union Hall, 86, 93
Imperials, The, 18–19, 26

Indescribable Wow, The, 227
Irwin, Billy, and Shara, 147, 150
'It Was I,' 147

Jagger, Bianca, 203
Jarvis, Felton, 36, 60, 61, 63
Jazz At The Philharmonic, 75, 80
Jimbo's Bop City (club), 85–6, 92, 135
John Denver & The Muppets (movie), 214
John, Little Willie, 83
Jones, Darryl, **127**
Jones, Quincy, 132, 157, 224
Jones, Tom, 25, 166

Kahane, Jackie, 9, 57–8
Kaye, Carol, 161–2
Keltner, Jim, **125**, 193–5, 210, 223, 225
Kennedy, John F., 139
Kennedy, Robert F., 182
Kershaw, Doug, 183
Kessel, Barney, 157–8, 179
Kevorkian, Dr, 73
King Jr, Martin Luther, 182
King Of America, 222–3, 225–6
King, B.B., 155
Kirkham, Millie, 18–19
Krieger, Bobby, **118**
Knechtel, Larry, 224, 226
Kniss, Dick, 217
Kojak Variety, 223, 225

LA Woman, **118**, 187–8, 192, 230
'Lady Of Spain,' 143
LaFaro, Scott, 159
Lambert, Hugh, 43–4
lang, kd, 227
Lanning, Bob, 39
LaRue, Florence, 166
Layla And Other Assorted Love Songs, 183
Le Chat Bleu, 210–11
Lefebvre, Gary, 131
Leim, Paul, 197
Lennon, John, 42, 132, 194
Let There Be Drums, 148
'Let Us Begin (What Are We Making Weapons For?),' 219
Lewis, Gary, & The Playboys, 31
Lewis, Jerry Lee, 194
'Light My Fire,' 187

Llewellyn, Roderick, 203
Longo, Al, 166
'L-O-V-E Love,' 187
'Love Me Tender,' 35–6
Lovello, Tony, 143
Lucas, Nick, 143

Maheu, Robert, 40–1
Mamas & The Papas, The, 156, 169, 187
Mansfield, David, 202
Manson, Charles, 184, 190
Marriott, Mark, 34–5
Martinis & Bikinis, 227, 228
Masi, Chic, 40
Mathis, Johnny, 194–5
McCartney, Paul, 194, 224
McCoo, Marilyn, 165–6
McGuire, Barry, 213
McLemore, Lamonte, 165–6
Melcher, Terry, 184
Memphis Mafia, the, 13, 15, 27, 63, 232
Midler, Bette, 194, 195, 196
Mighty Like A Rose, 223, 224
Miller, Glenn, 74
Miller, Roger, 30
Miller, Velna, 74
Mingus, Charles, 92
Mink DeVille, 210–11
Mitchell, Joni, 132, 190
Monk, Thelonious, 99, 132, 134
'Monster Mash,' 148
Montgomery, Monk, 75, 85
Moore, Archie, 134–5, 140
Morris, Bobby, 26, 27
Morrison, Jim, **118**, 188, 192, 229, 230
Mr Rose, 38–9
Muhoberac, Larry, 14, 25, 29
Muppets, The, 43, 44, 214
Murphy, Jerry, 76–9

Naval Amphibious Base, Coronado, 110, 129–31, 175
Naval Training Center, San Diego, 89–92
Navy School of Music, Washington DC, 93–4, 101, 102–5, 109–12
Nelson, Ricky, 12
Nelson, Sandy, 148
Nelson, Willie, 198

Nicholson, Jack, 203
Nilsson, Harry, 193–4
Nistico, Sal, 180
Nixon, Richard, 167, 179
Nunez, Flip, 85–6, 92

O'Connor, Kris, 218, 220
O'Day, Anita, 167
'Oh, What A Beautiful Morning!'
131
Ono, Yoko, 42, 194
Orbison, Roy, 33, 227
Osborn, Joe, 127, 161–2
Otis the parrot, 40, 41, 191
Owens, Buck, 184

Palacio, Gil, 140–1, 144, 146
Palmer, Earl, 132
'Papa-Oom-Mow-Mow,' 148
Parker, Butch, 147
Parker, Charlie, 79, 132, 151
Parker, Colonel Tom, 8, 19–22,
24, 38, 39, 51, 60, 61, 231,
232
Paxton, Gary, 30, 147–50, 157–8,
159–60, 184–7
Pello, Gene, 13, 14, 15–16
Phillips, Sam (female singer),
227–8
Phillips, Sam (Sun Records
founder), 14, 25, 231
Picasso, Pablo, 205
Picket, Bobby 'Borris,' & The
Crypt-Kickers, 148
Pico, Teddy, 134
Polanski, Roman, 184
'Polk Salad Annie,' 27, 60
Post, Mike, 162
Pour House, the (club), 131–2
Presley, Elvis, 7–10, 12–29,
31–7, 39, 42, 44–6, 49–53,
60–4, 70, 87, 114–15, 119,
159–60, 170–1, 187, 192–3,
197, 203, 214, 223, 229–30,
231–3; home life, 46, 47;
interest in guns and law
enforcement, 46, 51, 63–4;
'Jungle Room' sessions, 61–3;
song arrangements, 17–19;
Vegas shows, 9, 19, 25–8, 38,
49, 60–1, 232
Presley, Lisa Marie, 47
Presley, Priscilla, 44, 46, 52
Preston, Billy, 150–1, 154, 156

Pryor, Richard, 179, 195
Puente, Tito, 175

Radle, Carl, 183, 207
Raitt, Bonnie, 33, 227
Randi, Don, 43, 44
Raye, Martha, 167–9
Reese, Della, 100–1, 156
Ribot, Marc, 224, 225
Rich, Buddy, 179–80
Right Stuff, The (movie), 38
Rivers, Johnny, 165, 187
Riviera, Jake, 223
Rivingtons, The, 148
Roberts, Howard, 132
Robinson, Sugar Ray, 43
Roe, Tommy, 174
Rothschild, Paul, 187–8
Rude 5, The, 125, 224
Rundgren, Todd, 187

Sands, the (club), 150, 152, 155
Sgt Pepper's Lonely Hearts Club
Band, 176
Scheff, Bill, 69–70, 71, 73
Scheff, Darin, 138, 144, 149
Scheff, Gloria, 71, 146
Scheff, Jason, 138, 144, 192–3
Scheff, Jerry, childhood and
upbringing, 65–73; early
musical career, 131–6, 137,
139–41, 143–5, 146–152,
154–60, 171–2; early musical
influences and experiences,
69–70, 73, 74–82, 83–8, 92,
106–9; encounters with
racism, 84, 93, 95–8, 153–5;
fatherhood 138, 144; life in Las
Vegas, 19–20, 40–2; live
debut, 77–82; live debut with
Elvis Presley, 23–8; move to
Salt Spring Island, 50–1,
189–92; Naval career, 89–92,
102–6, 109–12, 113, 129–31,
133, 137–8, 175; playing
bass, 73, 76, 78–82, 85, 88,
103, 105, 108–9, 111,
113–15, 117–19, 121, 123,
126–8, 131–2, 135, 137–8,
141, 146–7, 149, 151–2, 157,
159, 161–3, 170, 179, 181,
193, 199, 217, 224, 225,
227–8; playing the bugle,
89–92; playing the tuba, 67–9,

71, 72, 90, 104, 125, 134;
playing valve trombone,
140–1, 151, 52, 156–7, 159;
politics, 138–40, 182–3, 190;
relationship with Elvis Presley,
44–7; relationship with Vivian
Varon, 16, 40–2, 144–5;
religion, 211–13; road trip to
Washington DC with Les Buie,
93–101; the Sanctified Boogie
Band, 213, 214; school, 66–8,
73, 75, 83; session work, 148,
150, 156–7, 159–64, 183;
treatment for cancer, 66–7;
use of and attitude toward
drugs, 29, 55, 109–10, 136,
164, 169–72, 175–6, 183–4,
211; working with Bob Dylan,
199–201, 203–5, 207,
208–10; working with Elvis
Presley and the TCB Band,
7–39, 48–50, 51–3, 60–4,
159–60, 170–1, 231–3;
working with Elvis Costello,
222–8; working with Gary
Paxton, 30, 147–9, 157–9,
160, 184–6; working with John
Denver, 66, 214–21, 224;
working with Nancy Sinatra
42–4; working with Tanya
Tucker, 197–8; working with
The 5th Dimension, 165–9,
175, 179–82; working with The
Association, 160–1; working
with The Doors, 187–8
Scheff, Lois, 67, 68, 71–3, 74–6,
81, 82, 85, 86, 88, 213
Scheff, Melva, 71, 72, 74
Scheff, Natalie, 65, 67, 233
Scheff, Walda, 71
Scheff, William Graham, 71–2,
93, 111
Seven Eleven Café, the (club), 88
'Shanghai Breezes,' 218
Sheldon, Jack, 134
Shore, Sammy, 9, 24, 25
Sinatra, Frank, 43, 61, 232
Sinatra, Nancy, 25, 42–4
Skip & Flip, 147
Sleet, Don, 131–3, 137
Slow Train Coming, 212
Smith, Myrna, 7
Soles, Steven, 33, 122, 202
'Song Sung Blue,' 162

Sounds Of Goodbye, 187
Spike, 223, 224
Springs, Helena, 201–2
Springsteen, Bruce, 33–4, 227
Stamps Quintet, The, 53, 64
Stevens, Connie, 201
Stoner, Rob, 199, 200
Strange, Billy, 43
'Straight, No Chaser,' 41, 134
'Strangers In The Night,' 61
Street-Legal, 200
Sumner, J.D., 50, 64
Swann, Virl, 65–6, 73
Sweet Inspirations, The, 7–8, 18, 24, 26, 53, 171

T-Bone Burnett, 226
Talking Animals, The, 226
Tate, Sharon, 184
TCB Band, the, 7–10, 13, 14, 15, 16, 17, 18, 19, 20, 21, 23, 25, 26–37, 39, 44, 48–50, 51–3, 61–4, **116**, 215, 231, 233
'Teen Beat,' 148
Tench, Benmont, **124**
'That's All Right Mama,' 51
That's The Way It Is (DVD), 17
Thomas, Pete, 224, 226
Thompson, Richard, 228
Thornton, Big Mama, 86–7
Three Tons Of Joy, The, 135–6

'Tiptoe Through The Tulips,' 143
TNT, 197–8, 199
Tomlin, Lily, 195
Tonight Show Starring Johnny Carson, The (TV show), 175
Townson, Ron, 165
Travis, Merle, 184
Tropical Cellar, the (club), 75–82
Tucker, Tanya, 197–9
Turner, Ike & Tina, 20
Turning, The, 227
Tutt, Ronnie, 15–16, 19, 25, 27, 28–9, 34–5, 39, 51–4, **116**, 209–10, 213, 223, 232
'Twilight Time,' 143

'Up, Up, And Away,' 166, 168

Valdy, 191
Vallejo Junior High School, 73
Varon, Marlon, 42, 169, 189
Varon, Vivian, 13, 16, 40–1, 42, 46, 47, 51, 144–5, 146, 150, 153, 170, 171, 173, 189, 191
Vaughan, Sarah, 77, 132, 167
Ventures, The, 183
Vicious, Sid, 202
Vincent, Gene, 83
Vineyard, the (church), 211–12
Waits, Tom, 195, 227

Walker, Billy, 197
Wallace, Ian, **120**, **122**, 200, 204, 205–6, 208, 209, 210
'Way Down,' 62
'We Are The World,' 219
Webster, Ben, 135
Weintraub, Jerry, 209
Weisberg, Steve, 217
West, Red, 13, 159
West, Sonny, 13
Westmoreland, Kathy, 42, 51–2
'(What's So Funny 'Bout) Peace, Love, And Understanding,' 213
White, Clarence, 164, 185
Whitlock, Bobby, 183
Wilkinson, John, 14, 32, **116**
Williams, Hank, 93–4
Wilson, Denny, 184
Wofford, Mike, 131–2, 137
Wolk, T-Bone, **124**
'Woman (Sensuous Woman),' 187
Wrecking Crew, The, 162
Wynne, Velna Lou, 74

Yeaman, Wilfrid, 73
'You've Lost That Lovin' Feelin',' 52–3, 132

Zaramby, Sid, 129–31, 134, 137

ACKNOWLEDGEMENTS

Thanks to Bill Scheff, my hearing aids hero Paul Higgins, Gillian G. Gaar, James Scileppi, and Tom Seabrook.

PICTURE CREDITS

Except where indicated, the pictures used in this book are from the author's archives. Every effort has been made to contact the original photographers where possible, but if you feel there has been a mistaken attribution, please contact the publisher. **114–15** *both images* Michael Ochs Archives/Getty Images; **119** *Dylan* Michael Ochs Archives/Getty Images; **120–1** *Dylan* Ebet Roberts/Getty Images; **124** *Costello* Estate Of Keith Morris/Getty Images.